Ten Lessons for a
Post-Pandemic World

Also by Fareed Zakaria

In Defense of a Liberal Education

The Post-American World:
Release 2.0

The Future of Freedom:
Illiberal Democracy at Home and Abroad

From Wealth to Power:
The Unusual Origins of America's World Role

(coeditor)
The American Encounter:
The United States and the Making of the Modern World

Ten Lessons for a Post-Pandemic World

FAREED ZAKARIA

ALLEN LANE
an imprint of
PENGUIN BOOKS

ALLEN LANE

UK | USA | Canada | Ireland | Australia
India | New Zealand | South Africa

Penguin Books is part of the Penguin Random House group of companies
whose addresses can be found at global.penguinrandomhouse.com.

First published in the United States of America by W. W. Norton & Company, Inc. 2020
First published in Great Britain by Allen Lane 2020
001

Printed and bound in Great Britain by Clays Ltd, Elcograf S.p.A.

A CIP catalogue record for this book is available from the British Library

ISBN: 978–0–241–49165–2

www.greenpenguin.co.uk

MIX
Paper from
responsible sources
FSC® C018179

Penguin Random House is committed to a
sustainable future for our business, our readers
and our planet. This book is made from Forest
Stewardship Council® certified paper.

To
Dan, Joanna,
and Gideon Rose

The Future never spoke—
Nor will he like the Dumb
Reveal by sign a Syllable
Of his profound To Come—

But when the News be ripe
Presents it in the Act—
Forestalling Preparation—
Escape—or Substitute

EMILY DICKINSON

Contents

Ten Lessons for a
Post-Pandemic World

INTRODUCTION

The Bat Effect

T HE *NEW YORK TIMES* called it "the spiky blob seen around the world." In late January, Alissa Eckert and her colleague Dan Higgins at the Centers for Disease Control and Prevention were tasked with creating an illustration of the novel coronavirus. What was needed was "something to grab the public's attention," Eckert later explained to the *Times*. What they produced was an image of a silvery globe with bright crimson spikes. It was evocative and disturbing, and it was soon everywhere, appearing in newspapers, magazines, and on television news. If right now you are imagining what a coronavirus looks like, then chances are you are thinking of the Eckert-Higgins rendering or a derivation of it. In the slightly macabre world of professional medical artists, the picture is known as a "beauty shot," an up-close depiction of a single viral particle, making it look menacing but also massive. In fact, the novel coronavirus is about 1/10,000th the size of the period that ends this sentence.

We are often advised to think big. But maybe we need to start thinking small. We're good at imagining the big, traditional dangers we face, however unlikely they have become, such as military attacks and invasions, and planning large-scale symmetrical responses to them. Governments spend trillions of dollars to build vast militaries, track the movement of armies across the planet, and practice war games against potential foes. The United States alone devotes almost three-quarters of a trillion dollars to its defense budget every year. And yet, we were unprepared to defend against a tiny microbe. It may well turn out that this viral speck will cause the greatest economic, political, and social damage to humankind since World War II.

This is a book not about the pandemic, but rather about the world that is coming into being as a result of the pandemic and—more importantly—our responses to it. Any large shock can have diverse effects, depending on the state of the world at the time and on how human beings react—with fear or denial or adaptation. In the case of the novel coronavirus, the impact is being shaped by the reality that the world is deeply interconnected, that most countries were unprepared for the pandemic, and that in its wake, many of them—including the world's richest nations—shut down their societies and economies in a manner unprecedented in human history.

This book is about a "post-pandemic world" not because the coronavirus is behind us, but because we have crossed a crucial threshold. Almost everyone alive had been spared from experiencing a plague, so far. But now we know what a pandemic looks like. We have seen the challenges and costs of responding to it. The Covid-19 pandemic could persist, but even if it is eradicated, new outbreaks of other diseases are almost certain to occur in the future. With this knowledge and experience, we now live in a new era: post-pandemic.

What exactly are the consequences of this pandemic? Some have suggested that it will prove to be the hinge event of modern history, a moment that forever alters its course. Others believe that after a vaccine, we will quickly return to business as usual. Still others argue that the pandemic will not reshape history so much as accelerate it. This last scenario seems the most likely outcome. Lenin is supposed to have once said, "There are decades when nothing happens, and then there are weeks when decades happen." The post-pandemic world is going to be, in many aspects, a sped-up version of the world we knew. But when you put life on fast-forward, events no longer proceed naturally, and the consequences can be disruptive, even deadly. In the 1930s, many developing countries were modernizing at a steady pace, moving people from agriculture to industry. The Soviet Union decided to brutally accelerate that process. This decision, the collectivization of agriculture, led to famine, the "liquidation" of millions of farmers, a hardening of dictatorship, and the deformation of Soviet society. A world on steroids can suffer unpredictable side effects.

Post-pandemic life will be different for countries, companies, and especially individuals. Even if economics and politics return to normal, human beings will not. They will have been through an unusual, difficult trial and have a sense of newfound, hard-won opportunity. Having survived the Spanish flu, a character in William Maxwell's 1937 novel, *They Came Like Swallows*, feels a sense of "wonder clinging to him (for it had been a revelation: neither he nor anyone else had known that his life was going to be like this)." As the worst passes, we emerge into the "dead cold light of tomorrow," as the writer Katherine Anne Porter put it in her 1939 semi-autobiographical novella, *Pale Horse, Pale Rider*, about surviving the same pandemic. Her last line: "Now there would be time for everything."

PLAGUES HAVE CONSEQUENCES

We should have seen it coming. The coronavirus may be novel but plagues are not. Western literature begins with one. In the opening verses of Homer's *Iliad*, the Greek armies are being ravaged by pestilence. It turns out to be divine punishment directed at their leader, the vain, avaricious, and quarrelsome King Agamemnon. The first serious history written in the West hinges on a plague. Thucydides' *History of the Peloponnesian War* chronicles the long conflict between the two superpowers of the age, Athens and Sparta. Toward the beginning of the war, Thucydides writes, a terrible plague swept through Athens, killing vast numbers of able-bodied citizens and, most significant, the city-state's peerless leader, Pericles. The two sides had very different political systems: Athens was democratic, Sparta a more rigidly run warrior society. Sparta eventually prevailed, and it's not a stretch to say that, had there been no plague, Athens might have won, and the course of Western history would have been different—with a vibrant democracy becoming a successful role model rather than a flame that burned brightly, but then flickered out. Plagues have consequences.

The most consequential by far was the bubonic plague, which began in Central Asia in the 1330s and spread to Europe in the following decade. One medieval chronicler accused the Mongols of introducing the disease to the continent by launching plague-ridden corpses into a Genoese fortress by catapult—an early bioweapon. More likely, the plague spread through global commerce, borne by the caravans and ships that plied goods from the Orient to major ports like Messina in Sicily and Marseilles in France. Also called the Black Death, it was carried by fleas on the backs of rats and attacked the lymphatic system of its victims, causing suffering and death on a scale that has never been seen since. Up to half of Europe's population was wiped out. The disease, like many, was never fully eradicated. The World Health Organization still reports a few hundred cases of bubonic plague every year, luckily now treatable with antibiotics.

The bubonic plague had seismic effects. Scholars believe that with so many dead, the economics of the time was turned on its head. Walter Scheidel explains that labor became scarce and land abundant, so wages rose and rents fell. Workers won more bargaining power and nobles lost out. Serfdom withered away in much of Western Europe. Of course, the impact varied from country to country based on each one's economic and political structures. Inequality actually rose in some places that took repressive measures. For example, noble landlords in Eastern Europe used the misery and chaos to tighten their hold and impose serfdom for the first time. Beyond these material effects, the plague prompted an intellectual revolution. Many fourteenth-century Europeans asked why God would allow this hell on earth and questioned entrenched hierarchies— which had the ultimate effect of helping Europe break out of its medieval malaise and setting in motion the Renaissance, Reformation, and Enlightenment. From death and horror came science, modernity, and growth. With Covid-19, thankfully, we do not face the same mass mortality. But might our era's pandemic provoke a similar spirit of societal introspection, an equivalent shock to our complacency?

The historian William McNeill, who wrote the seminal survey *Plagues and Peoples*, was drawn to epidemiology because he was trying to explain a puzzle: Why were small numbers of European soldiers able to quickly conquer and convert millions of people in Latin America? The Spanish explorer Hernán Cortés, for example, started off with 600 men facing an Aztec Empire of millions. The answer, McNeill found, involved plagues. The Spanish brought with them not only advanced weaponry but also diseases like smallpox, to which they had built up immunity but the natives had not. Estimates of the death toll of the ensuing outbreaks are staggering, ranging from 30% of the population at first to 60% to 90% over the course of the sixteenth century—all told, tens of millions of people. McNeill imagines "the psychological implications of a disease that killed only Indians and left Spaniards unharmed." One conclusion the natives drew, he speculates, was that the foreigners worshipped powerful gods. That might help explain why so many of them submitted to Spanish control and converted to Christianity.

The pandemic still lodged in our memory is the Spanish flu, which hit the world in the midst of World War I and killed some 50 million people, more than twice the number that died in the fighting. (It was called the Spanish flu not because it began in Spain, but because that country, being a noncombatant in the war, did not censor news. The outbreak of the disease was thus reported extensively out of Spain, which led people to assume it originated there.) Science has progressed enormously since the early twentieth century. Back then, no one had ever seen a virus, much less knew how to treat this new infection: electron microscopes had not been invented, nor had antiviral drugs. Still, the three most important guidelines from health authorities at the time—social distancing, masks, and handwashing—remain three of the four most important mechanisms used today to slow the spread of coronavirus, until the development of a vaccine. The fourth, regular testing, is the one modern addition.

In more recent decades, outbreaks of SARS, MERS, avian flu, swine flu, and Ebola spread quickly and widely, leading many experts to warn that we were likely to face a truly global epidemic soon. The public took note, too. In 1994, Richard Preston's best-selling book, *The Hot Zone*, detailed the origins of the Ebola virus. The 2011 film *Contagion*, inspired by the SARS epidemic of 2002–3 and the swine flu pandemic of 2009, imagined a virus that claimed 26 million lives around the world. In 2015, Bill Gates gave a TED Talk warning that "if anything kills over 10 million people in the next few decades, it's most likely to be a highly infectious virus." In 2017, he sounded the alarm louder, predicting in a speech at the Munich Security Conference that there was a reasonable chance that such a pandemic would erupt in the next ten to fifteen years.

By then, it did not take much foresight to imagine a pandemic and to argue for investing more time, resources, and energy toward stopping it. In June 2017, when President Donald Trump proposed budget cuts in the key agencies that dealt with public health and diseases, I devoted a segment of my CNN show to the topic, saying:

> One of the biggest threats facing the United States isn't big at all. Actually, it's tiny, microscopic, thousands of times smaller than the head of a pin. Deadly pathogens, either man-made or natural, could trigger a global health crisis, and the United States is wholly unprepared to deal with it. . . . One only needs to look back 100 years to 1918, when the Spanish flu pandemic killed an estimated 50 million people around the globe. In many ways, we're even more vulnerable today. Densely packed cities, wars, natural disasters, and international air travel mean a deadly virus propagated in a small village in Africa can be transmitted almost anywhere in the world, including the United States, within 24 hours. . . . Biosecurity and global pandemics cut across all national boundaries. Pathogens, viruses, and diseases are equal-opportunity killers. When the crisis comes, we will wish we had more funding and more global cooperation. But then, it will be too late.

It was too late. We had ample warning to gird ourselves for Covid-19. But beyond the specific dangers of a pandemic, we should have recognized the general possibility of a shock to our system.

After the Cold War, the world settled into a new international system marked by three forces, one geopolitical, one economic, and one technological—American power, free markets, and the Information Revolution. All seemed to work together to create a more open and prosperous world. But it was still a world full of crises—some of which would careen out of control. The Balkan wars, the Asian financial collapse, the 9/11 attacks, the global financial crisis, and now Covid-19. While they are all different, they have something crucial in common. They are all *asymmetric* shocks—things that start out small but end up sending seismic waves around the world. This is particularly true of the three that will be judged as the most enduring—9/11, the crash of 2008, and the coronavirus.

The 9/11 attacks shook the globe, focusing attention on a particular backlash to this new world, which many in the West had previously ignored. The attacks brought to center stage the furies of radical Islam, the tensions in the Middle East, and the West's complicated relationship with both. They then provoked a ferocious response from the United States. The country scaled up a vast domestic security apparatus—but also launched wars in Afghanistan and Iraq and targeted operations elsewhere, spending, by one estimate, $5.4 trillion on the "War on Terror." That campaign led to bloodshed, revolution, repression, and refugees, with millions of casualties and fallout that persists to this day.

The second shock was entirely different, a financial crash of a kind familiar in history. Good times led to rising asset prices, which led to speculation, then to bubbles, and finally, inevitably, to collapse. Although the crisis began in the United States, it spread quickly across the planet, plunging the world into the worst economic downturn since the Great Depression. The economy recovered slowly but markets boomed, heightening the divide between capital and labor. When it came to politics, the crisis had complex and corrosive effects. Even though the roots of the crash lay in the excesses of the private sector, in many countries, people did not move to the left economically; they moved to the right culturally. Economic anxiety bred cultural anxiety, hostility to immigration, and a nostalgic desire to return to a familiar past. Right-wing populism gained strength across the West.

The third shock is the one we are living through. It may be the biggest of them all, and it is certainly the most global. What began as a health-care problem in China soon became a global pandemic. But that was only the start. The medical crisis prompted a simultaneous lockdown of all business across the globe, resulting in a Great Paralysis, the cessation of economics itself. By some measures, the economic damage from this pandemic already rivals that of the Great Depression. The political consequences will play out over the coming years in different ways in different countries. The social and psychological consequences—fear, isolation, purposelessness—might endure even longer. Covid-19 is having deep and lasting effects on each of us, repercussions we cannot yet fully grasp.

And yet each of these three massive, global crises turned

on something small, seemingly trivial. Think about the 9/11 attacks, launched by nineteen young men, armed with the simplest and crudest of weapons, small knives, not so different from those used in the Bronze Age 4,000 years ago. But those nineteen men set in motion a wave of warfare, intelligence operations, revolts, and repression around the world. Or consider the origins of the global financial crisis—one obscure financial product, the "credit default swap," a kind of insurance policy mostly on mortgages, was bundled and rebundled, sliced and diced, sold and resold, until it became a $45 trillion market, three times larger than the US economy, and three-quarters the size of the entire global economy. And when that market crashed, it took the world economy with it and, in due course, triggered a wave of populism. Without credit default swaps, there might never have been a President Donald Trump.

And in the case of this pandemic, we now all recognize how a tiny viral particle, circulating in a bat in China's Hubei Province, has brought the world to its knees—a real-life example of the butterfly effect, whereby the flapping of a butterfly's wing might influence weather patterns on the other side of the world. Small changes can have big consequences. In power grids or computer networks, if one tiny element breaks and then shifts its load to another, which then breaks, it can produce a chain reaction that grows ever larger, like a ripple that becomes a roaring wave. It is termed a "cascading failure." A single software glitch or broken transformer can shut down an entire system. Something similar happens in biology. A minor infection in the blood can lead to a tiny clot that, through a chain reaction, can cause a massive stroke—a process called an ischemic cascade.

In earlier ages, epidemics were considered something outside of human agency or responsibility. The word *influenza*, for example, traces back to an Italian folk attribution of colds and fevers to the influence of the stars. In time, however, perceptions changed, and humans focused more on the features of the problem that were readily apparent, an important step toward then seeing what could be done about the problem. The French started calling influenza *grippe*, from the word for "seizure," likely referring to the tightness felt in the throat and chest. Ever since 1990, sudden, massive seizures have gripped the world—about one every ten years—with cascading effects. We will have more. They don't happen by conscious design, but neither are they entirely accidental. They seem to be an inherent element of the international system we have built. We need to understand that system—in other words, understand the world in which we live—in order to see the emerging post-pandemic world.

LESSON ONE

Buckle Up

T HE COVID-19 PANDEMIC is *new*, upturning many of our daily patterns and presumptions. But it has also revealed aspects of the world that are very old. This emergency has highlighted one of the oldest truths about international life—that ultimately, countries are on their own. When the pandemic struck, nations that had long cooperated—in Europe, for example—shut their borders and focused on their own survival. That would not surprise scholars of international relations, who have noted that the most important difference between domestic and international politics is that in the latter, there is no supreme authority, no world government, no Leviathan that maintains order. That basic condition has led many thinkers to conjure up an international realm of perpetual competition and conflict. Thomas Hobbes described countries as always "in the state and posture of Gladiators; having their weapons pointing, and their eyes fixed on one another." In fact, history is filled with periods of war *and* peace. Over the last century, countries have spent more time at peace than at war. Trade, travel, and investment across borders have soared. Nations have created mechanisms and institutions to cooperate and solve common problems. But in the end, in extremis, they walk alone.

Covid-19 hit a world that gained its essential structure in the years after the Cold War. With great-power rivalry subsiding and global trade booming, nations got linked by the strong bonds of interdependence. But economic integration also created countercurrents, as countries jockeyed for advantage and new economic competitors rose to become geopolitical challengers. In these same years, the Information Revolution ensured that everything—goods, services, culture, and ideas—moved around at warp speed. As did disease. All these tangible and intangible flows still course through every country on the planet, yet no one nation can shape them on its own. Everyone is connected, but no one is in control. In other words, the world we live in is open, fast—and thus, almost by definition, *unstable.*

It would be hard to bring stability to anything so dynamic and open. It turns out that in any system, of these three characteristics—open, fast, stable—you can have only two. An open and fast system, like the world we live in, will be inherently unstable. A fast and stable one will tend to be closed, like China. If the system is open and stable, it will likely be sluggish rather than dynamic. Think of the nineteenth-century Austro-Hungarian and Ottoman empires: vast, open, diverse—and decaying. This "trilemma" is an adaptation of an idea of Jared Cohen's, the technologist, who observed that computer networks must choose two of three qualities: openness, speed, and security. Economists have their own version of this idea, the "policy trilemma," which posits that countries can have two of the following three: free-flowing capital, independent central banks, and a fixed exchange rate. They're a bit wonkish, but all these trilemmas get at a simple notion— if everything is open and fast-moving, the system can spin dangerously out of control.

Consider our highly dynamic form of global capitalism, which can result in supercharged growth but also financial crashes and economic tailspins. From the mid-1930s to the early 1980s, when financial markets were more regulated, serious financial panics were few and far between. In recent decades, however, as governments deregulated finance, we have witnessed one crash after another: the Latin American debt crisis, the savings and loan collapse, the Mexican "Tequila" crisis, the Asian meltdown, the Russian default, the implosion of Long-Term Capital Management, the bursting of the tech bubble, and the global financial crisis. More open, more dynamic, more unstable.

We have created a world that is always in overdrive. Human development in every sense has dramatically accelerated over the last two centuries, and that pace has quickened further in the last few decades. People are living longer, producing and consuming more, inhabiting larger spaces, consuming more energy, and generating more waste and greenhouse gas emis-

sions. Just one example: a 2019 UN report, written by 145
experts drawn from fifty countries, concluded that "nature is
declining globally at rates unprecedented in human history."
It noted that 75% of all land has been "severely altered" by
human actions, as has 66% of the world's ocean area. Ecosys-
tems are collapsing, and biodiversity is disappearing. As many
as 1 million plant and animal species (of 8 million total) are
threatened with extinction, some within a few decades. All
these strains and imbalances produce dangers—some that can
be foreseen, and others that cannot.

ACTION AND REACTION

To understand this model of relentless action and reaction,
think about the three great crises of the twenty-first century—
9/11, the financial crash, and Covid-19—one political, one
economic, and one natural. In the first, 9/11, we saw that the
supposedly unstoppable march of capitalism, democracy, and
American hegemony had produced an angry, violent reaction in parts of the Muslim world. The West and its values
were sweeping the planet, but it turned out that not everyone
was happy about this. The backlash was that of a disgruntled
minority—after all, terrorism is the weapon of the weak—but
still it took the world by surprise.

The 2008 crash was the outgrowth of an economy in which
finance had run wild, so much so that financial engineering
was routinely more profitable than actual engineering. Wall
Street invented more and more esoteric products, derivatives
piled on derivatives, encouraging people to take more and
more risks for smaller rewards. Add to this the relentless focus

on home ownership, which led the government and private firms to lure more and more people to buy bigger houses and take on more debt. Ultimately, the system grew so complex that it took only a small shift in housing prices to unravel altogether. The crisis was the economic equivalent of a cascading failure.

The pandemic, for its part, can be thought of as nature's revenge. The way we live now is practically an invitation for animal viruses to infect humans. The Centers for Disease Control and Prevention estimates that three-quarters of new human diseases originate in animals. That was the case for AIDS, Ebola, SARS, MERS, bird flu, swine flu, and, most likely, the novel coronavirus. Why do diseases seem to be jumping from animals to humans at a faster pace in recent decades? Because in many parts of the world, people are living closer to wild animals. Developing countries are modernizing so quickly that they effectively inhabit several different centuries at the same time. In Wuhan and other such cities, China has built an advanced, technologically sophisticated economy—but in the shadows of the skyscrapers are wildlife markets full of exotic animals, a perfect cauldron for animal-to-human viral transfer. And the people who live in these places are more mobile than ever before, quickly spreading information, goods, services—and disease.

Our destruction of natural habitats may also be to blame. Some scientists believe that as humans extend civilization into nature—building roads, clearing land, constructing factories, excavating mines—we are increasing the odds that animals will pass diseases to us. Covid-19 appears to have originated in bats, which are hosts to many other viruses, including rabies and Ebola. Why bats? They have highly developed immune systems and defense mechanisms, such as a feverishly high body temperature when flying, which select for stronger viruses. Bats can endure viruses that might quickly debilitate other animals, giving the viruses greater opportunity to spread.* Bats also gather in large numbers in close proximity to one another, creating perfect breeding grounds for viral transmission. Just outside San Antonio, Texas, you can find the Bracken Cave Preserve, home to the world's largest colony of bats. Between March and October, over 15 million Mexican free-tailed bats congregate there and roam the skies at night, producing sights and sounds so dramatic that they are called a "batnado."

Bats used to live farther from humans. But as we encroached on their habitats, their diseases increasingly became our diseases. In Malaysia, rainforests have been cut down for decades in order to produce palm oil and lumber. Over time, this deforestation pushed fruit bats closer and closer to places where they could sustain themselves. Many clustered around pig farms, feeding off the mango and other fruit trees that grew there. And so in 1998, a virus called Nipah, hosted in

---

*This is why bats, as reservoirs for viruses (including a variety of coronaviruses), are studied at facilities like the Wuhan Institute of Virology. There are those who allege that the novel coronavirus was an accidental leak from this lab. This claim is as-yet unproven, but we should note that such facilities, even at the highest grade of biosecurity, BSL-4, have experienced leaks in the past, as with an outbreak of foot-and-mouth disease that escaped from a UK lab in 2007.

bats, appears to have infected pigs which then infected farm-workers. Something similar was probably at work with the novel coronavirus, which likely found an intermediate host—perhaps the pangolin, whose scales are used in traditional Chinese medicine—before infecting humans. "We are doing things every day that make pandemics more likely," said Peter Daszak, an eminent disease ecologist. "We need to understand, this is not just nature. It is what we are doing to nature."

As economic development moves faster and reaches more people, we are taking ever-greater risks, often without even realizing it. Think about meat consumption. As people get richer, they tend to eat more meat. When this happens globally, the effect is staggering: some 80 billion animals are slaughtered for meat *every year* around the world. (And that doesn't even count fish.) But supplying this enormous demand comes at great cost to the environment and our health. Animal products provide only 18% of calories worldwide, yet take up 80% of the earth's farmland. Meanwhile, meat is now produced as if in a nineteenth-century factory, with vast numbers of animals packed together in gruesome conditions. Most livestock—an estimated 99% in America, 74% around the world—comes from factory farms. (Organically farmed, grass-fed meat is a luxury product.) These massive operations serve as petri dishes for powerful viruses. "Selection for specific genes in farmed animals (for desirable traits like large chicken breasts) has made these animals almost genetically identical," *Vox*'s Sigal Samuel explains. "That means that a virus can easily spread from animal to animal without encountering any genetic variants that might stop it in its tracks. As it rips through a flock or herd, the virus can grow even more virulent." The lack of genetic diversity removes the "immunological firebreaks." Samuel quotes the biologist Rob Wallace: "Factory farms are the best way to select for the most dangerous pathogens possible."

The 2009 H1N1 swine flu outbreak seems to have arisen in North American pig farms, while many avian flus have been traced to poultry-producing factory farms in East Asia. Factory farms are also ground zero for new, antibiotic-resistant bacteria, as animals are bombarded with antibiotics that kill most bacteria but leave those that survive highly potent. Johns Hopkins professor Robert Lawrence calls antibiotic-resistant bacteria "the biggest human health risk of factory farms." Some 2.8 million Americans fall ill from antibiotic-resistant bacteria annually, according to the CDC, and 35,000 of them die a result. That's one person every fifteen minutes. Globally, the death toll is 700,000 a year. And yet, meat consumption keeps rising every year.

TEMPTING FATE

It's strange that in America we have not learned the lesson that hasty, unplanned development can provoke a backlash. After all, the country has experienced several, most notably the 1930s Dust Bowl, the greatest ecological disaster in North American history. The event is seared in the American imagination, depicted in novels and captured in movies. The bitter tale of desperate Dust Bowl migrants inspired John Steinbeck's *Grapes of Wrath*—describing the plight of people who could be called America's first climate refugees. And it is a story of human action causing a natural reaction.

The Great Plains are the semiarid places east of the Rocky Mountains and west of the Mississippi River. The wind blows fast over these lands, sometimes scarily so. Over centuries, probably millennia, nature's solution was to grow grass that held the loose topsoil in place. But by the late nineteenth century, as the pioneers headed west, lured by promises of fertile farmland, they tilled the prairies, turning the grassy plains into wheat fields. The farmers felled trees that served as windbreaks, and turned the soil over and over, until there was no grass and the topsoil had been reduced to a thin, loose layer just covering the hard land beneath.

Then came bad weather. Starting in 1930, the region was hit by four waves of drought. With the drought came winds— ferocious gales that blew off the entire layer of topsoil with a force that few humans had seen before and kicked up dust storms that blackened the sky. By 1934, the topsoil covering 100 million acres of land had blown away. The heat intensified the suffering—1934 was the United States' hottest year on record until 1998. Thousands died and millions fled. The farmers left behind were plunged into a decade of poverty.

We are tempting fate similarly every day. Climate change is a vast topic that deserves its own books and warnings. But suffice it to say that we are now watching its effects on almost every part of the natural environment. It is bringing a tropical climate to more of the world, thus creating more hospitable conditions for disease. It is also turning more land into

desert—twenty-three hectares every minute, by the UN's estimate. In 2010, Luc Gnacadja, who headed the organization's
effort to combat desertification, called it "the greatest environmental challenge of our time," warning, "The top 20 cen-
timeters of soil is all that stands between us and extinction."
Thirty-eight percent of the earth's surface is at risk of desertification, and some of it is caused less by global climate change
than by something more easily preventable: the over-extraction
of water from the ground. One of the world's most crucial
water sources is the Ogallala Aquifer, which sprawls through
the semiarid lands of South Dakota, Nebraska, Kansas, Oklahoma, and Texas and supplies about a third of the groundwater
used to irrigate American farms. This seemingly bottomless
well is in fact being emptied by agribusiness so fast that it is on
track to shrivel by 70% in less than fifty years. If the aquifer
ran dry, it would take 6,000 years for rainfall to refill it.

You may say that this is not new. Human beings have been
altering natural processes ever since they learned how to make
fire. The changes picked up speed with the invention of the
wheel, the plow, and most dramatically, the steam engine.
But they intensified, particularly in the twentieth century and
in the last few decades. The number of people on the planet
has risen fivefold since 1900, while the average lifespan has
doubled. The increase in lifespan goes "beyond the scope of
what had ever been shaped by natural selection," explained
Joshua Lederberg, the biologist who won the Nobel Prize at
age thirty-three for his work on bacterial genetics. In a brilliant, haunting speech in 1989 at a virology conference in
Washington, DC, Lederberg argued that we have changed

our biological trajectory so much that "contemporary man is a man-made species."

Lederberg called human beings' continued economic and scientific advancement "the greatest threat to every other plant and animal species, as we crowd them out in our own quest for *Lebensraum*." "A few vermin aside," he added, "*Homo sapiens* has undisputed dominion." But he pointed out that we do have one real competitor—the virus—and in the end, it could win. "Many people find it difficult to accommodate to the reality that Nature is far from benign; at least it has no special sentiment for the welfare of the human versus other species." Lederberg reminded the audience of the fate that befell rabbits in Australia in the 1950s, when the myxoma virus was unleashed upon them as a population-control measure. Eventually, rabbits achieved herd immunity, but only after the virus had killed over 99% of those infected in the first outbreaks. He concluded his speech with a grim image: "I would . . . question whether human society could survive left on the beach with only a few percent of survivors. Could they function at any level of culture higher than that of the rabbits? And if reduced to that, would we compete very well with kangaroos?"

If you aren't already worried enough, remember that we have considered the dangers only of natural reactions to human activity, from pandemics to global warming. But could humans use disease as a weapon? There are a few examples in history. The scholar Toby Ord has pointed out in his book *The Precipice* that, as far back as 1320 BC, sheep infected with the bacterial disease tularemia were driven from one kingdom to the next in Asia Minor. In modern times, the Soviet Union had a sophisticated bioweapons program, employing 9,000 scientists at its peak, to weaponize everything from smallpox to anthrax. Advances in biology and technology mean that today, it would take only a few trained scientists and a small investment to produce deadly pathogens.

I have always considered bioterror to be the most important under-discussed danger facing us. Since 9/11, the United States has focused much of its energy on stopping the spread of nuclear weapons. It went to war in Iraq chiefly to stop that country's supposed nuclear program, and it has threatened war with Iran and North Korea on the same grounds. Nuclear nonproliferation remains at the top of the US agenda; a vast body of arms-control treaties regulate these weapons internationally. But nuclear weapons are hard to build and relatively easy to detect. Bioweapons are far more practical to develop; they can be made cheaply and secretly in small laboratories on shoestring budgets. Their impact is almost unthinkably large: the death toll from manufactured pathogens could easily reach into the millions, even higher. And yet this danger gets little attention. The main international forum for preventing it, the Biological Weapons Convention, is an afterthought. As Ord notes, "this global convention to protect humanity has just four employees, and a smaller budget than an average McDonald's."

OUR RESILIENT WORLD

This is a gloomy compendium of threats. And given the unstable nature of our international system, it may seem that our world is terribly fragile. It is not. Another way to read human history is to recognize just how tough we are. We have gone through extraordinary change at breathtaking pace. We have seen ice ages and plagues, world wars and revolutions, and yet we have survived and flourished. In his Nobel acceptance speech, Joshua Lederberg acknowledged that nature usually seeks an equilibrium that favors mutual survival between the virus and the host—after all, if the human dies, so does the parasite. Human beings and our societies are amazingly innovative and resourceful. This planet is awe-inspiringly resilient. But we have to recognize the ever-greater risks we are taking and act to mitigate them. Modern human development has occurred on a scale and at a speed with no precedent. The global system that we are living in is open and dynamic, which means it has few buffers. That produces great benefits but also vulnerabilities. We have to adjust to the reality of ever-increasing instability—now.

We are not doomed. The point of sounding the alarm is to call people to action. The question is, What kind of action? There are those, from the right and left, who want to stop countries from growing economically and shut down our open world. But should we tell the poorest billion in the world that they cannot escape poverty? Should we close ourselves off from the outside world and seek stability in national fortresses? Should we try to slow down technology, or the global movement of goods and services? Even if we wanted to do any of this, we would not be able to arrest these powerful forces. We could not convince billions of people to stop trying to raise their standards of living. We could not prevent human beings from connecting with one another. We could not stop technological innovation. What we can do is be far more conscious of the risks we face, prepare for the dangers, and equip our societies to be resilient. They should be able not only to withstand shocks and backlashes, but learn from them. Nassim Nicholas Taleb suggests that we create systems that are "antifragile," which are even better than resilient ones. They actually gain strength through chaos and crises.

We know what to do. After the Dust Bowl, scientists quickly understood what happened. Franklin D. Roosevelt's administration produced a short movie to explain it to the country, *The Plow That Broke the Plains*. Government agencies taught farmers how to prevent soil erosion. The administration provided massive aid to farmers, established the Soil Conservation Service, and placed 140 million acres of federal grasslands under protection. In the last three-quarters of a century, there has been no second Dust Bowl, despite extreme weather.

"Outbreaks are inevitable but pandemics are optional," says Larry Brilliant, the American physician who helped eradicate smallpox forty-five years ago. What he means is that we may not be able to change the natural occurrences that produce disease in the first place, but through preparation, early action, and intelligent responses, we can quickly flatten its trajectory. In fact, the eradication of smallpox is a story that is only partly about science and mostly about extraordinary cooperation between rival superpowers and impressive execution across the globe. Similarly, climate change is happening and we cannot stop it completely. But we can mitigate the scale of change and avert its most harmful effects through aggressive and intelligent policies. It will not be cheap. To address it seriously we would need to start by enacting a carbon tax, which would send the market the right price signal and raise the revenue needed to fund new technologies and simultaneously adapt to the already altered planet. As for economic development, there are hundreds of ways we could approach the process differently, retaining traditional ingredients like growth, openness, and innovation while putting new emphasis on others like security, resilience, and anti-fragility. We can make different trade-offs, forgo some efficiencies and dynamism in some areas, and spend more money to make our societies prepared. The costs of prevention and preparation are minuscule compared to the economic losses caused by an ineffective response to a crisis. More fundamentally, building in resilience creates stability of the most important kind, emotional stability. Human beings will not embrace openness and change for long if they constantly fear that they will be wiped out in the next calamity.

And what about preventing the next pandemic? Again, we need to balance dynamism with safety. Much attention has focused on wet markets where live animals are slaughtered and sold, but these cannot simply be shut down. In many countries, especially in Africa and Asia, they provide fresh food for people who don't own refrigerators. (In China, they account for 73% of all fresh vegetables and meat sold.) These markets should be better regulated, but they pose limited risks when they do not sell wild animals like bats, civets, and pangolins. It is that exotic trade that must be outlawed. Similarly, getting the world to stop eating meat may be impossible, but promoting healthier diets—with less meat—would be good for humans and the planet. And factory farming can be reengineered to be much safer, and far less cruel to animals. Most urgently, countries need strong public health systems and those systems need to communicate, learn from, and cooperate with one another. You cannot defeat a global disease with local responses.

Human beings have been developing their societies at an extraordinary pace, expanding in every realm at unprecedented speed. It is as if we have built the fastest race car ever imagined and are driving it through unknown, unmarked terrain. But we never bothered to equip the car with airbags. We didn't get insurance. We have not even put on our seat belts. The engine runs hot. Parts overheat and sometimes even catch fire. There have been some crashes, each one a bit worse than the last. So we douse the vehicle, tune up the suspension, repair the bodywork, and resolve to do better. But we race on, and soon we are going faster and faster, into newer and rougher terrain. It's getting very risky out there. It's time to install those airbags and buy some insurance. And above all, it's time to buckle up.

LESSON TWO

What Matters Is Not the Quantity of Government but the Quality

IN OCTOBER 2019, just a few months before the novel coronavirus swept the world, Johns Hopkins University released its first Global Heath Security Index, a comprehensive analysis of countries that were best prepared to handle an epidemic or pandemic. The United States ranked first overall, and first in four of the six categories—prevention, early detection and reporting, sufficient and robust health system, and compliance with international norms. That sounded right. America was, after all, the country with most of the world's best pharmaceutical companies, research universities, laboratories, and health institutes. But by March 2020, these advantages seemed like a cruel joke, as Covid-19 tore across the United States and the federal government mounted a delayed, weak, and erratic response. By July, with less than 5% of the world's population, the country had over 25% of the world's cumulative confirmed cases. Per capita daily death rates in the United States were ten times higher than in Europe. Was this the new face of American exceptionalism?

It would be easy to blame President Trump, and he deserves a great deal of blame for downplaying the pandemic as it was arriving, remaining passive once it took hold, and continually undermining the guidelines of his own scientific advisors. He never was able to coordinate action across federal agencies and with the fifty states. But there is more to the story than just an inept White House. There were missteps across the government. The Centers for Disease Control and Prevention failed by sending out faulty test kits and initially discouraging the public from wearing face masks. The Food and Drug Administration dragged its feet on fast-tracking procedures that would have allowed private labs to bridge the gap in testing. The Department of Health and Human Services was unable to roll out its own system of mass testing. Many countries, from Germany to South Korea to New Zealand, emerged from their lockdowns with strong systems of testing and tracing in place. Not the United States.

In theory, America has formidable strengths. It is the world's richest country and boasts a scientific and technological establishment that is second to none. Its public health agencies, like the CDC, have been copied across the world, including by the Chinese. But years of dominance have led to complacency. All the while, Washington has loaded these agencies with mandates and rules while paring back their budgets—a recipe for dysfunction. Coordinating across a federal government as large and complicated as the United States' is always a hellish management challenge. Add to this an administration that openly regarded much of government as the enemy, a "deep state" to be dismantled, and the result was an across-the-board failure.

America's role as the global agenda-setter often masks its weaknesses. Americans and their institutions end up being the ones to set the standards and evaluate the world, just as Johns Hopkins did for global health. Inevitably, there is a home-team bias. Americans seem to focus on metrics that highlight the strengths of the US system while downplaying those that reveal its weaknesses. Before the pandemic, for example, Americans might have taken solace in the country's great research facilities or the huge amounts of money spent on health care, while forgetting about the waste, complexity, and deeply unequal access that mark it as well. Whatever the reason, few realized just how vulnerable the United States was. When Covid-19 hit, America's medical emergency system crashed. One month after Trump announced a warlike mobilization to fight the virus, the country's testing regime was still a fiasco, with dozens of tests of varying quality, a free-for-all as to who got them, and long waiting periods for the results. (It is telling that Great Britain ranked second on the Johns Hopkins list, being another country with superb high-end medical capabilities and also one that sets the global agenda. Like America, Britain performed miserably in confronting the pandemic, with its deaths per capita among the highest in the world.)

Initially, America's failures were set against China's successes, framed within a larger narrative about the decay of democracy and the rise of China's model of state capitalism. Despite being the first country to face the virus, China seemed to bring the disease under control with tremendous speed. Was this because it had a powerful, technocratic government, unencumbered by democratic constraints? At one point, the government put most of China on lockdown, shutting down almost all economic activity, including transportation, effectively quarantining about 750 million people. The gigantic China State Construction Engineering Corporation built two new hospitals in under two weeks. China isolated the sick, separated them from their families, and—using technology and detective work—tracked down those with whom they had contact.

But over time, it became clear that China had in fact botched the early response to Covid-19. Local officials in Hubei and Wuhan minimized the outbreak and silenced doctors who tried to sound a general warning. One of these whistleblowers, Dr. Li Wenliang, was arrested and, in a tragic twist of fate, died of the disease. Higher-ups in Beijing kept the World Health Organization and the rest of the world in the dark, delaying the release of vital information about the virus. Under Xi Jinping, the government and Communist Party have tightened their grip on the political system, the economy, and society—and in this atmosphere, local officials were reluctant to report bad news up the chain of command. Months after the outbreak, Beijing was still rebuffing international requests for information, even going so far as restricting the publication of scientific articles about Covid-19.

All this is inherent to the Chinese political system. Authoritarian regimes—always and everywhere—want to control information tightly. It is a source of their power. Looking at all epidemics recorded since 1960, *The Economist* found that dictatorships often mishandle outbreaks. In general, democracies have dealt with them better, resulting in significantly lower death rates compared to autocracies of the same income level. Likewise, the Nobel Prize-winning economist Amartya Sen found that democracies tend to respond to famines better than dictatorships do, because the key to preventing their spread is the free flow of information—and the pressure this puts on elected officials. It is also unclear that China's heavy-handed approach with total lockdowns and closures was the only path to success. Other countries managed the disease as effectively with far less coercive methods.

America, for its part, handled some parts of the crisis badly but other parts well. It allowed the disease to explode through neglect and mismanagement but then stepped in to cushion the economic blow with unprecedented support. Despite the most partisan climate since the Civil War, the administration and Congress came together and rolled out the largest package of financial relief in American history. The Federal Reserve, for its part, became the holder of last resort of virtually any asset, providing a floor for the economy as a whole. As of June 2020, the congressional bills, combined with the Fed's interventions, amounted to over $6 trillion to be spent—in absolute terms, the largest pandemic response in the world and one of the largest per capita (Japan, Germany, and others also enacted massive programs, in the trillions). Below the federal level, some American mayors and governors ramped up testing and expanded health-care facilities. America's large companies adjusted adroitly when asked, turning car production lines into ventilator factories. Silicon Valley's big technology companies became lifelines for people forced to work from home. And US pharmaceutical and biotech companies raced to find treatments and a vaccine with a speed that has surprised even optimists. This is not the picture of a country in irreversible decline.

America will always disappoint its most ardent detractors—and admirers. It's a big, complicated place, and you can always find in it what you want. But the pandemic laid bare fissures that have been persistently widening. They were best described decades ago by the economist John Kenneth Galbraith, who wrote that America was defined by "private opulence and public squalor." The United States has long had a dazzling private sector, but its public institutions, with a few exceptions—such as the independent, self-funded, and highly respected Federal Reserve—limp along. Washington can throw money at a problem, which often does the job eventually, but it cannot run a complex national program to serve a collective benefit. Social Security—whose job is mainly to write checks—works, while the Veterans Administration is a bloated, bureaucratic disaster.

Sometimes even writing checks goes badly. Washington spent trillions of dollars on pandemic relief, but much of it got snatched up by big companies and the rich, whose lobbyists skillfully wrote in provisions that sent money their way. Just getting the checks to individual Americans took longer than it should have, with bureaucratic hang-ups plus the last-minute insistence that the checks be printed with Donald Trump's name on them. In late April, at least 50 million Americans were waiting for their money while the Treasury Department had sent a million checks to dead people. Meanwhile, Canada's relief bill was simple and unencumbered by bureaucracy or politics—the money got to its citizens via direct deposits into their bank accounts within the first two weeks of the crisis. Similarly, Germany right at the outset expanded a program that guarantees furloughed workers 60% of lost wages, and 67% for workers with children, letting firms avoid mass layoffs. The speed and competence of these measures played a large role in their success, since the goal was to ease people's financial and psychological anxiety.

These ills of government are an American, not a democratic, disease. Many other democracies handled this pandemic effectively, better than any dictatorship. That list includes countries run by political parties of all stripes. The most aggressive responses were probably those undertaken by the left-of-center governments in South Korea, New Zealand, and Taiwan, but the right-of-center coalitions holding power in Germany, Austria, and Australia were not far behind. The governments with the most relaxed attitudes—which didn't work well—were countries like Brazil and Mexico, run by fiery populists, but also Sweden, run by left-of-center leaders. Does this muddle tell us anything? Mostly that the old ideologies are obsolete. The divide that has organized politics for centuries has been between left and right. The Left has advocated a larger role for the state in the economy. The Right has staunchly defended free markets. For the twentieth century, the great political debate was about the size and role of government in the economy—the quantity of government. But what seems to have mattered most in this crisis was the *quality* of government.

Take the countries that responded early to the pandemic, tested widely, tracked the infected, slowed down the spread, and did all that with limited lockdowns. At the top of the list are Taiwan, South Korea, Hong Kong, and Singapore—which is remarkable because all of them receive millions of Chinese travelers annually. These are not places with big states. Government expenditures as a percent of the economy are relatively low. Hong Kong was long touted by American conservatives as an ideal free-market economy, regularly topping the list of the Heritage Foundation's Index of Economic Freedom. Public spending as a share of its economy is astonishingly low—a mere 18%, a third of France's figure. And yet Hong Kong registered just eighteen deaths as of late July. At the same point, Taiwan, with 23 million people, had only seven deaths. It spends a mere 6% of its GDP on health care, one-third the American number. On the other hand, Germany, Denmark, and Finland also handled the pandemic extremely effectively, and they have large states by most measures. The same is true of Canada. In other words, some of the countries that beat the virus had big governments, while others had small ones. What was the common element? A competent, well-functioning, trusted state—the *quality* of government.

A BRIEF HISTORY OF GOOD GOVERNMENT

Why do some states have governments that work well and others don't? It's a puzzle that scholars have studied for centuries. To answer it, let's start at the very beginning. All societies from the earliest of times began with political systems that Max Weber famously described as "patrimonial," meaning simply rule by a strongman. The regime was just his family, friends, and allies. Political power and economic power were fused, creating a system that was deeply unrepresentative yet effective. Francis Fukuyama describes the strength of patrimonial systems: "They are constructed using the basic building blocks of human sociability, that is, the biological inclination of people to favor family and friends with whom they have exchanged reciprocal favors." The patrimonial system has deep roots in human society and has lasted through the millennia. The Mafia still runs this way, and many modern regimes maintain some of its basic features. Brazil, Greece, and India have all adopted formally modern political institutions, but scratch deeper, and you'll find a strong underlay of patrimonialism, with family ties being a crucial component of political power.

Even the United States still retains elements of an old patronage, if not a patrimonial, system that operates basically as legalized corruption. I once asked a senior official in the Treasury Department whether it made sense for banks to be overseen by five or six different congressional committees, in addition to various state regulators. It adds endless and conflicting complexity to routine oversight. His response, of course, was no, but it will never change: "Each of these committees, plus politicians in the states, all raise funds for their electoral campaigns by asking these very banks for money. Take away their oversight and you take away their fundraising." Ever since a Supreme Court ruling in 1976, *Buckley v. Valeo*, the United States has adhered to the view that spending money is an act of free speech and thus cannot be regulated in any serious way. This view of speech, later affirmed and expanded in the notorious *Citizens United* decision of 2010, is held in no other advanced democracy on the planet, most of which routinely regulate how politicians raise and spend money—with no adverse effects on the quality of their free speech or democracy. As a result, at the heart of American government, there is a ceaseless series of quid pro quos—money raised for favors bestowed. The American tax code is one of the world's longest for a reason. The thousands of amendments to it are what politicians sell when they raise campaign money.

Intellectuals have always imagined a better system run by experts of some sort—people we would now call technocrats. In *The Republic*, Plato describes five basic types of regimes: aristocracy, timocracy, oligarchy, democracy, and tyranny. The best regime, he believed, was an aristocracy led by philosopher-kings. The ruling class would be educated rigorously enough to appreciate the greatest goals for a society—the Platonic ideal of "the Good." They could not own property lest that make them pursue their own petty, personal interests. They were incentivized to think only of what was best for the entire society. A timocracy, in which only property owners can vote, was what happened once an aristocracy degenerated and men—then always men—of middling character and education became rulers. They would be greedy and power-hungry, soon leading the regime into pure oligarchy, the naked rule of the rich whose sole purpose was to preserve their own advantages. For Plato, democracy—the rule of the masses— and oligarchy—the rule of the rich—were dangerous because these were forms of government motivated by self-interest, lacking a higher purpose. They were also unstable, almost always degrading into the worst kind of regime, tyranny.

The initial efforts to create competent bureaucracy were decidedly mixed. The notion of a ruling class trained to govern found its earliest Western expression in the Roman Empire, which came to be run through a large administrative network of officers, mostly military. Its most famous reforms took place under the emperor Diocletian, who ruled in the third century AD. He decentralized the empire and devolved power to three other commanders, creating a regime that was called the "tetrarchy," or rule by four. It did not produce great military or economic success and is often seen as a failure. After the fall of Rome to barbarian invaders in the fifth century, the Eastern Roman Empire, ruled from Byzantium (renamed Constantinople and later Istanbul) became legendary for its ever-expanding set of laws and layers of administration—so much so that to this day an overly complicated system of any kind is labeled "byzantine."

Far from the West and a century before Plato, Confucius praised rulers who governed not by brute force but with a sense of morality and whose goal was to inculcate in their people a code of honor and a sense of shame. Influenced by Confucius' thinking, China established one of the first examinations to recruit government officials. It had precursors in the Han dynasty but was properly established in the Tang, which ruled between AD 618 and 907. Students were tested on their knowledge of the Confucian canon as well as military history and strategy. Successive dynasties expanded the exams, which in addition to staffing the imperial administration also served as a way to center power on the emperor and clip the wings of local chieftains. The idea of these exams and some kind of a merit-based process spread across East Asia to Japan, Korea, and Vietnam, each of which created its own version of a scholarly bureaucracy. During the Ming dynasty, visiting Portuguese travelers began referring to high-level Chinese officials as "mandarins," and to this day that word is used to describe powerful bureaucrats anywhere.

These technocracies were not always successful at creating highly competent states largely because the experts did not actually wield power. Political leaders and their cronies were always in charge. The officials who passed the exams were often subordinated to the ruler's relatives and courtiers. The impressive-sounding bureaucracies were limited in scope and often lacked authority. But in places as disparate as China and Germany, they did lay the groundwork for future political development.

What really made governments increasingly powerful and effective was something else: conflict. The scholar Charles Tilly famously noted that "war made the state and the state made war," and you can see how the size and scope of the state enlarged as countries engaged in military competition. War almost always meant taxation, which ended up putting pressure on government to provide more services for its people. One of the reasons that tiny Britain became such a formidable modern state and then built a global empire was that its many conflicts in the seventeenth and eighteenth centuries helped it develop not only a superb navy but also an impressive fiscal machine. By the late 1700s the average Briton paid taxes almost three times higher than a Frenchman's. As the historian John Brewer put it, these taxes were the "sinews of power"—which, even more than its navy, enabled Britain to defeat France repeatedly and achieve global hegemony. Sometimes the pressure that galvanized the system was not military but natural. The historian Frank Snowden has suggested that medieval plague was part of the cocktail of state formation because it demanded a powerful government to enforce quarantines.

But catastrophe was not the only driver of change. Government also grew more effective because of reformers from above and below. Their motives varied. Machiavelli and Hobbes wanted government simply to produce order. By the eighteenth century, Frederick the Great of Prussia sought to bring Enlightenment rationalism to bear on politics. In the nineteenth century, Napoleon was determined to unify Europe under a modern code of laws. Britain's Northcote-Trevelyan reforms created the permanent and apolitical British civil service that was copied across the world. The Chartists, socialists, and liberals all agitated to open up politics in various ways but all with the hope of empowering people based less on their position in the social order and more on their talent or need. The places that began these kinds of reforms early and saw them to their successful conclusion, mostly in Northern Europe, have maintained a long tradition of effective government across various political and ideological systems through the centuries. Even under communism, East Germany was always more efficient than the rest of Eastern Europe.

Non-Western countries did not modernize as rapidly, though some, especially in Asia, began to do so in the late nineteenth century. Most copied certain Western institutions and practices and—combined with their long traditions of merit-based exams and bureaucracy—created effective states. This is true of Japan, South Korea, and, decades later, China. Japan consciously copied the Prussian bureaucracy during its nineteenth-century modernization and for generations was the most effective government in Asia. In Latin America, Chile stands out from the other countries in the region for its deeply rooted, well-functioning government, which later on helped produce sustained economic growth. (The reasons for this "Chilean exceptionalism" are much debated, probably a mix of culture, leadership, and luck.) Singapore is the model example of this phenomenon—drawing on its cultural roots for social cohesion, the mandarin tradition of an elite bureaucracy, and the British legacy for more open and transparent systems (though still under a somewhat authoritarian framework). It also benefited from highly disciplined and focused leadership. Today Singapore is often ranked as the most effective government in the world.

AMERICAN EXCEPTIONALISM

And then there is America, which has long charted its own course. Was this exceptionalism the cause of the country's inability to tackle Covid-19? Does that failure shed light on broader weaknesses of the world's most powerful country? It certainly highlights a specific American vulnerability. The United States has always had a deep anti-statist tradition, which began with the ideas and practices of its first English settlers. Insulated from Europe's conflicts, the thirteen colonies never faced the pressure to strengthen their states for a war footing. They fought for independence from an empire ostensibly over the issue of the power of government to tax. As a result, America began its national experiment with a central government so weak that it collapsed in ten years. The new constitution, adopted in 1789, gave more powers to the federal government but still constrained it in many ways. Even a century later, when America was exploding with economic growth and industrialization, it had a small state. The president was weak, Congress rarely acted in unison, federal income taxes were unconstitutional, and the military was puny compared with those of European rivals.

Reformers could see that the only way to modernize America was to create a strong and efficient national state. But until the Civil War, efforts were limited: the country was paralyzed by the question of slavery and its potential expansion. After the war, a national economy arose and with it the need for national government, and one more professional in nature. In 1883, Congress required that many positions within the federal government be given on the basis of merit, doing away with the system of patronage that had dominated the political system. One reformer, a young scholar, Woodrow Wilson, went a step further, arguing that as America industrialized, the states would yield power to Washington and in that city, the presidency would inevitably become the most powerful branch. He expressed frustration with Congress's foot-dragging, infighting, and "petty barons," lamenting that the American constitutional structure has "no one supreme, ultimate head . . . which can decide at once and with conclusive authority what shall be done." Decades later, as president, Wilson expanded the power of the federal government, which was now breaking up trusts, taxing income, and intervening in labor disputes. (Wilson, it must be said, was also an unabashed racist, and he pointedly did not use this power to improve the plight of Black people.) His predecessor Theodore Roosevelt had also favored a stronger state that could regulate the excesses of big business. For all these reforms, however, the United States entered the industrial world with a preindustrial state.

The seismic shift came with Franklin Roosevelt. Roosevelt's predecessor, Herbert Hoover, had been deeply suspicious of government intervention in the economy and, as a result, led a passive response to the Great Depression. Roosevelt's strategy was different: Try everything. One of his chief advisors, Rex Tugwell, framed the approach in more consciously ideological terms. The goal of the New Deal reforms, he said, was to replace the laissez-faire maxim of "competition and conflict" with one of "coordination and control." Under Roosevelt, the president became the undisputed head of government—and FDR, far more than any other president, became the architect of modern America. Virtually every task that American government handles today can find its roots in the Roosevelt era. But even during his administration, there was pushback. The Southern states always resisted the encroachment of Washington, for fear that it would mean the end of the Jim Crow laws. They were right, as it was the power of the federal government that eventually did away with segregation.

America's statist experiment was relatively brief, about fifty years—most of it, it should be noted, marked by roaring economic growth, rising productivity, and high levels of entrepreneurship. The Roosevelt revolution ended with the presidency of Ronald Reagan, who famously said, "Government is not the solution to our problem. Government is the problem." And he said it in 1981, in the midst of what was then the worst recession since the 1930s. In other words, Reagan was dismissing the role government might play even in a calamitous crisis. Although he actually increased federal spending, the numbers are deceptive. The Defense Department and large entitlement programs like Social Security and Medicare held steady or grew during his tenure, but most everything else shrank. In the 1950s, federal civilian employees made up more than 5% of total employment. That figure has now dropped below 2%, despite a population that is twice as large and an inflation-adjusted GDP that is seven times as large. Government investments in science, technology, and infrastructure have slumped sharply from their levels in the 1950s. Twenty-first-century America is living off that old capital.

Today, the United States has fewer government officials per capita than most other advanced democracies. Public service is no longer the prestigious career it once was. Hiring freezes and budget cuts have had their effect. As a Brookings analysis has pointed out, "one third [of the federal workforce] will be eligible to retire between now and 2025, and only 6% of federal employees are under 30 years old." From Reagan onward, people have tended to assume that government causes more problems than it solves, that all federal agencies are bloated, and that most tasks are best handled by the private sector. Politicians on the right often used the phrase "starving the beast" to describe their strategy toward the government. The anti-tax crusader Grover Norquist put it in even more pungent terms: "I don't want to abolish government. I simply want to reduce it to the size where I can drag it into the bathroom and drown it in the bathtub." Steve Bannon, the ideologist of the Trump revolution, made clear that one of his central goals was the "deconstruction of the administrative state." For four decades, America has largely been run by people who openly pledge to destroy the very government they lead. Is it any wonder that they have succeeded?

To these factors, add American federalism. Many of America's dysfunctions are multiplied because they are replicated at the state and local levels. The creation of a national strategy for the pandemic, for example, was complicated by the existence of 2,684 state, local, and tribal health departments, each jealously guarding its independence. To make matters even messier, the US has 90,126 units of state and local government, many of which were tasked with devising their own rules on mask-wearing and public gatherings. Unemployment payments were similarly delayed by the many varying state requirements. We like to celebrate American federalism. And it does allow for useful and important experiments; what Louis Brandeis called "laboratories of democracy." States compete against each other for investment and workers, which can spur growth. But this patchwork of authority is a nightmare when tackling a disease that knows no borders. The fragmentation of standards is especially acute when handling Covid-19 tests. Results are reported via a bewildering mishmash of old and new technology—by phone, data feed, email, snail mail, and even fax, producing mountains of paper that leave out essential patient data. (It is a far cry from Taiwan's system of "health cards," which link up with a single database for all relevant medical information.) Beyond the pandemic, the federal system has hampered American efforts to create uniform access to health care and voting. It has made something like police reform dependent on the actions of 18,000 separate police departments across the country. It has contributed to the paralysis and gridlock in government. Some countries with deep traditions of consensual government and strong social capital—Germany, Switzerland, and the Netherlands most prominently—have managed decentralized government well. In the United States, that has rarely been achieved.

HOW TO BUILD A BETTER BUREAUCRACY

To understand how a healthy distrust of government can turn into toxic cynicism, look across the Atlantic. Britain has historically had a strong, effective, and open government at every level, though with a robust anti-statist tradition of its own. In general, it has shared much of the historical development and strengths of the Netherlands and the Nordic countries, with strong political institutions and well-regulated markets. Its imperial administrative and legal systems were the envy of other European powers. Scholars have often noted that the majority of politically stable democracies in the developing world are former British colonies, a legacy of British institutions and culture. Singapore's founding father, Lee Kuan Yew, considered the British tradition of effective, clean bureaucracy to be one of the key reasons for his city-state's success, despite other onerous aspects of colonial rule. And yet, Britain has adopted the same anti-government ideology as the United States since the 1980s. It, too, has starved its domestic agencies in the name of efficiency and, in Boris Johnson, is run by a populist leader who scorns experts and views beureaucrats with great skepticism. His government, presiding over a state hollowed out by austerity, fared unusually poorly in its initial battle against Covid-19, far worse than Northern Europe did. By contrast, Greece, a young and still-developing democracy, with a legendarily dysfunctional bureaucracy, handled the pandemic exceptionally well. Why? It was led by an able, technocratic leader who believed in science and good management. Sometimes the tone from the top makes all the difference.

The assault on good government has come not only from the Right. Over the years, left-wing politicians have added layers upon layers of bureaucracy and regulation. One scholar who has long studied this topic, Paul Light, notes that under President John F. Kennedy, the cabinet departments had seventeen "layers" of appointees in their hierarchies. By the time Trump took office, there were a staggering seventy-one of them. Most of these meddlesome mandates were designed for some worthwhile purpose. The Food and Drug Administration's cumbersome rules and bureaucratic checks have good intentions behind them. But they accumulate into hundreds of requirements, often at cross purposes with each other, making speed and efficiency an impossible dream. Every time an abuse of power is discovered, a new, additional set of rules is put into place. Often there are separate sets of rules at the federal, state, and local levels, which must all be dutifully followed. Government agencies must pass every project through stringent environmental and labor reviews, and all kinds of other objectives must be addressed. Officials have little discretion; for example, they are often pressured to take the lowest bid for a tender, no matter if they think the work will be shoddy and delayed. Congress loves to micromanage agencies and rarely wants to grant them the independence and flexibility that are routine in places like Germany, Japan, and South Korea. In fact, people who work across many Western countries are often struck by the fact that in laissez-faire America, there is far more red tape than in supposedly statist countries like Canada, Denmark, and Germany. Whatever the size of their states, those countries believe in creating independent agencies, giving technocrats power and autonomy, and ensuring that the system works effectively. There is pride in good government.

The technology entrepreneur Marc Andreessen responded to the pandemic of 2020 with a long blog post declaring, "It's time to build." He begins with the failure of American government during the pandemic but goes well beyond it, asking why the United States can no longer imagine and execute large projects—building more housing and better infrastructure, reviving manufacturing at home, expanding higher education to millions more people, and so on. He offers some theories: inertia, a lack of imagination, and the influence of established incumbents wary of competition. But the real reason is much deeper than that. America has become what Francis Fukuyama calls a "vetocracy." The system of checks and balances, replicated at every level of government, ensures that someone, somewhere can always block any positive action. The United States has become a nation of naysayers.

Marc Dunkelman, a tenacious researcher, spent years digging into the history of efforts to renovate and rebuild Manhattan's Pennsylvania Station. The need is obvious. Penn Station is the second-most trafficked transit hub on the planet, handling more passengers every day than all three New York-area airports combined. It is also a monstrously ugly, poorly designed, badly maintained facility that would be an embarrassment were it a regional facility in a poor country, let alone the main transport hub for America's leading metropolis. Over the last thirty years, powerful politicians have championed a series of efforts to rebuild it and yet nothing substantive has happened. Dunkelman explains that in each effort, it turns out one group or interest found a way to derail the project. "In a dynamic where so many players can exercise a veto, it's nearly impossible to move a project forward," he writes. "No one today has the leverage to do what seems to be best for New York as a whole. And ultimately, government is rendered incompetent." This problem goes beyond Penn Station. One version of the vetocracy, NIMBYism—named for the rallying cry of those opposed to local construction, "not in my backyard"—hobbles worthwhile projects across the country. In California, it has stymied new housing for decades, and greatly exacerbated the state's spiraling cost of living, which forces hundreds of thousands of workers to commute for hours to get to work.

America is, in its DNA, an anti-statist country. The Right comes at it by defunding government. The Left does it by encumbering it with so many rules and requirements that it has a similar dysfunctional effect. As the political theorist Samuel Huntington once explained, power in America is not divided, as is often said, but rather shared and contested, so that you need broad agreement and compromise to get anything done. It is possible to overcome this dilemma, but it takes skillful and persistent leadership, on the scale of a Roosevelt or a Johnson. It also takes, for the most part, a single party in control. The writer Ezra Klein has observed that during those years when government seemed to function and things got done— say, the 1930s to the 1960s—one party often held the White House and both houses of Congress, and the parties encompassed many ideologies. Nowadays, neither party has a lock on political power and both brook less internal dissent, which means that everything becomes partisan and most efforts end in stalemate. That, in turn, reinforces the deep anti-statism at the heart of American political culture. Having voted in ways that ensure gridlock, Americans point to that very gridlock and despair that any good can come from Washington.

Covid-19 has changed some of this, accelerating trends that were already afoot. Trump has no ideological commitment to laissez-faire economics and eagerly signed off on a $2 trillion stimulus. His party now supports tariffs, mercantilism, restrictions on immigration, and massive federal spending to cushion the blow of economic downturns. Could this mark the beginning of a new attitude toward government? The arch-conservative Missouri senator Josh Hawley has proposed a Denmark-style plan to reimburse employers 80% of their payroll, a remarkable turnaround that, in the writer James Traub's words, "removed the mark of the devil from the Nordic model." It is not that surprising that Hawley, despite being far right on social issues, is comfortable with spending. After all, his hero, and the subject of a 2008 biography he wrote, was the Republican leader of the Progressive Era: Theodore Roosevelt. But within much of the Republican Party, anti-statism remains powerful and virulent, and in some ways has become nastier and more conspiratorial. Armed protesters in Michigan who were fed up with public-health restrictions occupied the statehouse and forced the legislature to adjourn. Similar groups in Ohio hounded the state health director into stepping down. Conspiracy theories about the "deep state" abound, often encouraged by President Trump. In some quarters on the right, the case against government has become a dark and desperate effort to rage against the tides of demography and culture, against modernity itself.

Early on, the United States laid the foundations for a uniquely powerful society and dynamic economy with a limited state, though one that, given its British origins, functioned effectively. It ensured that liberty flourished. In the twentieth century, progressive reformers created a modern government that helped America weather the Great Depression and fight World War II and the Cold War, all while rising to economic supremacy. But that state, battered and creaky, needs renovation and improvement for the twenty-first century. Look around. There are now many liberal democracies that are just as free as America but with governments that are far more competent. In tackling the pressing challenges of our time—infrastructure, job training, climate change, public health—there is ample evidence that American government has been failing for a generation. Covid-19 is only the latest, though perhaps the most serious, of many warnings.

I am not a fan of big government. I grew up in India, a country with a large, ambitious state that was a model of incompetence and inefficiency. It destroyed India's prospects for decades and still holds the country back. Simply enlarging the size of government does little to solve societal problems. Good government is about limited power but clear lines of authority. It is about giving officials autonomy, discretion, and the ability to exercise their own judgment. It requires recruiting bright, devoted people who are inspired by the chance to serve their country and earn respect for doing it. This is not something that can be created overnight, but it can be done. Taiwan and South Korea were not born with good government. On the contrary, they began as corrupt dictatorships but they developed their own models over decades, learning from others. In fact this is a common trait of almost all the countries that handled the pandemic well—they learned from history. They saw that capitalism worked and adapted it to their own societies. Many of them embraced the latest technologies so that they could leapfrog stages of development. Most recently, some experienced SARS and MERS, learning from those epidemics, preparing well for the next outbreak. But in general, their mindset has been to look around and find best practices to emulate. Historically these countries often learned from the United States.

Over the last few decades, America's extraordinary position of power has shielded it from the consequences of a government that consistently executes badly. So many of America's recent efforts—from the occupation of Iraq to the simple extension of subway lines—have been costly disasters. For decades now, compared with citizens of other advanced countries, Americans have put up with a government that is second-rate at all levels. The country can compensate. Washington has the world's reserve currency and can print trillions of dollars. It still boasts the largest military on the planet. America has a huge tech industry, dominating the digital world. The country's vast internal market means that it can ignore many of the pressures of trade and external competition. But these are crutches. They prop up the country, allowing it to escape penalties, never really experiencing the true costs of its mistakes—until now.

America is successful enough never to collapse, but it could slowly edge downward, muddling along with a haphazard mix of dynamic economics and dysfunctional politics. While American military power might still outrank all others, the lives of average Americans would continue to slip behind, oblivious to the improvements abroad. The country could become more parochial and less global, losing influence and innovation, all the while consoling itself with fantasies that it is utterly exceptional. For many decades, the world needed to learn from America. But now America needs to learn from the world. And what it most needs to learn about is government— not big or small but good government.

LESSON THREE

Markets Are Not Enough

THE *FINANCIAL TIMES* is a paper for the elite. Founded in London in 1888, its inaugural issue promised to be the friend of "the honest financier, the bona fide investor, the respectable broker, the genuine director, [and] the legitimate speculator." Through world wars and depression, fascism and socialism, it has been a consistent advocate of capitalism. It supported the free-market reforms of Margaret Thatcher and Ronald Reagan that ushered in the economic era we live in today, as well as the broad expansion of free trade that has brought virtually every country on the planet into a single world economy. Core to its identity is the belief that most problems in the world can be solved by more open markets and greater liberalization.

So the *FT*'s readers must have been startled on April 3,

2020, when they opened the newspaper to a lead editorial that broke with much of its orthodoxy. The short essay began by noting that the coronavirus pandemic would call on people to make collective sacrifices, and that "to demand collective sacrifice you must offer a social contract that benefits everyone." But, it continued, "today's crisis is laying bare how far many rich societies fall short of this ideal." It declared a need for "radical reforms—reversing the prevailing policy direction of the last four decades. . . . Governments will have to accept a more active role in the economy. They must see public services as investments rather than liabilities, and look for ways to make labour markets less insecure. Redistribution will again be on the agenda; the privileges of the elderly and wealthy in question. Policies until recently considered eccentric, such as basic income and wealth taxes, will have to be in the mix."

These were strong words coming from a surprising place. But many in the Western world were already welcoming even more radical ideas. In America, for example, 43% of those surveyed in a May 2019 Gallup poll agreed "some form of socialism" would be good for the country. In 1942, only 25% did. There seemed to be a quiet revolution afoot. The country that defined itself by its unapologetic advocacy of capitalism now appeared to be increasingly embracing an ideology that it had fought against for most of the twentieth century. Covid-19 appears to have only accelerated this trend.

The Gallup poll marked a sharp shift from the previous four decades—particularly in the Anglo-American world, which had often defined the world's ideological landscape. The 1980s had been dominated by Reagan and Thatcher, who spearheaded a wave of free-market reforms in their countries that were emulated in some fashion across the world, even by their ideological opponents. For example, in 1981, French president François Mitterrand was elected as a committed socialist—but quickly abandoned most of his old leftist agenda in favor of austerity and tight money. In the 1990s, the rise of Bill Clinton and Tony Blair represented the Left's acceptance of the new capitalist consensus. Gerhard Schroeder, another left-wing leader, entered office in 1998 and presided over the most thorough market reforms of the German economy in decades. In 1991, India, which had long practiced socialism and protectionism, faced an economic crisis that forced it to liberalize. The next year, with Deng Xiaoping's "Southern Tour," China revived its stalled capitalist reforms.

The financial crisis of 2008 began the process of reevaluation—on both right and left. Steve Bannon argues that the seeds of Trump's takeover of the Republican Party were sowed by that crash. In the years since, the Right has veered away from its devotion to markets, instead espousing protectionism, subsidies, immigration controls, and cultural nationalism—ideas championed by Trump in the United States, Boris Johnson in the United Kingdom, and other populists around the world. On the left, meanwhile, two trendsetters have been Bernie Sanders and Jeremy Corbyn, both self-described "socialists." They have been joined by energetic newcomers on the political scene such as New York congresswoman Alexandria Ocasio-Cortez, who seems just as comfortable with the label. And in several polls, Americans between eighteen and twenty-nine show significantly higher support for socialism than their elders. In fact, in some surveys, less than half of them express support for capitalism. Does all this add up to a turn toward socialism?

On closer examination, the picture looks fuzzier. Pollsters have not consistently posed questions about capitalism versus socialism over the decades, so there is no clear trend line. It's true that during the Cold War, people professed greater hostility to socialism—but the explanation might lie in definitions. In those days, the term "socialism" was often used interchangeably with "communism," and frequently to describe the system practiced by the Soviet Union, the West's mortal foe—and a dictatorship. Many of the people who claim to support socialism today in fact have in mind something entirely different from what the term has meant in its historical origins.

The textbook definition of socialism is government ownership of the means of production—factories, farms, and enterprises. That was the plan pursued by the socialist politicians of the twentieth century, from India's Jawaharlal Nehru to Israel's David Ben-Gurion to Britain's Clement Attlee. In these countries, the state usually owned and ran the electricity, telephone, water, and gas utilities; airlines, trains, and bus services; coal, oil, and steel companies. These leaders implemented democratic versions of Lenin's vision of a socialist economy, one in which the state sat atop "the commanding heights" of the economy.

But when you ask what people mean by socialism now, it is not really that system at all. Today's self-professed socialists want greater government investment, new and expanded safety nets, a "Green New Deal" to address climate change, and higher taxes on the rich. Bernie Sanders himself makes clear his dream country is not Cuba but Denmark. You can see how amorphous the label is by the fact that Elizabeth Warren supports many of the same policies as Sanders, but has also called herself "a capitalist to my bones." Any program that can be described as both capitalist and socialist probably lies somewhere in between. And yet it says something that Sanders would campaign openly as a socialist and that young people do not run away from that label. Meanwhile, on the right, prominent politicians think nothing of proposing large government relief programs. Self-described libertarian tech entrepreneurs embrace the idea of a universal basic income to ensure that even if robots and software leave most people jobless, they won't be broke. Many taboos have been broken—and they have been broken because American capitalism itself is broken.

THE PENDULUM SWINGS

We often make the mistake of thinking that people support a political party because of deep-rooted agreement with its basic principles, values, and logic. In fact, most scholars who have studied this phenomenon have concluded that people tend to choose parties more as one would a social club. They support their chosen party for a mixture of reasons—chiefly a sense of belonging, affinity, and identity with others in it, some of which is based on class and ethnicity. As a result, their ideological commitment is often less pure than one might imagine. Consider how Republicans, who a few years ago identified as staunchly free-market, now enthusiastically support protectionism and closed borders. Tucker Carlson, the Fox News host most in tune with this shift, declared in a striking 2019 monologue, "Republican leaders will have to acknowledge that market capitalism is not a religion. . . . You'd have to be a fool to worship it. Our system was created by human beings for the benefit of human beings. We do not exist to serve markets. Just the opposite. Any economic system that weakens and destroys families is not worth having. A system like that is the enemy of a healthy society." Bernie Sanders could not have said it better.

Ideologies gain appeal because they seem to address the crucial problems of the moment. In the 1930s, capitalism had run aground, causing financial panic, collapse, and mass unemployment—and it seemed unable to right itself anytime soon. Along came Franklin Roosevelt, who let the government step in where the market was failing and got the country moving again. In the 1970s, as inflation took off and growth slowed, Western societies seemed to have fallen victim to excessive state intervention in the economy, embracing wage and price controls and other supposed remedies that only made things worse. As a result, there was an appetite for a fresh approach to open up the economy and unlock the potential of the private sector. In many Third World countries, likewise, state socialism had produced utter stagnation, and by the 1980s, the Reagan-Thatcher reforms seemed the way out. Now the pendulum has swung back, and there is a pervasive sense that markets alone cannot solve the widening inequality and rampant job insecurity that have been sparked by relentless technological change and foreign competition. These problems require government solutions.

Has the pandemic changed society's mood in ways that were not possible before? Previous shocks to the system occasioned a sense of foreboding and predictions of wholesale change—only to be met with cosmetic changes in policy. During the Asian financial crisis of the late 1990s, the economist Paul Krugman warned in a *Fortune* essay that unless Asian countries took drastic measures (like putting controls on their currency), "we could be looking at a true Depression scenario—the kind of slump that 60 years ago, devastated economies, destabilized governments, and eventually led to war." When the dot-com bubble deflated in 2000, wiping out $5 trillion in wealth, many predicted the end of the obsession with technology and the Internet. In the wake of the global financial crisis, Martin Wolf, the *FT*'s chief economics commentator, declared, "Another ideological god has failed," and Tim Geithner, the secretary of the treasury, promised, "Capitalism will be different." But after each crisis, the economy was patched up and we muddled along. Could we do so again?

It is certainly possible. But this pandemic has come along at a moment in history when there is much greater dissatisfaction with the economic system. Krugman, Wolf, and Geithner were all accurately describing the fragility of that system, pointing to cracks and worrying that one of them would cause the entire edifice to collapse. But despite their concerns, few structural repairs were ever undertaken. There was a pervasive sense that, in the phrase Margaret Thatcher famously used to shut down debate over free-market economics, "there is no alternative." She used the slogan so much that some of her cabinet colleagues began to call her "TINA."

That phrase captured the spirit of the times, an almost Marxist idea of historical inevitability—except that capitalism, rather than socialism, was the ideology lying at the "end of history." And it wasn't just Thatcher. Nearly every Western leader believed that global capitalism had become ubiquitous, like the air we breathe. You could not fight it, you simply had to accommodate yourself to it. The collapse of communism only strengthened this case. "We cannot stop global change," President Bill Clinton explained to the American people when signing the North American Free Trade Agreement into law in 1993. "We cannot repeal the international economic competition that is everywhere. We can only harness the energy to our benefit."

When Thomas Friedman's book *The Lexus and the Olive Tree* was published in 1999, capitalism was riding high. This was the era of the dot-com boom and the Washington Consensus, a set of free-market reforms that rich countries were prescribing to poorer ones. Friedman explained that most developing countries viewed the new formula for economic prosperity as a "golden straitjacket." The carefully thought-out reforms left little room for deviation, but if countries played by the rules and did what was asked of them, they would reap great rewards. In Friedman's formulation, with the straitjacket on, "your economy grows and your politics shrinks." But over the years, people have chafed at that straitjacket. More importantly, they have noticed that some countries did things differently and managed to get ahead anyway.

Take China, the fastest-growing economy on the planet over the last twenty years—indeed the fastest-growing major economy in history. That country followed its own particular mix of capitalism, state planning, openness, and dictatorship. Its economy grew, but so did its political controls. (The *New York Times*'s Nicholas Kristof described it as "Market-Leninism.") And in charting its own path, China has become the second-largest economy in the world, dominating traditional industries like steel and cement but also becoming a leading player in the world of computers, telecommunications, social media, and even artificial intelligence. Watching Beijing's rise, it's easy to see why many leaders around the world might think Margaret Thatcher was wrong. There is an alternative.

As important as China's successes have been America's failures. The liberation of markets over the last decades has produced growth and innovation but it has also produced an impoverished public sector, rising inequality, a trend toward monopolies, and a political system that has been bought by the rich and powerful. And many Americans have now seen these shortcomings laid bare during the pandemic. A weak, malfunctioning state, highly unequal access to health care, relief mechanisms that help people with capital and connections much more than those who work for their wages. The disillusionment began with the global financial crisis. The system broke, and the people who were punished seemed to be the most vulnerable, not the guiltiest. Those who were rewarded were disproportionately rich or connected. Twice in recent years, in 2008–9 and 2020, the federal government spent several trillion dollars to rescue large companies and prop up the assets of the richest Americans. And yet calls to spend a few billion on preschool or low-income housing are repeatedly met with grave concerns about the cost or the harmful effect of giving people handouts. (Why is that effect not a concern when the Federal Reserve provides support to those with stocks and bonds?) We have gotten used to an American capitalism that is now riddled with special rules and emergency exceptions. And yet we have been told that all's well. The system works fine.

PAY TO PLAY

At the start of the pandemic, the Norwegian University of Science and Technology made a Facebook post urging any of its students studying abroad to return home, adding, "especially if you are staying in a country with poorly developed health services and infrastructure and/or collective infrastructure, for example, the USA." The university later deleted the reference to America because it recognized it had made a gaffe—as the joke goes, it had accidentally told the truth.

By late March 2020, when Americans realized that the virus had hit hard, it should have been easy to ensure that every American would get a test instantly. After all, America spends almost twice as much per capita on health care as most other advanced countries. But the United States was desperately short on tests, and because American health care is organized as a for-profit enterprise, many people faced prohibitive costs even if a test was available. If you were rich and connected, you had no such problems. In mid-March, all the players on eight NBA teams were tested. Celebrities and politicians with no symptoms got tested, all while health-care workers had to wait for weeks, sometimes longer. The failure to test large numbers of vulnerable people left everyone unsafe.

The health-care system in the United States is a vast, complex, and expensive one, but it responds to market incentives. Facilities for testing and treatment are concentrated in wealthy areas, forcing people who live elsewhere to find their way to substandard facilities. Doctors must spend large amounts of time making the business end of their practice work, giving priority to the procedures that generate the most revenue. Hospitals are run like hotels, aiming to fill their beds and leave little spare capacity. Bill Budinger, a highly successful entrepreneur who is in his eighties now, reflected on the change in mentality. "I grew up when things were different, a time when profits were to be reasonable, not maximized," he recalled. "For hospitals, a high occupancy rate was a call to action. They would need more beds to cover possible emergencies. Now the objective is to trim beds to ensure high occupancy." Spare supplies, empty beds, extra staff—these were all inefficiencies that got weeded out over time.

The highly unequal access to health care is part of a larger dynamic of a "pay-to-play" society, in which everything has become dominated by the market. Hospital executives and university presidents are seen not as societal leaders but as CEOs, and are paid to behave like them as well. Professions like law, banking, and accounting used to be guided by principles that required that they not maximize profits if it came at the cost of sacrificing their independence and integrity. Once upon a time, these people would tell their clients *not* to do deals rather than eagerly lap up all business. Groups that served as gatekeepers and mediators in society and the economy have become profit-driven enterprises selling their seals of good housekeeping to anyone who will pay—no matter the conflicts of interest or broader risks. Before the 2008 financial crisis, the rating agencies—supposedly independent and impartial— eagerly put their stamps of approval on shoddy, risky financial products because they were paid handsomely to do so.

Perhaps most important, politics itself has been taken over by markets. In a 1993 essay, the political scientist Robert A. Dahl explained why almost all democratic countries had chosen not to organize themselves as purely market-driven but instead left a large role for the state. He pointed out that there were many things in society that one would want to insulate from market forces—politicians' and citizens' votes, for example. But even those have now become a tradable good, with money dominating politics to the extent that the rich— companies and people—can effectively buy votes, writing and rewriting rules to suit them.

Thomas Philippon, a French economist, arrived in America in the 1980s, amazed by how competitive the economy was, offering an array of choices in products—from airline tickets to banking to phone services—at low prices. Today, however, it is Europe that has the cheaper goods and services and a greater variety of them. Over the last twenty years, Europe broadened its offerings while the United States narrowed them. Philippon's research shows that some of the forces behind this shift are structural—in the digital economy, any given market tends to be dominated by one or two players, which then have the ability to raise prices. But a crucial cause, his scholarship revealed, is industries' political power. Companies are able to write the rules in a way that shuts out competition and keeps their profits high.

I have always appreciated the power of markets, perhaps because I grew up in sluggish, socialist India. They are incredibly dynamic and can transform stagnant societies. In India and China, they have lifted hundreds of millions of people out of poverty. They produce extraordinary innovations and give people from all backgrounds a chance to better their lives. But free markets also have flaws. Because they offer the possibility to create so much wealth and inequality, people find ways to subvert the market itself. This problem may be an inevitable consequence of the workings of capitalism. Markets always generate unequal returns. And as Peter Thiel, the Silicon Valley venture capitalist, has admitted, every company's goal is to be a monopoly. It then follows that successful companies will try to use their resources to eliminate the competition. They can be blocked in their attempts only if the political system can monitor them, and to do so, it must have some insulation from business. That means curbs on private spending for elections and a bureaucracy that is truly independent. That combination—real open markets and a strong state—is a tough balancing act. Perhaps it is not surprising that, as Philippon shows, the European Union does a better job at enforcing open competition than America. The "Eurocrats" in Brussels might be arrogant and officious, but they do not sell waivers to regulations in return for campaign contributions.

There is a larger critique of markets, though, that goes beyond economics. Market-centric thinking has invaded every area of human life, leaving little space for other values like fairness, equality, or intrinsic value. People across the world woke up during this pandemic to a realization that should have dawned on them much earlier—that people should be honored for the work they do, even when it does not bring great material rewards. We have watched health-care workers put themselves in harm's way to fulfill their fundamental mission of healing others. We have seen people pack themselves onto buses and trains to keep the lights on, the water flowing, the garbage picked up, and the grocery stores stocked—all so others can work from home. This should remind us to value the many people whose jobs do not generate huge incomes but are worthwhile, essential, even noble—from scholars and teachers to janitors and street cleaners. The market may not reward them, but we should respect them.

THE GREAT DANES

Americans, not having large government programs as supports and buffers, have always been taught to rely on themselves to achieve "the American Dream." If there is an iconic idea at the heart of the country, it is that America is a place where anyone can make it, where children grow up expecting to do better than their parents, where a person from any background can become president, or even better, a billionaire. America still has plenty of spectacular examples of such success stories, from Barack Obama to Steve Jobs. But they turn out to be brilliant exceptions, not representative of the fate of most Americans.

The studies on this topic are so numerous and convincing that even the staunchly conservative *National Review* published an essay that concluded, "What is clear is that in at least one regard American mobility is exceptional . . . where we stand out is in our limited upward mobility from the bottom." A Stanford study set out to quantify the American Dream, defining it as "the probability that a child born to parents in the bottom fifth of the income distribution makes the leap all the way to the top fifth of the income distribution." The aggregate data shows that low-income Americans have a 7.5% chance of moving that far up the economic ladder, compared to 11.7% for low-income Danes and 13.5% for Canadians—almost double the chance of their Americans counterparts.

One of the traditional American responses to these comparisons has been that the United States faces the unique challenge of absorbing large numbers of poor immigrants. But in that respect America is no longer unique. Many European countries have large numbers of immigrants, and Canada has an even larger percentage of its population that is foreign-born—22%, compared to 14% in the United States. And while these other countries have all struggled to integrate immigrants, they have still been able to keep offering their residents—of all backgrounds and creeds—a way to move up the escalator of opportunity and income.

The American Dream, in other words, is alive and well, just not in America. In his ambitious two-volume work, *Political Order and Political Decay*, Francis Fukuyama writes that the fundamental question for every human society is simple: How do you get to Denmark? "By this I mean less the actual country

Denmark," he writes, "than an imagined society that is prosperous, democratic, secure, and well governed, and experiences low levels of corruption." Fukuyama is speaking more of a political than an economic system, but the two are deeply connected. Indeed, one reinforces the other. Denmark is successful politically because it is successful economically—and vice versa.

Denmark is somewhat different from what its admirers and detractors imagine. Bernie Sanders sees it as a socialist paradise, repeatedly referring to it as an example of the type of system he wants to emulate. This led the prime minister of the country to publicly contradict Sanders. "Denmark is far from a socialist, planned economy. Denmark is a market economy," Lars Løkke Rasmussen explained in 2015. The facts bear him out. Denmark ranks higher than the United States on the free-market Heritage Foundation's Index of Economic Freedom (eighth for Denmark, seventeenth for the US). In general, Denmark, like most Northern European countries, has an open, low-tariff, competitive economy. In some ways it better incentivizes the accumulation of capital than America does, with lower taxes on capital gains and inheritance (the estate tax is 15% in Denmark and zero in Sweden and Norway). Years ago, I met Poul Nyrup Rasmussen, who enacted many reforms in Denmark as the country's prime minister in the 1990s, creating what is now called the "flexicurity" model. He emphasized that the first half of the term was key: ensuring employers had the flexibility to hire and fire workers easily, without excessive regulation or litigation, in an economy that's open to the world and competitive—but all within a system that provides the security of a generous safety net.

What distinguishes Northern European countries from the United States are their high levels of general taxation and redistribution. In other words, the system is designed to make it easy to generate wealth through free markets and free trade. Then, the state collects much of that wealth and spends it to ensure that its citizens have equal and abundant opportunities. Denmark's taxes add up to 45% of its GDP, whereas in the United States the figure is 24%. And Denmark doesn't just tax the rich. Like other European countries, Denmark collects a large part of its revenues from a national sales tax. Its sales tax rate is 25%, in line with the European Union's overall average of 20%. In the United States, state sales taxes average just 7%. Denmark's consumption taxes on everything from beer to eggs to smartphones naturally fall more heavily on the poor, who spend a larger share of their income on purchases. This regressive system of taxation is more than made up for, however, by the fact that government expenditures and programs disproportionately help the poor and lower middle class. One additional advantage of a commonly shared tax burden is greater solidarity: everyone supports the government programs because they feel that everyone has contributed to them.

Imagine that you're an average family. You and your spouse have a child, and make the mean household income. You could choose to live in either America or Denmark. In high-tax Denmark, your disposable income after taxes and transfers would be around $15,000 lower than in the States. But in return for your higher tax bill, you would get universal health care (one with better outcomes than in the US), free education right up through the best graduate schools, worker retraining programs on which the state spends seventeen times more as a percentage of GDP than what is spent in America, as well as high-quality infrastructure, mass transit, and many beautiful public parks and other spaces. Danes also enjoy some 550 more hours of leisure time a year than Americans do. If the choice were put this way—you can take the extra $15,000 but have to work longer hours, take fewer vacation days, and fend for yourself on health care, education, retraining, and transport—I think most Americans would choose the Danish model. More than just the free education and nice trains, the overwhelming advantage of Nordic flexicurity is that it embraces the dynamism at the heart of the modern, globalized world and yet eases the anxieties it produces. And these anxieties, of course, have reached new heights amid the pandemic.

It's easy to understand why people get jittery these days. An open world of fast-moving markets and technological change is scary. One answer is to close it down. Populists like Donald Trump want to keep out immigrants, restrict the flow of goods and services, and somehow preserve in amber the existing culture of their nation. They seek a return to some of the ways of the past—usually an imagined time of greatness. The reality is, there was never a Garden of Eden, and the periods that people recall nostalgically were actually far more difficult than is remembered. Think of what life was like in the 1950s if you were a woman or a minority or gay. (And life was no picnic even for white men working as steelworkers and coal miners.) The path to making America—or any country— great again is to move forward, not backward.

We cannot close down the world. We cannot—nor should

we—stop emerging powers from growing nor prevent technological progress. We can only navigate through the times and
trends we face, and do it poorly or well. We will face tough economic headwinds in the future. New trends—pandemic fears
and protectionism—will compound deeper structural shifts
like demographic decline and "secular stagnation," so that
growth, at least in the developed world, is likely to stay slow for
the foreseeable future. But there are ways to encourage dynamism and also spread opportunities around to more people.

Regulations, properly tailored, can ensure that competition is free and fair. Tax policies can be geared to help workers more and capital less. The government must get back to
making major investments in science and technology. Education and retraining also need more funding, which should go
hand in hand with restructuring these government programs
to minimize bureaucracy and focus on the goal—providing
the best education. The challenge is to make it possible for
citizens to face that environment of global competition and
technological dynamism *armed*—with the tools, training, and
safety nets that will allow them to flourish. In staying open to
the world and yet arming its people, the countries of Northern
Europe, such as Denmark, have found a path that is dynamic,
democratic, secure, and just. They understood that markets
were amazingly powerful, yet not sufficient; that they need
supports and buffers and supplements. We should all adapt
their best practices to our own national realities. There really
is no alternative.

People Should Listen to the Experts— and Experts Should Listen to the People

I N MARCH 2016, with Donald Trump poised to secure the Republican nomination, he was asked which foreign policy experts he was consulting with. "I'm speaking with myself, number one, because I have a very good brain," he said. "My primary consultant is myself, and I have a good instinct for this stuff." He later explained why he didn't rely on experts. "The experts are terrible," he said. "Look at the mess we're in with all these experts that we have." A couple of months later, the British politician Michael Gove was quizzed about his advocacy for Brexit and asked to name a few economists who supported his view that leaving the European Union would be good for business. His response: "People in this country have had enough of experts."

Now that the world has experienced a global pandemic, it

should have become painfully clear that people need to listen to experts. But that is not exactly how things have worked out. To be sure, in many countries, particularly in East Asia, there was a strong, instinctive deference to authority, especially scientific authority. Taiwan's near-flawless response was overseen by its vice president, a Johns Hopkins-educated epidemiologist who previously steered Taiwan through the SARS epidemic as health minister. In Germany, with former scientist Angela Merkel at the helm, the approach was particularly sober and fact-based. The Greek prime minister, when asked what explained his country's success at handling the outbreak, answered, "We listened to the experts."

But there were also places where, after an initial period of deference, people questioned the recommendations of medical professionals and, in some cases, refused to comply with them. In Brazil, this attitude was encouraged by the country's president, Jair Bolsonaro, who dismissed Covid-19 as a "measly cold" and railed against medical experts' advice on how to slow the pandemic. He fired one health minister and caused his replacement to resign. Despite government regulations, he refused to wear a mask, leading a Brazilian judge to order him to wear one. Bolsonaro ended up a victim of his own careless attitude: he announced in July 2020 that he had tested positive for the coronavirus. Boris Johnson conspicuously did not socially distance in the early stages of the outbreak, and ended up in the ICU with Covid-19. In Mexico, President Andrés Manuel López Obrador encouraged people to go out, attend rallies, shake hands, and hug—all in direct contradiction of his own public health officials. López Obrador urged Mexicans to move on with their lives, and to be happy and optimistic, as if positive thinking could cure the virus. Some American governors insisted on fully reopening their states despite experts' warning that without good testing and mask-wearing mandates, the infection would spread rapidly—which it then did.

For his part, Trump tweeted his support for right-wing movements to "LIBERATE" states suffering from the apparent tyranny of Democratic governors, who were enforcing the very lockdowns that Trump's administration recommended. In fact, Donald Trump consistently undermined his own experts' guidance. For months on end he refused to wear a mask publicly, signaling that in his view, face-covering was for weak liberals. He recommended his own dubious medical treatments and cures, most of which were directly contradicted by the US government's public health officials. He even went so far as to raise the possibility of injecting cleaning products into people, prompting the makers of Lysol to warn customers not to drink bleach. Trump touted the malaria drug hydroxychloroquine, which he called a "game-changer," and announced in May 2020 that he had been taking it for more than a week, despite FDA warnings that it may cause fatal arrhythmia. "I feel good about it," he said. "That's all it is. Just a feeling. You know, I'm a smart guy. I feel good about it." It was life imitating art, mirroring what the comedian Stephen Colbert called "truthiness" in the first episode of *The Colbert Report*. "Who's *Britannica* to tell me the Panama Canal was finished in 1914?" his character asked. "If I wanna say it happened in 1941, that's my right. I don't trust books—they're all fact, no heart . . . Face it, folks, we are a divided nation . . . divided between those who think with their head and those who know with their heart . . . Because that's where the truth comes from, ladies and gentlemen—the gut."

HOW SCIENCE WORKS

For those of us watching in horror at these abject displays of know-nothingism, the solution seemed obvious: Just follow the science. But what does science tell us? Dr. Anthony Fauci, the US government's top infectious disease expert, initially downplayed the dangers of the novel coronavirus, saying in late January, "It's a very, very low risk to the United States. . . . It isn't something the American public needs to worry about or be frightened about." A few days later, Alex Azar, the secretary of health and human services, also reflected the prevailing view of government public health officials when he said, "The risk of infection for Americans remains low." This mirrored the conclusions of the World Health Organization, which also downplayed the chances of a pandemic until the end of January. The US Centers for Disease Control and Prevention initially recommended that people to stay indoors and not use masks and then, months later, reversed itself and urged the opposite. Some countries locked down fully, while others—using their own epidemiologists and models—did not. What should we make of all this?

The reality is that science does not yield one simple answer, especially not with a new phenomenon like the coronavirus. Fauci, the head of the National Institute of Allergy and Infectious Diseases, came to a reasonable conclusion given the initial evidence. Many scientists at first believed that the coronavirus was not a significant danger—but everyone was making quick judgments with little data. The novel coronavirus was just that, novel. Its transmission rates and lethality remained unclear. As the evidence changed, Fauci and others changed their minds. This is normal. No expert is infallible. Some of the early models' projections for Covid-related hospitalization rates were far too high, causing hospitals to stop performing non-urgent care in order to conserve beds. This seems to have dissuaded many non-Covid patients from going to the emergency room under the mistaken notion that they would not get care—not to mention worries over contracting the virus at an overwhelmed hospital. Some hospital systems saw a 50% drop in heart attack patients, which means many people likely died at home, unnecessarily. Later estimates of hospitalization rates proved more accurate.

We tend to think of science as providing a single, definitive answer, but that isn't really how it works. Science is, above all, a method of inquiry, a process of posing questions and rigorously testing these hypotheses. With new and better data, we arrive at new and better conclusions. Scientists still have many important questions about Covid-19, and they will be answered—but over the next few years, not months. There are certain fields of study (climate change, for instance) in which experts have researched the topic for decades, collected mountains of data, published numerous peer-reviewed studies, and arrived at a consensus—though almost always a provisional one that can be revised or even overturned. A strong consensus holds for much of the science we learned in school.

Covid-19 is entirely different. When public health officials like Fauci had to make immediate judgment calls about
how seriously to take the virus, it had existed for barely two
months and had surfaced in just a few countries. Within a few
weeks, more information became available, and now there is
a considerable body of research on the topic that grows by
the month. But in the initial stages of an epidemic, doctors
and scientists are like generals immersed in war. They have
incomplete and often erroneous information. Even worse,
they know this. And yet they have to make huge, consequential
judgments—well before much clarity is achieved.

Operating in the fog of a pandemic creates a dilemma.
In the early stages of the crisis, some scientists felt the need
to speak more boldly than the evidence at hand warranted.
Sometimes this was done to encourage people to take their
guidelines seriously. That approach might have short-term
benefits, but it has a long-term drawback that is dangerous.
If predictions prove to be off the mark or if new data changes
the picture, that undermines the authority and integrity of
these experts and of science more generally. We have seen
this before with prior epidemics. For example, Neil Ferguson—the epidemiologist whose research shaped the British
lockdown—had predicted in 2009 that swine flu could kill
65,000 in Britain, panicking politicians like Boris Johnson,
then serving as mayor of London. In the end, some 450 Britons died from H1N1. But the damage from the faulty model
was done. A decade later, with Johnson in the prime minister's
office, the memory of this overblown panic may have contributed to his delayed and botched Covid-19 response. Now,

other politicians who don't want to listen to the experts point to a statement here or there, or produce their own "experts" to vindicate the course of action they want to follow.

What, then, is the best course for the real experts? To help the public understand how their field works, in particular how science works. Most Americans think of science by its endpoints—a discovery or breakthrough or invention. They look at dazzling pictures of galaxies and read of miracle drugs. But science is really all about the process of learning and discovering, with many failures and disappointments. The Harvard scholar Steven Pinker warned in an April 2020 interview that scientists' "earned authority" may be breaking down, so that much of the public may "think that those people in the white coats are just another priesthood." Pinker called on advocates of science to start "lifting the hood and showing how it works," through a process of "open debate and attempts at falsification." When announcing her plans for reopening Germany, Angela Merkel took to national television to give a science lesson. The virus was reproducing at a rate of 1, she explained, which meant that each infected person was infecting one other person before recovering—and thus not increasing the net numbers infected. This gave her cautious optimism about reopening. But the country was on "thin ice." If that reproductive rate grew to even 1.1 or 1.2, the country's health-care system would soon be overwhelmed and the lockdowns would have to be reinstated. Merkel was letting the public understand the key measure that would determine her decisions. It has not been the case that simply imposing the harshest possible lockdowns produced the best

results. Many of the governments that handled Covid-19 suc-
cessfully, as in Germany, South Korea, and Taiwan, were able to
do so with relatively brief or partial lockdowns, combined with
widespread testing and tracing.

The public can grasp nuance if it is presented honestly. But
too often, elites have a patronizing attitude toward laypeople.
Western experts at first overlooked the mounting evidence
that in East Asian countries "universal masking" was a key
component of their successful response. Even if the data on
their efficacy was not entirely clear, the public narrative about
mask-wearing from the US government was fundamentally
disingenuous. Officials actively discouraged the use of masks,
claiming both that they were ineffective at protecting ordinary people and that they should be reserved for doctors and
nurses. But if the true purpose was to avoid the hoarding of
surgical masks, couldn't the government at least have encouraged the public to make simple cloth masks at home, when no
more was needed than a T-shirt and scissors? Officials like
the US surgeon general later admitted they had feared the
public would engage in panic buying and hoarding masks,
exacerbating the shortage for doctors and nurses—evidently
they saw it as too complicated to explain to people that certain
kinds of masks should be saved for health-care workers while
other kinds were fine to wear.

This tradition goes back decades. In his memoirs, Secretary of State Dean Acheson explained why, in the early days
of the Cold War, he had to scare the American public about
worldwide Soviet expansionism. His justification is dripping
with condescension:

Qualification must give way to simplicity of statement, nicety
and nuance to bluntness, almost brutality, in carrying home
a point. . . . In the State Department we used to discuss how
much time that mythical "average American citizen" put in
each day listening, reading, and arguing about the world outside his own country. Assuming a man or woman with a fair
education, a family, and a job in or out of the house, it seemed
to us that ten minutes a day would be a high average. If this
were anywhere near right, points to be understandable had to
be clear.

Acheson understood the complexity of the struggle against
the Soviet Union. But in making his case to the public "clearer
than truth," as he put it, he and other officials conjured up an
existential and global danger to the United States that had to
be countered everywhere, from Latin America to Indochina,
and by any means necessary, from coups to covert wars. More
nuance might have prevented much bloodshed.

More explanation from experts would help—and so would
less hypocrisy. The United Kingdom provides two striking
examples. In May 2020, Neil Ferguson was forced to resign
his government post after he was found to have broken his
own social distancing rules by meeting up with his lover. An
even bigger outpouring of public anger followed later that
month, with the revelation that Boris Johnson's top advisor
Dominic Cummings had flouted stay-at-home orders by driving hundreds of miles across England to visit family, while
his wife was sick with Covid-19. Backed by the prime minister, he defended his actions as necessary to ensure his young

son received childcare. Cummings refused to step down. The British people, who had been asked to make great sacrifices in their own family lives—missing weddings, births, and funerals—were livid. In the wake of these scandals, trust in the Conservative government plummeted, and lockdown breaches soared.

Across the Atlantic, expertise has been undermined even more purposefully. But Trump's foolish attitude toward experts and his own incompetence does not change the reality that no one area of expertise can settle the question of how to handle a broad national challenge. This is especially true when considering something as enormous as shutting down an economy, plunging millions into unemployment, putting firms out of business, and then trying to start it all up again. Scientific data is crucial, but so is economic analysis. Public health officials cannot know the costs and benefits of various approaches to economic lockdowns. City planners should be consulted when closing and opening vast metro areas. The greatest theorist of warfare, Carl von Clausewitz, observed that "war is not just an act of policy but a true political instrument." By that, he meant that it could not be fought using military expertise alone; other perspectives had to be integrated, too. This is particularly true of modern warfare, which is "total" in nature, involving all of society. In these kinds of conflicts, the scholar Eliot Cohen has shown, the leaders who succeed—Lincoln, Churchill, Georges Clemenceau, David Ben-Gurion (and, I would add, Franklin Roosevelt)—are the ones who question and overrule their generals, factor in other views and disciplines, and forge a comprehensive political-military strategy.

Leading a country through a pandemic has many similarities to leading it through a war. Both have huge impacts on the economy and society. There are often terrible trade-offs that have to be made, substituting one set of risks for another. Perhaps that is why one of those legendary wartime leaders, Clemenceau, once remarked, "war is too important to be left to the generals." He didn't mean that one could win a war by dispensing with generals, but rather that you had to supplement them with other kinds of professionals to arrive at the broadest possible understanding. In that spirit, one could say that pandemics are too important to be left to the scientists. They are essential—but so are experts in other fields.

THE CRISIS OF KNOWLEDGE

The fundamental reason many people refused to heed expert advice on Covid-19, however, might have little to do with the complexity of science or the limited initial data. There are many people who distrust experts, no matter how highly credentialed, even in matters of their own health. In a study done a week after Donald Trump declared the pandemic a national emergency, three political scientists surveyed a representative group of Americans about their behavior during the crisis. Their findings were striking. They found that the single best predictor of whether you washed your hands, avoided contact with others, or self-quarantined was not where you lived or how old you were but *your party affiliation*. "Republicans are less likely than Democrats to report responding with CDC-recommended behavior, and are less concerned about the pandemic," they concluded. The report went on: "Partisanship is a more consistent predictor of behaviors, attitudes, and preferences than anything else that we measure." Since then, a slew of other studies have come to a similar conclusion. Several, using cell phone and debit card data, determined that people in counties that voted for Donald Trump were less likely to shelter in place than those that voted for Hillary Clinton, even after controlling for geographical differences in Covid-19 cases. Worse than mere passive disregard for public health measures, officials have encountered active hostility. On the Internet, ever-wilder conspiracy theories have proliferated, blaming the disease on everything from a Chinese world-domination plot to Bill Gates to 5G wireless technology. In just ten days during the pandemic, Britain saw more than thirty incidents of arson or vandalism against telecommunications equipment like cell towers.

It's easy to make fun of these findings. Even on the life-or-death matter of the virus, people were viewing experts' advice through the prism of their politics. They trusted their party leader (Trump) and their partisan sources of news and analysis (Fox News), rather than public health officials like Fauci, who had spent decades studying infectious diseases. This has led some critics to fume about "low-information voters," but the problem is not ignorance. The social psychologist Jonathan Haidt and others have emphasized the power of "motivated reasoning," whereby people construct their arguments to arrive at a preferred conclusion. Some studies have found that "high-information voters," those who read widely and follow news carefully, are in fact *more* guilty of this kind of partisan thinking. As two political scientists who have studied this phenomenon, Christopher H. Achen and Larry M. Bartels, have argued, the more appropriate term might be "rationalizing voters"—smart people who read the facts and follow the debates, but use their knowledge to justify and support their preexisting biases.

This research echoes an insight from the Enlightenment philosopher David Hume, who called reason "the slave of the passions." We use rationality as a means to an end—but our gut tells us where we want to go in the first place. And so, America faces what the *Vox* writer David Roberts has called an "epistemic crisis." As Roberts explains, "Epistemology is the branch of philosophy having to do with knowledge and how we come to know things; the crisis is that, as a polity, we have become incapable of learning or knowing the same things, and thus, incapable of acting together in a coherent fashion." Today, listening to experts, reading the news, and getting facts are no longer neutral acts but rather are loaded with political meaning.

This is not just an American story. In many countries, you can see the same dynamics at work, with people suspicious of the establishment, relying on their own sources, doubting credentialed authorities, and placing partisanship ahead of the truth. The Brexit debate was characterized by just this sense of two sets of facts. The phenomenon extends to Brazil, Mexico, Turkey, and India, all places where one side of the political divide has come to see itself as representing the experts while the other deeply distrusts that establishment. The increasing hostility between these two groups is one part of the most significant political trend of the last decade—the rise of populism worldwide.

At the core of the new populism is a deep antipathy toward the establishment. You can find left-wing versions, from Bernie Sanders's faction of the Democratic Party to the Greek political party Syriza, all demanding more government intervention and spending. The right-wing versions, from Trump to Boris Johnson to Italy's Matteo Salvini, are concerned chiefly with immigration. And then there are the developing world's populists: Brazil's Jair Bolsonaro, India's Narendra Modi, Turkey's Recep Tayyip Erdoğan, and the Philippines' Rodrigo Duterte. Immigration is less central to their messages, but their appeal is also based on a mix of cultural chauvinism and religious nationalism. Almost always they demonize some "other," from minorities to urban liberals. All these divergent movements share the populist hostility toward the elite. The pandemic has heightened this tendency to fever pitch.

Cas Mudde, a Dutch political scientist, provides the most useful definition of populism: an ideology "that considers society to be ultimately separated into two homogenous and antagonistic groups: 'the pure people' and 'the corrupt elite,' and argues that politics should be an expression of the *volonté générale* (general will) of the people." As if to prove his point, Donald Trump declared during his 2016 campaign, "The only antidote to decades of ruinous rule by a small handful of elites is a bold infusion of popular will." The practical effect of implementing Trump's "bold infusion" has been to denigrate expertise entirely. Michael Lewis's chilling account of maladministration under Trump—*The Fifth Risk*—warned of the intentional sidelining of professionals in obscure but crucial government institutions such as the National Oceanic and Atmospheric Administration. The agency, which is responsible for extreme weather forecasting, came to the forefront of the battles over expertise and truth during Hurricane Dorian in 2019. Trump's attitude toward experts was vividly on display when he falsely claimed the storm would hit Alabama. When NOAA experts publicly issued a correction, Trump displayed a map that had been altered. Someone—most believe Trump—had redrawn the storm's path in black marker, to show its trajectory reaching into the state. On top of this cartoonish undermining of their work, the government meteorologists who had contradicted Trump's false claim were rebuked.

THE NEW RULING CLASS

For many of us, experts in various fields are seen as just that, *experts*. Through education, hard work, and experience, they have developed a mastery of a specific topic. They've demonstrated their talent by acing tests, graduating from the best colleges, and working in places that value excellence. Surely when they speak about the issues they know well, they should expect to be trusted. Not so, writes the scholar Michael Lind in his book *The New Class War*. Quoting 1960s radicals, he explains: "The issue is not the issue," meaning the real conflict is not over any particular matter or dispute. "The issue is power." In any society, he argues, power exists in the political, the economic, and the cultural arenas. "All three realms of Western society today are fronts in the new class war." For many people, "advice from experts" is part of a larger strategy of domination by the new ruling class—the meritocrats.

All advanced countries are now run by a meritocracy. Schools admit applicants based largely on their test scores, and companies hire and promote people based mostly on credentials of one sort or another. Most leaders in government, business, arts, and culture have a college education, and many also have a postgraduate degree. Some societies take this to an extreme, as in East Asia. In the late 1990s, Taiwan boasted a cabinet in which some 70% of ministers held a postgraduate degree—60% of which were from American universities. Yet consider how exclusive higher education is. In America and the European Union, around a third of the public have college degrees. An even smaller share get postgraduate education, barely 13% in the United States. And yet most of the leadership positions in Western societies are held by people who have at least a college education and usually some postgraduate training. In other words, about two thirds of people stand by and watch as the other third run everything. (In large Asian countries, which have a smaller share of college graduates, the divide is arguably much greater. Just 10% of China's population attended some college and yet virtually every member of the Communist Party's Central Committee has—99% as of 2016. Ironically, this makes the Chinese Communist Party in some ways the world's most elitist organization.)

The meritocrats form a distinct class, separated from the

rest of society. For one thing, they earn much more: according to the US Census, the incomes of Americans with postgraduate degrees are 3.7 times as high as those of high school dropouts. These uber-educated Americans usually live in cities, hold professional jobs, and tend to be socially liberal. The non-college-educated public, by contrast, is more rural, has fewer professionals, and is generally more socially conservative. In 2016, Hillary Clinton won most of the first group, while Trump got most of the second. The urban-rural divide, which is growing every year, might be the most significant fault line in America electorally speaking—more so than race or gender. Polls show that about two-thirds of rural Americans approve of Trump and two-thirds of city-dwellers loathe him. A 2019 study noted that this sorting process "has progressed to the point that there is now essentially no such thing as a Republican city"—Republicans now control only 6% of "pure urban" districts in the House of Representatives.

This pattern is replicated across Europe. In the United Kingdom, those without university degrees were far more likely to vote for Brexit. In France, the "yellow vest" protests were powered largely by non-college-educated people living in the countryside. The gear that gave the movement its name was itself a symbol of anti-urban sentiment: as they protested rising fuel taxes, drivers donned the vests they had to wear when pulling over in an emergency, signaling the revolt of car-dependent rural-dwellers against a green agenda designed by metro-riding Parisians. The divide shows up in German politics as well, with support for the far Right coming from the rural areas with aging populations. And in Tur-

key, authoritarian-populist Recep Tayyip Erdoğan finds his
warmest support in the ethnic Turkish heartland of Anatolia,
and his strongest opposition along the urbanized west coast of
the country and in minority regions.

The pandemic has widened these divisions. Rural areas
have watched as a disease that came from cosmopolitan cities
spread into their communities. And yet the city-dwellers have
ways to function despite its ravages. That is because the Covid
divide is also a class divide. In 2019, the Bureau of Labor
Statistics released a report looking at how much job flexibility Americans enjoyed. Of those with a bachelor's degree or
higher, almost half reported working from home at least occasionally. For those with a high school diploma, fewer than
10% ever worked from home—for high-school dropouts, 3%.
Not surprisingly, then, when Covid-19 hit and the lockdowns
started, it was those who couldn't work from home who were
hurt most. Only 13% of people in households making over
$100,000 were laid off or furloughed, compared with 39% in
households making less than $40,000. Across the world, as the
economy recovers, those with college degrees and advanced
training are likely to fare better than those without, and big
businesses will do better than mom-and-pop enterprises. The
gap between credentialed elites and others will widen.

At his rallies, Donald Trump has found a reliable applause
line to attack America's elites. After bragging about his own
schooling and wealth, he says to the crowd, "They're not elite.
You're the elite." Trump has tapped a genuine vein of disgust
among many Americans at the way their more successful fellow citizens have mismanaged the country and yet still want

to manage their lives. The voters who chose Brexit resented smooth-talking technocrats who allowed Polish workers into the country to—in their minds—"take their jobs." France's yellow vest protesters believe that the metropolitan elites run the country for their own benefit and look down on the country bumpkins. At some level, this anti-elitism is a reflection of the feeling of powerlessness that many people experience when navigating the modern world—one in which experts and intellectuals seem to hold the keys to knowledge and power. Reflecting on this reality decades ago, the great American historian Richard Hofstadter wrote, "Once the intellectual was gently ridiculed because he was not needed; now he is fiercely resented because he is needed too much."

EMPATHY AND EXPERTISE

We have discussed how people think about elites. But how do elites think about people? What does having power do to a person's sense of themselves? Nothing good, say the experts. Henry Kissinger once claimed, "Power is the ultimate aphrodisiac." As seductive as power can be, psychological studies have shown it deadens the sensitivity of those who wield it. In short, power kills empathy. The UC Berkeley scholar Dacher Keltner ran studies finding that participants raised in greater wealth, power, and prestige showed fewer neurological signs of compassion when confronted with images of suffering, like cancer-stricken children. Beyond the deep roots of social class, the effect of dampening empathy and heightening selfishness is seen even with recently acquired power. In one experiment, Keltner arbitrarily designated one member of a group of three undergrads as the supervisor for a group proj-ect. Within thirty minutes of the study beginning, this newly minted "boss" began showing greater entitlement, snatching an extra cookie off a plate twice as often as the "followers." In his book *The Power Paradox*, Keltner likened these effects of power to "a form of brain damage, leading us to self-serving, impulsive behavior"—which paradoxically undermines the very compassion and empathy needed to wield power effec-tively. One of the deepest students of human psychology has described this process with great literary skill. Shakespeare's *Macbeth* is a story of a man who, as he gains power, loses empathy, to the point where, by the end of the play, he is even unable to feel sorrow for the death of his wife. King Lear, having been in power for decades, can no longer hear any-thing but flattery, banishing the one person—his own daugh-ter Cordelia—who dares to speak to him truthfully.

There are, however, many examples of people who develop empathy despite being in positions of great power. The two Roosevelts came from American aristocracy, and yet were both able to develop bonds with ordinary people. When Theodore went to the Dakota Badlands to escape New York after the deaths of his wife and mother, he lived for three years amid cowboys, ranch hands, saloon owners, and horse thieves—and enjoyed their company and learned from all of them. Franklin Roosevelt, whose upbringing was even more gilded than his distant cousin Theodore's, became an unex-pected champion of the poor and dispossessed. People often note that his battle with polio must have given him a sense of life's hardships. But his biographers, Jean Edward Smith and Doris Kearns Goodwin, make an additional crucial observation. To aid his recovery, Franklin regularly headed to Warm Springs, Georgia, where the naturally heated mineral waters seemed to ease the effects of the disease. He spent about a month every year in that small town, swimming and picnicking with other polio victims, most of them from modest backgrounds, and learning of their troubles. He never forgot them to his last breath, which he drew with them in Warm Springs. FDR understood in his bones what it felt like to be powerless. A story, perhaps apocryphal, captures the essence of how this WASP aristocrat, the most powerful man of his age, was nonetheless able to connect with ordinary people. During FDR's funeral procession, a mourner collapsed, overcome with grief. Someone helped him up and asked why he was in such pain. Did he know the president? "No," the man replied. "But he knew me."

The world has gotten very complicated. We will need more experts, not fewer, to manage the affairs of nations—from big companies to small counties—through these times. That inevitably makes them an elite of some kind, a group whose knowledge lends them authority and power. The alternative is unthinkable in the modern age: government by gut and the celebration of ignorance. To the extent it has been tried recently—in America, Brazil, and elsewhere—the results have been dismal. But experts and elites should take greater pains to think about how to connect with people and keep their needs front and center. The greatest moral failing of meritocracy is the belief that your success, your higher perch in society, makes you superior in any fundamental sense. After all, in democracies, at least, the people's wishes are the ultimate source of authority. So, let's be clear, as we navigate this pandemic and future crises, people need to listen to the experts. But the experts also need to listen to the people.

LESSON FIVE

Life Is Digital

COULD WE BE EXAGGERATING the consequences of this pandemic? Could the Covid effect be smaller than imagined? It's possible. Human beings have an extraordinary capacity to absorb pain and loss—and move on. Events that seemed permanently scarring can sometimes prove transitory. Consider the Spanish flu. After a pandemic that killed some 50 million people worldwide, including almost 700,000 Americans, the US settled into the Roaring Twenties and the Jazz Age. During Prohibition, there were thought to be up to 100,000 speakeasies—illegal bars—in New York by the middle of the 1920s. Was that pent-up desire? Or a devil-may-care attitude born of the great losses from World War I and the influenza? Whatever the reason, there is little evidence that people worked differently or socialized less after that gruesome outbreak. There was no new normal, just normal. The first post-pandemic US president, Warren G. Harding, even campaigned on the theme of a "return to normalcy."

But history doesn't always repeat itself. Sometimes one is struck as much by the discontinuities as the continuities. And that might be the case when comparing the Spanish flu to the novel coronavirus. In the 1920s, people went back to their farms, factories, and offices because there was no alternative. To work, you had to be at work. If you sought entertainment, you would find it only in theaters and music halls. If you wanted to buy food or clothing, you needed to go to a brick-and-mortar store. That is no longer true. Over the last two decades, we have seen the rise of a digital economy that makes it possible for people to do most of these things without having to cluster together, battle traffic, pack into trains, and spend hours commuting. In recent years, the changes go well beyond videoconferencing and e-commerce. Today, life can be lived digitally.

When did we transition to a digital economy? It was a process, naturally, and there was no single turning point. First came computers, initially developed during the Second World War for the military. The invention of the integrated circuit produced the personal computer, which is often dated to 1971 (the year of the production of the Kenbak-1). The Internet also developed slowly, beginning with the Defense Department's ARPANET in the 1960s, then steadily expanding to more universities in the '70s and '80s. The World Wide Web was born in 1990. Its largest company, Amazon, got its start in 1995, just selling books. In its early days, the Seattle-based company installed a computerized bell that was set to ring every time a sale was made. When it rang, as the journalist Brad Stone writes, "everyone in the office would gather around to see if anyone knew the customer." As sales increased, the bell tolled so often it had to be removed. Fast forward to the first quarter of 2020, and Amazon was making $10,000 in sales—every second. Had that bell survived, it would now emit a constant ring, as if an alarm bell warning of a new age.

There have been many waves of technological change. To understand the most recent one, you have to go back to August 2011. That might seem an odd choice. It was a gloomy month, not ideal for techno-optimism. Economies around the world were still suffering through the aftershocks of the global financial crisis. Europeans worried that Spain and Italy would default on their debt and spark a crisis across the continent. In the United States, unemployment remained stubbornly high, over 9%. Stock markets in Europe and America reflected these fears. On August 8, "Black Monday," the Dow Jones Industrial average dropped 635 points, the sixth-largest drop in its history up to that point. It was in this uneasy environment that Marc Andreessen, the inventor of Mosaic, the first major web browser, published an essay in the *Wall Street Journal* under a perplexing headline: "Why Software Is Eating the World."

By this point, there were really two economies: the digital economy and the material economy. Andreessen's point was that the digital economy was becoming so powerful that it was dominating—eating up—the material economy. Increasingly, new companies were finding that they could use software to enhance their profits dramatically, expand their reach, and sell digital services rather than physical products. Incumbents that didn't jump on board were replaced outright. Kodak missed the revolution in digital photography, and had to file for bankruptcy. Record stores virtually disappeared once people started buying online subscriptions for streaming services like Spotify. Uber transformed a physical industry—taxicabs—into one whose essence was an information network, created and maintained by software. The fastest-growing entertainment companies, Andreessen pointed out, were not movie studios or theme parks but software companies that sold online video games. (For at least ten years, the revenues of the video gaming industry have exceeded those of Hollywood and the music business put together.) As Covid-19 accelerates the trend of digital retail overtaking real-life retail, over the next five years, by one estimate, around 100,000 brick-and-mortar stores in the United States will close—three times the number shuttered during the recession of 2007–9.

Even the most seemingly traditional companies are taking advantage of software. Microsoft CEO Satya Nadella gave me the striking example of Thyssenkrupp. The company is one of Germany's great industrial giants, a top steel producer and the fourth-largest elevator manufacturer on the planet. Although it continues to make elevators, it now finds that its greatest added value is not in charging ever-higher prices for them, but in selling service contracts to maintain them with maximum efficiency. Its smart, software-enabled elevators, which are connected to the cloud, constantly send out performance data, which the company rigorously analyzes and then uses for "predictive maintenance"—repairing a problem before it gets worse. The software is built by Microsoft, which is why Nadella tells the story.

Klaus Kleinfeld, when he was CEO of the aluminum company Alcoa, put it this way: "We have furnaces. In the old days, we could improve their efficiency a little bit every few years when we built a new one. Now, the furnaces are run using software, and they get relentlessly more efficient every year, like software." The software revolution created a new world in which there is increasingly little distinction between the digital and material economy. Almost everything today runs on software, which has spurred other breakthroughs such as cloud computing, which in turn has produced the drive toward big data. People speak of data as the new oil, the main resource fueling modern business, but without software that can refine it, data is useless. For every business, software has become the key to growth.

A parallel revolution, also enabled by software, has been the mobile revolution. The iPhone was launched in 2007, and smartphones now connect the majority of the world to the Internet. For most people, their phone is their computer. To best understand this shift, look at India. Like the citizens of most poor countries, Indians until recently had largely been left behind by the Information Revolution. Computers are expensive and Wi-Fi is rare. Ravi Agrawal tells the story in his book, *India Connected*: "In 2000, only 20 million Indians had access to the Internet. Ten years later, that number grew to 100 million." Even then, in 2010, the majority of India's billion-plus people couldn't go online with their phones, which were usually simple handsets. Then along came 4G, which allowed a $30 smartphone to connect easily to the Internet. Now over 550 million people in India have a minicomputer in their hands. They use it to buy and sell products, watch the news, entertain themselves, join groups, and work remotely.

India leapfrogged the digital divide with astonishing speed. In 2015, it ranked 155th in the world in mobile broadband penetration. By 2017, it was consuming more mobile data than any other country on earth. And by 2025, hundreds of millions more Indians are expected to have handheld computers connected to the Internet. This move has been given a massive push by Mukesh Ambani, the chairman of Reliance, India's largest company, who invested a staggering $37 billion in creating a new wireless network and offering it to consumers at giveaway prices. Ambani told me that he believes digitization will transform India like nothing before it. "In the next 20 years, in a networked society, we are going to have change much more than we have seen in the last 100 years," he predicted. The mobile revolution is accelerating modernization in places like India at a startling pace. Not all the changes will be positive. Smartphones are already proving to be a dangerously efficient way to mobilize people along ethnic lines. Baseless rumors spread over messaging groups like WhatsApp have triggered mob killings in India in recent years. And for many, smartphones offer their first jarring introduction to endless streams of pornography and brutal violence.

BACK TO THE FUTURE

By 2018, you could finally say that the majority of the world was connected. Covid-19 came onto this stage and obliterated the one remaining obstacle to a digital future—human attitudes. Many people were stuck in their old ways. Some were still reluctant to send credit card information over the Internet. Others would never think of taking a class online. Most would not have agreed to a doctor's appointment via video chat. The pandemic and the lockdowns that followed compelled changes in behavior, and not just from people but businesses, too. Hollywood studios would never have dreamed of debuting a big-budget movie through a streaming service. Michelin-starred restaurants thought they were above takeout and delivery. Health clubs didn't want to be in the business of creating YouTube videos. But all these taboos have been broken, the barriers crossed, and now a new normal exists. It is unlikely that we will ever fully go back to the past. The pandemic served as a forced mass product testing for digital life—and for the most part, our technological tools passed.

The single most significant economic trend resulting from the Covid-19 crisis is likely to be in the nature of work itself. An MIT report a few weeks into the crisis found that about a third of Americans who previously commuted were working from home. Around the same time, one of India's largest companies, Tata Consultancy Services, announced that, because of the crisis, it had decided that 75% of its employees would be working remotely by 2025. "We don't believe that we need more than 25% of our workforce at our facilities in order to be 100% productive," said TCS's chief operating officer, N. G. Subramaniam. When the media began reporting that the new policy would affect some 250,000 of TCS's 350,000 employees in India, the company issued a correction: the policy would in fact apply to its 450,000 employees across the globe. Surveys of American and European firms reveal that most intend to permanently shift some of their jobs off-site, in the belief that they can maintain productivity while giving workers more flexibility and cutting office-space costs.

In some ways, this future takes us backward. The modern office is a straightforward application of the model of an early twentieth-century factory. Everybody arrives and leaves at the same time, Monday through Friday. People work in large central areas, often eating in communal cafeterias. That made sense in an industrial operation, because all hands had to be on deck, doing their part on the assembly line. But in a modern, service-oriented economy—which is what most developed countries have nowadays—people work very differently. Collaboration involves teamwork that is intellectual, not physical, and can be carried out by email, group chat, and videoconference. The new work model might be one in which people do much of their day-to-day work remotely, and come into the office only for meetings, presentations, and brainstorming sessions. Routine group meetings might go virtual, but conferences that are about networking, deepening connections, providing intellectual stimulation, or simply offering entertainment might continue to be in person. Most likely, there will be new hybrid models. Far from devaluing personal ties or unpredictable interactions, this new setup would make them more prized because they would happen less often.

In a sense, work would return to what it was like for much of history, more closely tied to life at home. A farmer lived and farmed on his land, a craftsman worked next to his house, and a merchant had his shop on the ground floor of his home. The personal and the professional were intermingled; children saw their parents not simply as family members but also as workers. Over the last 200 years, with the rise of the factory and the office, home life and work life bifurcated sharply. If you had a job, you left your domestic world behind every morning as you walked out your door and traveled to the entirely different universe of work. Your colleagues saw one side of you and your family saw another. It was a *Mad Men* world. In the twenty-first century, we might find a way to blend the two and allow both groups to see you whole.

The jobs that the pandemic has transformed the fastest are in medicine. The benefits of using technology to provide health care are obvious. Patients don't need to make trips to doctors' offices, wait, and return, all to get a routine exam or prescription. Many symptoms can be described over the phone or displayed on a video call. The technology has been with us for a while—the obstacles have been human and organizational. Patients didn't want to do consultations over the Internet. Doctors were reasonably reluctant to conduct telehealth visits when they wouldn't get paid as much. Covid-19 changed all this. US states relaxed licensing requirements in order to facilitate care across state lines. Lacking other options, patients agreed to have video consults rather than nothing—and then found them to be more convenient. Providers saw advantages, too. Much attention has been paid to the triage that hospitals had to do when confronting a surge of patients with the disease. But the real triage in the system has been that telehealth has allowed doctors to handle many less serious medical problems online, freeing up time, resources, and personnel to tackle the more serious cases, Covid-related or not. It has been estimated that in 2020, Americans will rack up one billion virtual health-care interactions.

The pandemic has opened the door to a much broader transformation. Every time a task moves to the digital realm, it becomes easier to use software to automate and optimize it. The same is true for medicine. Machines and software are already helping with diagnosis, surgery, treatment, and therapy. Meanwhile, small wearable devices can constantly monitor a person's vital functions and transmit the data to the cloud, where it can be analyzed and, if something irregular is detected, sent to medical specialists. Apple CEO Tim Cook has said he believes that his company's "greatest contribution to mankind . . . will be about health"—through the increasingly sophisticated medical use of products like the Apple Watch.

Ideally, the pandemic-induced move online will shift the entire focus of medicine away from treating diseases and toward preventing them, which is a far more effective way to keep us all healthy. Unfortunately, the obstacle to that shift lies in an inconvenient truth: there is much less money in prevention than in treatments and cures. As a result, experiments with a new preventive model will probably work best in countries with government-managed health systems. In those where the private sector dominates, as in America, doctors and hospitals have little incentive to embrace this model. That is not to suggest that these people and organizations are dishonorable. But in any market system, economic incentives matter, so resources and technologies will be devoted to the areas that produce the most revenue.

THE AI REVOLUTION

The technology that will transform medicine the most over the long run is artificial intelligence. In fact, it could well be the most profound shift we are undertaking as human beings. Its consequences will likely prove more significant than the dominance of software. Artificial intelligence could eat not just the world but the humans in it, too.

In some parts of medicine, machines are already on par with, or even outperforming, doctors. One study determined that AI programs trained to read pathology images can now diagnose certain kinds of lung cancer with 97% accuracy. Another study found that AI had up to 11% fewer false positives in reading radiology scans than human experts in some situations. During the pandemic, the IBM and MIT team behind the AI system Watson put the technology to a number of different uses: identifying Covid-19 patients at high risk for sepsis, designing proteins to block the virus from bonding with human cells, testing the efficacy of face mask materials, predicting if already approved drugs will help fight the virus, and planning for the large-scale manufacture and supply of vaccines. Although many of these applications are experimental, the results are impressive. Why, for so many tasks, does AI work better than a human being? Because a process like diagnosis is fundamentally about collecting, organizing, and analyzing information, which computers can do far better than the human brain. Over the course of a thirty-year career, a seasoned doctor might have seen several tens of thousands of patients and have read hundreds of journal articles. An AI program will analyze tens of millions of patients' data and hundreds of thousands of studies—in minutes if not seconds. This is why computers now help fly planes and trade stocks. They can beat world champions at chess, *Jeopardy!*, and video games. Put simply, AI can, in theory, do complicated analytic tasks better than humans—the more complicated, the greater the advantage for the computer.

Right now, computers do have limits. When the Covid-19 outbreak began, many observers hoped that AI might find solutions that humans could not. The results were mixed. Numerous obstacles got in the way. For one thing, computers need mountains of data to see patterns, and with the novel coronavirus, there was little data at the start, and for months afterward, the information continued to be incomplete. Historical data on other viruses hasn't been of much use either because the many differences—in lethality, how the viruses mutate, and so on—are crucial.

Location-tracking data has also failed to live up to its promise. Although East Asian countries found some success in using it to predict hotspots and identify superspreaders, the technology has its shortfalls. Installing a location-tracking app is voluntary, and since not everyone does so, the data gives only part of the picture. Even in Singapore, where social cohesion and trust in government is high, by June 2020 only some 30% of the population had downloaded the government's Covid-19 tracking app. Requiring everyone to supply their health data, as in China, is not an option in most democracies. At any rate, it's mostly a moot point. China, South Korea, and Singapore do not owe their success in fighting Covid-19 to invasive new technology. Rather, what made the difference were the hallmarks of a proper pandemic response: fast, widespread testing and old-fashioned contact tracing, conducted through in-person interviews.

The stumbling blocks that AI has faced in the fight against the novel coronavirus do not reflect some underlying flaw with the technology; they just reveal its limits in a special situation where much is unclear and good data is hard to come by. With time, there will be more and better data about the disease and innovative ways to use it—from mass thermal scanning for temperatures to facial recognition, both of which could be put to use in quickly detecting potential illness among large crowds in public spaces. It is already possible for AI to predict which patients will get worse and which will get better based on observed patterns. There is also the ongoing use of AI in pathbreaking medical research—in mapping the three-dimensional structure of proteins, for example—which will continue to yield impressive results that could help in treatments and vaccines. And of course, as the research on Covid-19 proliferates, AI is already helping scientists make sense of it all, analyzing the thousands of new studies being produced each week around the world far more efficiently than humans could. However, all in all, the experience of this pandemic has highlighted not just the strengths but also the limitations of AI—as of now.

The most lasting effect of Covid-19 on AI will likely have less to do with any particular medical breakthroughs than with the rise of robots. More robots in more settings will allow the economy to function while minimizing the dangers of infection. A study published in *MIT Technology Review* finds that "between 32 and 50 million US jobs could be increasingly assisted by technology to reduce health risks posed by human interaction and safeguard productivity in a time of crisis." Some of those jobs are obvious candidates for replacement, like cashiers. Others are more complicated, like cooks, but there are already robots that can do that work effectively.

And the more robots there are, the more they can tap into artificial intelligence to boost their productivity. In the same way that once you attach software to a machine, it becomes the controlling factor, once you introduce artificial intelligence into any system, it gradually does the same, becoming a generalized force multiplier. We are on track to introduce AI into most of our institutions and organizations for the simple reason that it makes them work better. But that will surely mean fewer humans are needed to work because AI will make things much more efficient—for blue-collar and white-collar work alike. You don't need as many paralegals or young lawyers if the machine can scan documents for cases, facts, and patterns.

And you certainly don't need as many drivers if computers can control cars, buses, and trucks. Autonomous driving will be a huge boon to safety. Over a million people around the world die every year in vehicle accidents, and according to the US Department of Transportation, some 94% of crashes in America occur because of driver error. But in a driverless world, what happens to the almost 4 million Americans—mostly men, mostly without college degrees—who work as drivers? For now, their career prospects are on the upswing as Amazon and other digital retailers boom. Frederick Smith, the CEO and chair of FedEx, said in May that his company was hiring "prolifically," adding about 4,000 drivers a week. In the long term, while drivers might not lose their jobs, they will lose their ability to command livable wages—because their jobs become less prized. Computers are quickly shrinking the human role down to the last mile. Autopilot already flies many commercial planes much of the time. AI-driven long-haul trucking is already being tested on public roads, even as local delivery vans and workers are still used for the final leg of delivery. Even that limited role, too, may fade as the "last mile" problem is increasingly taken over by AI drones. AI may not always produce unemployment, and it might have effects on a longer time horizon, decades from now. But it will be the game-changer of our lifetimes.

Leave it to a profession that has not yet been threatened by robots to sketch out the AI future. In his 2019 novel, *Machines Like Me*, the writer Ian McEwan describes a world in which automation is becoming part of everyday life. In London, there are mass unemployment protests. The main character notes,

I went on one march, then gave up after I read about a new car factory starting production outside Newcastle. It built three times as many cars as the factory it replaced—with one-sixth of the work force. Eighteen times more efficient, vastly more profitable. No business could resist. It wasn't only the shop floor that lost jobs to machines. Accountants, medical staff, marketing, logistics, human resources, forward planning. Now, haiku poets. All in the stew. Soon enough, most of us would have to think again what our lives were for. Not work.

Such prospects seem closer than ever amid the pandemic. (Even McEwan's prediction about poets is coming true: computer scientists are developing algorithms that can write literature.) Discussions about the "future of work" should recognize that the future is already with us. Philosophers used to theorize about how to keep people afloat once technology replaced a critical mass of jobs. Now, Covid-19 has forced countries to experiment with some kind of near-universal basic income. In the United States, this idea went mainstream in a matter of months—no longer just the quixotic quest of the underdog presidential candidate Andrew Yang but a proposal that, in a temporary form, was passed by Congress to stave off economic disaster. During the pandemic, governments concluded that, through no fault of their own, people could not earn money and so deserved to be paid for not working. Further down the line, could the state decide that people forced out of work by AI similarly deserve to be compensated?

In his 1930 essay, "Economic Possibilities for Our Grandchildren," the economist John Maynard Keynes pondered this exact question. He looked forward to a world of fifteen-hour workweeks made possible by technology. But even if such a world materializes, we will need to find a way to give people things to do. That could involve creating extra jobs in a variety of fields, from education to public works projects to park and wilderness maintenance—just as FDR's celebrated Works Progress Administration and Civilian Conservation Corps hired millions of Americans to expand infrastructure and beautify the country. Some of these jobs would involve work for work's sake. As Keynes wrote, "we shall endeavour to spread the bread thin on the butter—to make what work there is still to be done to be as widely shared as possible."

The full-color example of this future is George Jetson of the 1960s cartoon show. George's job at Spacely Space Sprockets, Inc., is to push a few buttons three hours a day, three days a week. Everything else is automated. But it is still a job, and it gives him and his family the contours of family and social life that were more or less recognizable to someone in the 1960s. That's one vison of our automated, digital future—one in which the center more or less holds. Patterns of life are readjusted but not destroyed. You see early examples of this possible world in the Finnish prime minister's call for a four-day workweek consisting of six-hour days. You see it in the flexible jobs that characterize the gig economy, such as driving for Uber or DoorDash, where workers can choose their own hours. You see it in the ever-greater number of hours people spend in the office futzing around on social media. And you see it in the rise of what the anthropologist David Graeber colorfully calls "bullshit jobs." He describes several types, including "box tickers," who generate lots of paperwork to suggest that things are happening when things aren't, and "taskmasters," who manage people who don't need management.

A big problem with technological revolutions, Keynes said, was that with so much of the work increasingly being done by technology, humans would have to find a sense of purpose. For human beings, especially men, work has historically given them an identity, a sense of accomplishment, and dignity. These are not irrelevant attributes. That's why I have always found the idea of a universal basic income unsatisfying, preferring the expansion of a program like the Earned Income Tax Credit, which essentially tops up the wages of low-income workers. It incentivizes work but guards against immiseration. It's an idea that has attracted support from the far Left as well as from libertarians. I'm convinced it is not as popular as other, less effective policies—like raising the minimum wage—because it is difficult to express simply and symbolically. Expanding it substantially, as we should, would be very expensive. But if we recognize the scale of this problem—potentially permanent mass unemployment or underemployment—it seems money well spent.

Keynes also worried that with the decline of work, all that free time would be a problem because people were not good at leisure. He noted that the indolence of much of the aristocracy, which already faced this problem, was a gloomy omen of what might come to the larger public eventually. In his novel, McEwan muses on this "problem of leisure," describing humanity in an AI-run world:

> We could become slaves of time without purpose. Then what? A general renaissance, a liberation into love, friendship and philosophy, art and science, nature worship, sports and hobbies, invention and the pursuit of meaning? But genteel recreations wouldn't be for everyone. Violent crime had its attractions too, so did bare-knuckle cage-fighting. VR pornography, gambling, drink and drugs, even boredom and depression. We wouldn't be in control of our choices.

This scenario is the logical endpoint to the rise of robots and AI. Automation would make less work, but there would still be new jobs generated. For those unable to find good work, government assistance would expand significantly. There would also be more time and more technological access to seek fulfillment in recreation and leisure. People would naturally adapt to this new world differently, some feeling liberated, others trapped. But a darker alternative future is one in which the trends gradually deepen, and yet the government doesn't respond with a large-scale program. Inequality gets worse, more jobs disappear, real wages stagnate, the quality of life for most people falls. This is a future in which wealth moves into the hands of a rich few, while everyone else is left behind, the worst crippled by alcoholism, drug addiction, and suicide. The demand for populism increases. We're currently in the foothills of each of these futures, but it is unclear which one lies ahead.

ONLY HUMAN

The decline of work is a massive problem, but even if we can solve it, AI confronts us with an even larger one: Will we lose control of the machines? The crucial shift that is taking place right now is from "weak" or "narrow" AI to "strong" or "general" AI. In the first, a machine is programmed to complete a specific task—say, win a game of chess—which it then does superbly. The second is the broader development of the kind of intelligence that can think creatively and make judgments. That leap in cognitive capacity was a watershed moment for AI. The board game Go is considered to be the most complex in the world, with vastly more potential moves than there are atoms in the observable universe. Google's AlphaGo learned the game, and in March 2016, consistently beat the eighteen-time world champion, Lee Sedol. (In 2017, its successor program, AlphaZero, taught itself Go in just three days and defeated AlphaGo, one hundred games to zero.) AlphaGo was seen by computer scientists as a mark that machines could teach themselves and also think in nonlinear, creative ways. In March 2020, its makers revealed that another one of their programs merely watched the screen as a series of Atari video games were played—and then mastered all fifty-seven games, outperforming humans in every single one.

This more powerful form of AI mimics human mental capacities. But the programs will not stop at mere mimicry. Soon they will vastly exceed our abilities. Machines can already outsmart humans at many analytic tasks. And they will get better and better with more and more data, and through new mechanisms of learning such as neural networks. The University of California, Berkeley, computer scientist Stuart Russell has a way to explain this trend. He points out that modern computers read without really understanding. They can translate because they look at previously translated material and match words, phrases, and sentences. But now they are learning to understand. Once computers can do that, they will quickly read and absorb everything that human beings have ever written on every subject. At that point, they will be vastly more knowledgeable than any human, indeed than all humans on the planet.

Will these computers be conscious in the sense that human beings are? Will they have morals? Russell gives the example of what could happen if you asked a computer to end cancer. It might conclude that the easiest way to do so would be to kill all human beings since that would certainly kill the disease too. I have always thought that at the end of the day, the human being is still in control because she can unplug the machine. But what if the computer knows this and believes that, to fulfill its mission, it must stay operational—and finds ways to keep itself on? That was the dilemma explored fifty years ago in Stanley Kubrick's *2001: A Space Odyssey*. The movie was stunningly prescient in understanding the greatest dilemma posed by artificial intelligence. In the film, the computer, HAL, chooses to kill its human masters so that it can proceed with its mission. In the end, the human, David Bowman, was able to outsmart the machine—but in real life it seems far more likely that the opposite would happen. That is why Bill Gates, Elon Musk, and a slew of other luminaries, usually optimistic about technology, have echoed the warnings of Oxford philosopher Nick Bostrom: they now worry that the development of general AI could threaten the human species itself.

AI-powered computers are already black boxes. We know that they get to the right answer, but we don't know how or why. What role does that leave for human judgment? Henry Kissinger has asked whether the rise of artificial intelligence will mean the end of the Enlightenment. That eighteenth-century movement elevated human reasoning above age-old superstitions, dogma, and worship. Immanuel Kant called the Enlightenment "man's emergence from his self-imposed immaturity." Humanity had to grow up—we had to understand the world ourselves. But if AI produces better answers than we can without revealing its logic, then we will be going back to our species' childhood and relying on faith. We will worship artificial intelligence that, as was said of God, works in a mysterious way, his wonders to perform. Perhaps the period from Gutenberg to AlphaGo will prove to be the exception, a relatively short era in history when humans believed they were in control. Before that, for millennia, they saw themselves as small cogs in a vast system they did not fully comprehend, subject to laws of God and nature. The AI age could return us to a similarly humble role. This time, though, humans may work hand in hand with a higher intelligence, not subservient to it but not entirely above it, either. In some ways that is a more accurate reflection of our actual place in the vast, unfathomable universe.

It is worth keeping in mind that along with the AI revolution, we are witnessing another one that is also likely to have transformational effects—the bioengineering revolution. To put it simply, we are getting better at creating better human beings—stronger, healthier, and longer-living. With gene selection, parents can already choose fertilized eggs that are free of known genetic diseases. (Many fear that soon they will also select for babies that are, say, blond, blue-eyed, and male.) The scholar Yuval Noah Harari argues that for all the social, political, and economic changes over the millennia, human beings have not changed much physically or mentally—until now. The combination of these twin revolutions—in biology and computing—will allow human beings to expand their physical and mental capacities. The result, he says, will be the creation of a god-like superman: Homo Deus.

Perhaps that is what lies in store for us. The future of artificial intelligence and biotechnology is the subject of great debate and is beyond the scope of this book, and this author. I believe that we have a long way to go before we reach truly general intelligence in a machine—one that can, for example, not just solve a scientific problem, but grasp the underlying logic of innovation, the very notion of science itself. Could it really invent new modes of inquiry and new fields of knowledge in all areas, as humans have done repeatedly? In any event, one thing seems clear: so far, this technological revolution has had the effect not so much of replacing humans but rather of refocusing them. When I speak with people who run hospitals in the developing world and have deployed AI extensively to make up for the shortfall of doctors, they point out that the machines' superior ability to make diagnoses has allowed doctors and nurses to focus on patient care. These professionals are now more deeply engaged in helping patients understand their conditions, ensuring that they take their medicines, and convincing them to change their diets and habits. They also act as coaches, providing the moral and psychological support that is key to recovery. In many ways, these are more essentially human tasks than purely analytic ones like reading X-rays or interpreting lab results. This development represents a new division of labor, with machines and humans each doing what they do best.

The pandemic has shown that these technological revolutions are further along than we might have thought—but also that digital life can feel cramped, a poor simulacrum of the real world. For many people, these shifts will be scary. Some jobs will go away, but overall productivity will rise, generating greater wealth that could help all. Everyone's quality of life could improve. There are real concerns about privacy, handling data, and the role of the government in regulating companies and itself in this domain. But these are not insoluble problems; we can have the benefits of digital life and also protect our privacy. And if we can take care as we develop the rules around the AI and bioengineering revolutions, we will not lose our humanity either. Indeed, we could enhance it.

People worry that as AI becomes more highly developed, we will rely on our computers for so much that we will end up thinking of them as friends and becoming unable to function without them. But already, my phone can give me more information than any human I know. It can solve complex tasks in a nanosecond. It can entertain me with content from across time and space. And yet, I have never mistaken it for a friend. The smarter a machine becomes at calculating data and providing answers, the more it forces us to think about what is uniquely human about us, beyond our ability to reason. In fact, intelligent machines might make us prize our human companions even more, for their creativity, whimsy, unpredictability, warmth, and intimacy. This is not such a strange thought. For much of history, humans were praised for many qualities other than their power to calculate—bravery, loyalty, generosity, faith, love. The movement to digital life is broad and fast and real. But perhaps one of its deepest consequences will be to make us cherish the things in us that are most human.

Aristotle Was Right— We Are Social Animals

THE REAL PUZZLE about pandemics is why they don't happen more often. Covid-19, along with the bubonic plague, SARS, MERS, Ebola, and certain other diseases, are known as zoonoses—infections that jumped from animals to humans. (*Zoonosis* comes from the ancient Greek words for "animal" and "disease.") HIV, the virus that causes AIDS, is thought to have hopped species when a hunter in equatorial Africa killed an infected chimpanzee and was exposed to the animal's blood through a cut. But here's the frightening question: Given that there are untold thousands of these viruses in thousands of animal species, why don't they infect humans more often? In fact, they do. The viral leap from chimp to human "likely had happened many times before," Craig Timberg and Daniel Halperin explain in their book on the origins of the AIDS epidemic.

Similar scenarios in Asia, with bats, civet cats, and pangolins causing local instances of influenza-like viruses, go back decades and probably even centuries. So why are there not more epidemics and pandemics? And not just more, but *many* more? Writing of HIV, Timberg and Halperin explain: "To fulfill its grim destiny the virus needed a kind of place never before seen in Central Africa but that now was rising in the heart of the region—a big, thriving, hectic place jammed with people and energy, where old rules were cast aside amid the tumult of new commerce." In short, it takes a city.

"We predict between 1 [million] and 7 million people a year actually get infected by these bat coronaviruses," says Peter Daszak, the "virus hunter" I introduced in lesson one. But, Daszak notes, "it's only occasionally that that unlucky person happens to go to a market or the animal infects someone in a wildlife market, and then the virus can spread and become a pandemic." For a virus to become a full-blown pandemic, it has to find its way to an urban setting. Covid-19 illustrates this principle perfectly. When we think of the disease, certainly in the United States, we remember how New York City, with its crowded streets and packed twenty-four-hour subways, became the biggest epicenter.

It's not just New York, of course. The intermingling of people in cities everywhere has always made these places vector-rich venues for disease. The connections within cities, and those between cities, have always been a source of vulnerability to infection. When railways and telegraphs knitted cities together in the latter half of the nineteenth century, it heralded a new era both for humans and for diseases. In late 1889, when an outbreak of influenza was first reported in Saint Petersburg, Russia, the news spread across Europe via telegram.* At first, the newspaper reports triggered more curiosity than concern. Londoners read in *The Times* how the apparent reemergence of the illness after decades without an outbreak would amount to little more than an academic oddity. The paper explained that the new cases might afford pathologists a "most lively interest," akin to the thrill felt by a sportsman hunting rare game or an archaeologist uncovering Egyptian mummies. But soon, city-dwellers read with increasing dread as the lethal contagion swept through metropolises on the European continent and eventually into London and beyond. In a world of connected cities—linked through railroads and steam-powered shipping—the virus circled the globe in just four months. Today, widespread air travel, combined with increased urban density, seems to make cities even more of a magnet for disease. The initial hotspots for Covid-19 were all major cities. At first these epicenters were big cities unknown to most Westerners—

---

* It is worth noting there is some evidence to suggest that this 1889 pandemic, thought to be influenza by contemporaries, might have actually been a zoonotic coronavirus—perhaps a bovine strain that jumped from cows. See Leen Vijgen et al., "Complete Genomic Sequence of Human Coronavirus OC43," *Journal of Virology* 79(3): 1595–1604, https://www.ncbi.nlm.nih.gov/pmc/articles/PMC544107/.

Wuhan, Daegu, Qom—but soon the virus struck closer to home, overwhelming Milan, London, and New York.

By April 2020, many of the world's most glamorous cities had become shells of their former selves. Paris, with its pretty cafes lining the empty sidewalks, looked like a movie set. Even after the lockdown, the city only inched back to some semblance of normalcy. Pre-pandemic, each of Paris's commuter trains could carry some 2,600 passengers—after Covid, that number was slashed to 700 as a result of new social distancing guidelines. Separating people in cities, especially during rush hour and on public transportation, proved immensely difficult. The energy and synergy of people all pressing against each other had vanished. So had the spontaneity of urban life. London partially reopened in July, but the adventure of pub-crawling must have felt different, since before serving you a pint, the bartender took down your name and phone number—for possible testing and tracing by the National Health Service. Some of Asia's large cities have experimented with even more intrusive monitoring via smartphone tracking. Users who opt into using the Singaporean government's app receive alerts if Bluetooth data shows contact with a Covid-positive individual, and the app then prompts the possibly infected person to get tested. All the while, the pandemic has bankrupted many restaurants, theaters, galleries, bars, music venues, and retail shops, depriving cities of most of their top attractions.

With no certainty about when or if things would return to normal, many city-dwellers did what they have done throughout history when confronting disease—they fled. Some went on long visits to family and friends. Others, especially those with means, moved to country houses, or rented or even bought them. An analysis of smartphone data found that between March 1 and May 1 as many as 420,000 people moved out of New York City. Wealthy neighborhoods such as the Upper East Side, the West Village, and SoHo saw residential population declines of 40% or more. Remote work has made this option more feasible, but only for professionals. California cities are facing a similar exodus on the horizon: Facebook's CEO, Mark Zuckerberg, remarked that, since the pandemic, three-quarters of his employees have signaled some level of interest in leaving the Bay Area. Reports from France suggested a similar trend, with Parisians decamping to rural regions they once scorned as "the provinces"—with many locals suspicious of these unwelcome, potentially infected visitors.

For centuries, denizens of cities have abandoned their homes in times of trouble. In the fourteenth century, the bubonic plague hit Florence hard, killing more than half of the city's population, by some estimates. In his collection of stories from that time, *The Decameron*, Giovanni Boccaccio offered advice that sounds remarkably current: flee the city; isolate with a few friends; and gather in the evenings to eat, drink, and tell stories (their version of Netflix). And yet this outflow proved temporary. Cities came back. After this worst plague in human history, Italy's city-states, Florence above all, launched the Renaissance.

Great cities have often emerged stronger from catastrophe. Surveying London in the year 1666, an observer could be forgiven for thinking that it truly was the devil's year—the city had been doubly destroyed, first by plague and then by the Great Fire. Tens of thousands lay dead from disease, and 80% of the city had been razed to heaps of smoking rubble. This seemed to be the end. Reports of London's death were, needless to say, greatly exaggerated. That year marked England's last plague outbreak. And crucially, Londoners chose—in modern parlance—to "build back better." The old city, mostly wooden, had been a tinderbox. The new city recreated itself in brick and stone. London as we know it today rose from the ashes.

The journalist Clay Jenkinson points to a New World example of this tendency to declare the death of cities. In 1793, when Philadelphia was America's leading metropolis— the nation's capital and most populous city—it experienced a gruesome yellow fever epidemic that literally decimated the population, killing 5,000 of the city's 50,000 residents. Secretary of State Thomas Jefferson, who had always disliked urban centers, lived in the city's outskirts and continued to commute to work. "Most evils are the means of producing some good," he later wrote. "The yellow fever will discourage the growth of great cities in our nation." It didn't quite work out that way.

NEVER-ENDING URBANIZATION

For those who stayed behind in 2020, it was like living in a strange, spooky version of your city—all the energy had been let out. I first visited New York in the 1970s, when it was a rough, dirty place, but filled with vigor. To a boy from India, it felt like the most dazzling metropolis in the world. I moved there in the early 1990s, when it was reveling in a new Gilded Age, but still never losing its chaotic spirit. Contrast that with April 2020. The confinement, the empty streets, the stilled heart of the city, the silence punctuated only by the Doppler effect of ambulance sirens passing—all of it was alien and unnerving. Alan Weisman's 2007 nonfiction book, *The World Without Us*, imagines how cities would crumble and the wilderness would return if humans were suddenly to disappear. Fairly quickly, Weisman writes, the sewers would clog, the subways would flood, and buildings would collapse. Without people providing food and warmth, rats and cockroaches would die. All that would remain would be the mementos of modern civilization—the aluminum bits of appliances, stainless steel pots and pans, and, of course, plastic.

If city-dwellers are in danger, that would be a lot of us. The worldwide movement of people into cities over the last few decades is perhaps the most consequential demographic shift in our lifetime. Since human beings first settled down about 10,000 years ago, the vast majority lived on farms and in the countryside. No more. In 1950, less than a third of the world's population lived in cities, but by 2020, the share has pushed past a half. It is growing and growing—at a clip equivalent to adding a new Chicago to the planet every two weeks. By 2050, the UN estimates, more than two-thirds of humans will live in cities. To accommodate this influx, not only are new cities rising up, but existing ones are getting bigger. In 1800, there were just two cities with at least one million inhabitants, London and Beijing. In 1900, there were around fifteen. By 2000, the number had soared to 371. And by 2030, it is projected to surpass 700, of which 125 will be in China. By then, the world can expect to have over forty mega-cities, those with 10 million inhabitants or more.

All past prophecies of the decay of cities have proved wrong. Cities will endure. Urbanization, especially in developing countries, will likely recover and continue at more or less its pre-pandemic pace. No rural awakening is at hand. Most of the people who leave one city will simply move to another, perhaps smaller one. Others will buy homes in the suburbs, still centering their lives around a city, and many more will decide to stay put.

Critics say this time is different. New technologies make it much easier for people to work from home, and the danger of disease will keep them away. And it's true that there will be some significant changes in the nature of work and the old requirement that people be at the office week in and week out. But today's urban problems seem tame compared with previous eras'. The Harvard economist Edward Glaeser points out that US cities faced a bleak future in the 1970s—far bleaker than today. Globalization and automation had killed off many of the great urban industries, from textile manufacturing to shipping. The car had proved to be a life-changing technology in allowing people to live farther from the office—much more transformative than Zoom. Phone service had become cheap and easy. Add in race riots and crime and you had a Molotov cocktail of factors that wrecked city life.

And yet, cities came back. They found new economic life in the service sectors, from finance to consulting to health care. Despite the rise of fax machines, email, cheap phone calls, and videoconferencing, cities reinvented themselves in myriad different ways, drawing on a simple asset: human beings like to mingle. Glaeser notes that in industries such as finance and technology, people gain huge advantages by being close to the action, meeting new people, learning day-to-day from mentors, and comparing notes—much of which happens accidentally. He points to the data: "Americans who live in metropolitan areas with more than a million residents are, on average, more than 50% more productive than Americans who live in smaller metropolitan areas. These relationships are the same even when we take into account the education, experience, and industry of workers. They're even the same if we take individual workers' IQs into account." Globally we see the same effect: the world's 300 biggest metropolitan areas produce half of global GDP and two-thirds of GDP growth.

Cities are an ideal way to organize human beings for modern life—allowing them to mingle, work, and play, all in the same place. They help build the economic and social capital upon which healthy societies rest. They are also the most adaptive geographical units, capable of constantly responding to the pressures placed on them by broader trends or by their inhabitants. While some aspects of digital technology provide alternatives to city life, like teleconferencing, most of them—from rideshare to meal deliveries—actually make city life easier and richer. Today you can use your smartphone to get around a city quickly and cheaply, order in from hundreds of restaurants, get alerts about events in your neighborhood, and swipe for a date. Technology has enhanced the core reason people live in cities—to meet others. Indeed, cities have long promised and delivered a more engaging and exciting lifestyle—and at least in the past century, a measurably higher quality of life for their inhabitants.

Modern cities have afforded people a healthier life. Our image of urban pollution and disease comes from an image of industrial cities of another era. Researchers have described a "mortality penalty" paid by people who lived in such places, one that became severe with the onset of the Industrial Revolution and the mass urbanization that followed. In 1890, for example, death rates in America's urban areas were around a third higher than in rural areas. The young had it worst. For children aged one to four, mortality was 94% higher in urban areas. But over time, that penalty disappeared. Paved roads, sewers, streetlights, trash disposal, professional fire departments, building codes, hygiene laws, public parks—all improved health and safety. One of the drivers of the open space movement for parks and playgrounds was the idea that foul air caused disease. The creator of New York's Central Park, Frederick Law Olmsted, captured the prevailing wisdom, writing in 1870 that "air is disinfected by sunlight and foliage," so parks served as the "lungs of the city." In the developed world, the filth and squalor rampant by the mid-nineteenth century, the pall of Dickensian grime, gave way to cleaner, safer, and better cities in the twentieth century.

New Yorker writer Adam Gopnik calls the accrued advantages of liberalism "a thousand small sanities." An equivalent description for modern urbanization might be "a thousand small sanitations," but that might be an undercount. The cleanup process kicked off in nineteenth-century London.

Dirty water had become a crisis in the unprecedentedly populous cities of the industrial age. The author Steven Johnson describes London in 1851: "without infrastructure, two million people suddenly forced to share ninety square miles of space wasn't just a disaster waiting to happen—it was a kind of permanent, rolling disaster." Cholera stalked the streets, killing tens of thousands. John Snow, a pioneering epidemiologist, theorized that the disease was waterborne, and blocked a local pump to prove it. Lo and behold, the outbreak stopped raging in that neighborhood. But this dramatic experiment failed to convince the authorities to systematically implement Snow's recommendations—until his ideas became consensus decades later, after thousands of unnecessary deaths.

Across the Atlantic, turn-of-the-century America forged its own path to healthier cities. In 1908, Jersey City implemented the first large-scale use of water chlorination. The effects were miraculous. Mortality rates from diseases like typhoid cratered, and so other cities adopted the practice—among them Baltimore, Chicago, Cincinnati, Cleveland, Detroit, Philadelphia, and Pittsburgh. Cities made other changes to the way they supplied water: they filtered it, they constructed drainage canals to shield it from contamination, and they drew it from deep underground sources rather than from polluted rivers. These and other simple advances in sanitation had astonishing effects. Mortality rates in the United States fell by 40% from 1900 to 1940 and life expectancy rose from forty-seven to sixty-three, note researchers David M. Cutler and Grant Miller. They add that during that period, clean water alone "was responsible for nearly half of the total mortality reduction in major cities." For children, the reduction was higher still.

Time and again, cities the world over adopted the policies that worked, and improvements spread and built on one another. This included new ideas that we might not immediately associate with cities. For example, Boston and Philadelphia began providing school lunches late in the nineteenth century. Reform movements of all kinds gained purchase in cities, and when a new idea succeeded in one, it spread to others. In this way, urban life became better, safer, healthier, and longer. Cities haven't stopped experimenting. Leading causes of death today include noncommunicable illnesses, such as heart disease and chronic respiratory disease, ailments caused by an unhealthy diet and physical inactivity. In response, modern cities have launched all kinds of initiatives: building bicycle paths, expanding public parks, and increasing access to nutritious food sources to curb malnutrition. Even New York mayor Michael Bloomberg's much-maligned proposal of a soda tax was part of an effort to tackle the toxic rise of obesity. In 2011, Bloomberg could boast that residents of his city had a life expectancy that was two full years higher than the national average. "If you want to live longer and healthier than the average American, then come to New York City," he urged. "If you have friends and relatives that you deeply care about and they live elsewhere, on average, if they move to New York City, they will live longer."

Cities are also a much more sustainable way to live on Earth. That a city is environmentally friendly might clash with the image of concrete, tar, garbage, and smoke that we associate with it—but the facts are hard to dispute. First, city-dwellers use much less space. Urban areas take up less than 3% of the earth's surface while housing a majority of its inhabitants. City-dwellers have fewer children, and they consume less of virtually everything, from energy to food. In fact, pollution is sometimes worse in rural areas because of industrial activity or reliance on dirty fossil fuels—consider Louisiana's notorious "Cancer Alley," a region along the Mississippi where predominantly Black residents live amid a scattering of petrochemical plants. Transport is cleaner in cities since urbanites use buses, trains, subways, and bicycles. Even those mountains of garbage on New York's streets are misleading. The average urban resident recycles more while consuming less water and electricity than those in the countryside and suburbia. Major European and Asian cities are the world leaders in efficiency and sustainability.

THE POST-PANDEMIC CITY

But does a respiratory virus change all this? Actually, no. One of the myths about this pandemic has been that cities are uniquely susceptible. True, the disease will always hit cities first because they are the most globalized parts of any country. But in most nations, it soon spreads through sprawling suburbia and the countryside. Many rural areas in the United States and Europe face worse per capita death rates from Covid-19 than big cities. Within cities, some of the densest neighborhoods were the least infected—in New York, suburban Staten Island suffered more than super-dense Manhattan. Most important, good public policy can make city life safe even during an influenza-type epidemic. If you look abroad, massive cities have handled the virus stunningly well. Hong Kong, Singapore, and Taipei are all dense cities with packed mass transit systems, and yet their death tolls from Covid-19 have been amazingly low. By late July 2020, despite being exposed to millions of travelers from mainland China annually, Hong Kong had 2,100 cumulative cases of the disease and just eighteen deaths. These cities succeeded in tackling this virus because they were prepared. The SARS epidemic had taught them some painful lessons. They invested in health care and hygiene and reacted to the coronavirus early, aggressively, and intelligently. For any city with good leadership, density was not destiny.

Many developing countries have fewer resources and many more problems. In their cities, with the poor packed into crowded neighborhoods, sanitation services are severely stressed or entirely overwhelmed. Their residents rarely see the doctor. As the pandemic spread, it became apparent these cities would be the most vulnerable. Under pressure, some became inventive. Officials in Mumbai, for instance, launched new initiatives to aggressively trace, track, test, and isolate people in Dharavi, one of Asia's largest slums, to halt the spread of infection. "Private doctors have joined the fever camps," reported Soutik Biswas, the BBC's India correspondent. "The cash-rich municipality, politicians, and non-profits have provided tens of thousands of free meals and rations. Bollywood actors and businessmen have donated gear, oxygen cylinders, gloves, masks, medicines and ventilators." Before the crisis, most of the city's elite had never given much thought to—let alone visited—the poverty in their midst.

In the late nineteenth century, outbreaks of cholera and popular reports of "how the other half lives" in overcrowded tenements spurred urban reform movements in Europe and the United States. Today, the developing world's cities face issues of exponentially greater size, but, ultimately, they could easily apply some of the solutions Western cities did a century ago—centering on sanitation and clean water. And the pandemic might spur measures to protect against other calamities. The United Nations estimates that 59% of the world's cities with a population of at least half a million are at high risk from natural disasters—from cyclones to floods, droughts, earthquakes, landslides, or volcanic eruptions.

Cities still have their problems, of course. In American cities, life expectancy gaps reveal discouraging racial and economic inequalities. Newborns in Chicago's majority-White, upscale Streeterville neighborhood can expect, on average, to live to be ninety years old. That is three decades more than those born in Englewood, a predominantly African American neighborhood to the south. Meanwhile, police treat Blacks and Whites deeply unequally—and this cruel reality is most glaring in cities. These disparities have no single solution and many deep reforms are needed. But cities often highlight national problems and concentrate them in a single space. America suffers from inequality and racism everywhere—cities just force us to confront these issues rather than walling them off with gates and private security guards.

We know that cities have always been the centers of ideas, innovation, and action. They are also fonts of political progress. As John Ibbitson and Darrell Bricker explain in their study of global demography, "As a society urbanizes, and women gain more power, the ties of kin, the power of organized religion, and the dominance of men decline, along with the fertility rate." In rural areas, having many children is seen as desirable, since it means extra workers. In cities, huge families are a burden, especially for women. Cities free women from restrictive village life, providing them with new opportunities. Urban centers are also the starting points of social activism. Almost every important political, social, and economic movement began in a city. Even many of the most effective environmental groups were founded by city slickers—from the Sierra Club to Greenpeace. And it was in America's cities that protesters gathered to demand policing reforms after the murder of George Floyd.

Urbanization will continue apace in developing countries. In fact, by 2030, they will be home to some 80% of the world's megacities. But in the developed world, urbanization has probably peaked. In the United States, the share of the urban population is currently 83%. It may creep up to 89% by 2050, but the share seems to be approaching a natural limit. Researchers note that some big cities, such as New York, Los Angeles, and Chicago, have seen some recent slippage in population, and some worry about a repeat of the 1970s, when New York lost 10% of its residents. Other cities, such as Houston, Washington, DC, and Miami, have seen slower growth rates in recent years, too. Yet much of this relates to the high cost of living in cities—a symptom of success, not failure. After all, the cities of 1970s America were hollowed out by "white flight"—today's cities face gentrification, a problem arising from too many affluent people wanting to live there.

In any case, most of those leaving cities are not headed for small towns. They are relocating within their metro region, or moving to other metros, sometimes smaller ones. What's clear is that established cities are increasingly vying *with one another* to keep residents.

THE NEW METROPOLITAN MODEL

What will the city of the future look like? It could be reimagined one more time. Paris is the place to watch in this regard. In January 2020, before the full force of the coming pandemic was known, Mayor Anne Hidalgo proposed a bold new plan that could gain momentum in the post-pandemic world. As part of her reelection campaign, she announced the goal of turning Paris into a *"ville du quart d'heure"*—a fifteen-minute city. The idea is to make almost everywhere one might need to go in a typical day accessible by a short walk or bike ride. Grocery stores, work, parks, schools, cafes, gyms, doctors' offices, all would be reachable within a quarter of an hour. It sounds pleasant and obvious enough, but the idea is revolutionary. "This really goes against a hundred years of urban planning orthodoxy, the idea being that you want to separate the functions of the city," says Samuel Kling, an expert on cities at the Chicago Council on Global Affairs. The prevailing idea has long been to differentiate between the residential, commercial, entertainment, and industrial areas of a city. Nowhere have these principles been implemented more aggressively than in America. Restrictive zoning has distorted development by forbidding density, cramping construction, and pushing housing costs through the roof. Influential homeowners' associations block all change they see as infringing on their turf or threatening to attract "the wrong people" to their neighborhood—often code for minorities. Recently, this NIMBYism has provoked a countermovement in California and beyond. These activists instead say *YIMBY*, Yes In My Backyard, and advocate for zoning reform, better mass transit, and more development to spur vibrant urbanism.

Mayor Hidalgo's plans follow this same vision of diversity, both in amenities and experience, as she strives to integrate all the varied functions of the city. The new proximity of the fifteen-minute city would encourage bicycle rides and reduce car traffic. (She has already transformed the famous highways alongside the Seine into bike and walking paths.) Defying the pro-car backlash of the yellow vest movement, Hidalgo was resoundingly reelected during the pandemic and is steaming ahead with her agenda. Her popularity is understandable— even driving a brand-new Peugeot loses some of its appeal if everything you need is within walking distance. Public transportation, too, might become less crowded, a welcome outcome amid lingering concerns about social distancing. If the Paris plan moves forward, other mayors may try to make their own megacities work and feel more like small, walkable communities. To provide safety for the greater numbers of runners, walkers, and bikers who now avoid the subway, cities like Barcelona and New York banned cars from some streets. Parking spaces were converted into outdoor seating for socially distant dining. The moves have proved so popular that in some European cities these zones reclaimed by pedestrians may remain car-free after the virus recedes.

Far from downtown, cities remain the hub, with suburbs and exurbs arrayed around it. Some people like the density of city life, others prefer to live farther out in larger homes, but come and go into the city constantly for work and entertainment. This constellation of activity will vary from place to place, but everywhere, the city is the center of the solar system around it. The author Parag Khanna notes that economically, America has really turned into a collection of interlinked metro regions that he dubs, "The United City-States of America." Big, developed cities are beginning to think of themselves as independent actors on the world stage. As major metro areas have seen their economies and populations grow, mayors have sought to exercise greater political power at the national and even international levels. When President Trump announced his intention to withdraw the United States from the Paris climate accords in 2017, the leaders of Atlanta, Pittsburgh, New York, Chicago, Salt Lake City, and Los Angeles pushed ahead with the agreement anyway. Climate change, terrorism, and, yes, the pandemic have driven home the notion that cities face common challenges and should work together to tackle them.

While the biggest cities receive much of the attention, a lot of the action is happening in smaller cities. In the United States, state capitals and cities that can attract graduates of nearby universities seem especially well suited to thrive in the modern economy. That's why Denver, Oklahoma City, Austin, Nashville, and Columbus have seen notable population growth in recent years. Around 40% of students at The Ohio State University—one of the biggest schools in the nation—

say they plan to stay in Columbus after graduation. Older people, too, are choosing to live in smaller cities, often university towns that have a mix of culture and access to top-notch medical facilities.

Of course, the fact that cities in general will thrive does not mean all cities will. New York and London both bungled Covid-19 early on, despite having tremendous resources. Those cities that use the pandemic as an opportunity to make long-overdue changes will rebound. Those that handle the crisis badly will get mired in a downward spiral. But when cities decline, most often they do so for the same reasons that countries decline—bad government and mismanagement—not some broad structural trend against cities.

THE DEATH AND LIFE OF GREAT CITIES

I love cities. I grew up in a big, boisterous, dirty one, Mumbai, that was viewed with suspicion by much of the country, and today I live in one, New York, that is similar in many respects. But I like smaller, quieter cities as well. I spent seven years in Boston, living in the oldest, quaintest part of town, Beacon Hill, utterly seduced by its old-world charm. I like Los Angeles, for sure a very different place, with its brash, self-assured spirit and defiant air of modernism. I love Paris and London, Vienna and Berlin, Istanbul and Cairo, Singapore and Tokyo. I like them when they are bustling and even when they quiet down. Maybe it takes a romantic to see the beauty in an empty city. William Wordsworth was mesmerized by a seemingly uninhabited London on an early morning in September 1802. "This City now doth, like a garment, wear / The beauty of the morning; silent, bare," he wrote. "Dear God! the very houses seem asleep; / And all that mighty heart is lying still!" Wordsworth saw something peaceful and joyous even in the empty urban expanse. The sky was clear; the river ran smooth. "Ne'er saw I, never felt, a calm so deep!" he exclaimed.

My experience of New York has always been closer to that of the writer E. B. White in his 1949 paean, *Here Is New York*. For White, the people and their frenzied activities were what gave the city its vitality. This was true even as most New Yorkers were oblivious to the spectacles happening a block away. White found proximity exciting. He was thrilled to sit "eighteen inches" from a famous actor at a restaurant for lunch, and, again, "eighteen inches" from a spirited young couple at dinner. Alas, the pandemic has made a distance that felt electric now feel dangerous—at least for now. Nonetheless, for White, "The city is like poetry: it compresses all life, all races and breeds, into a small island and adds music and the accompaniment of internal engines. The island of Manhattan is without any doubt the greatest human concentrate on earth, the poem whose magic is comprehensible to millions of permanent residents but whose full meaning will always remain elusive."

That captures the essence of what the great urban theorist Jane Jacobs loved about cities—their diversity. It's why she believed that the architecture of cities should grow organically in an unplanned, haphazard way. As she put it, "Genuine, rich diversity of the built environment is always the product of many, many different minds, and at its richest is also the product of different periods of time with their different aims and fashions." She also celebrated the diversity of a city's pop-ulation. What attracted so many people to cities through the centuries was that they would meet people unlike them and see the world through different eyes. The best city, Jacobs thought, was a mosaic, "the idea being that each piece of the mosaic helps compose the overall picture, but each piece nevertheless has an identity of its own."

The world we are entering is going to be far more diverse than ever before, with ever more types of ideas, industries, jobs, companies, and people. And these people are going to be of all backgrounds, races, colors, and creeds, believing in all kinds of gods or none at all. To succeed in this world, we will have to learn to manage diversity and gain strength from it, rather than feel threatened by it. Cities do that better than anyplace else. They are built to be factories of assimilation and amalgamation.

Prophets of cities' inevitable decline have pointed to Zoom and other tools that allow work from home. But it is becom-ing increasingly clear that remote work is a fantastic tool but an imperfect substitute for actual human contact. To be sure, colleagues with established relationships can continue work-ing together smoothly by chatting online. Yet bringing on new coworkers, and establishing trust and teamwork with them, is extremely hard to achieve on video. Not to men-tion that remote work leaves out all the spontaneous water-cooler conversations and accidental meetings that ultimately create greater productivity and innovation from the collision of minds. When you teleconference, you are spending social capital rather than building it. Education by video has left students drained and uninspired, craving the actual human contact, with professors and peers, that is at the heart of learning. The technology is transformative but clearly the best model is a hybrid one that puts value on both the ease of virtual interaction and the greater resonance of actual physical contact.

Those who think that digital life renders cities obsolete should look no further than E. M. Forster's science fiction story "The Machine Stops." Written in 1909, it feels eerily prescient in 2020. In Forster's dystopia, humanity almost never experiences the real world. The "clumsy system of public gatherings had been long since abandoned"—instead, everyone lives in a small private room, "hexagonal in shape, like the cell of a bee," where all food, goods, and entertainment are automatically delivered to them by an Amazon-like "pneumatic post" and everyone talks only via videoconferencing. In this world, cities from England to China have been ironed out into uniformity:

> Few travelled in these days, for, thanks to the advance of science, the earth was exactly alike all over. Rapid intercourse, from which the previous civilization had hoped so much, had ended by defeating itself. What was the good of going to Peking when it was just like Shrewsbury? Why return to Shrewsbury when it would all be like Peking? Men seldom moved their bodies . . .

But even in this fictional vision of the future, Forster correctly anticipates that no technology can truly substitute for face-to-face connection. Subtleties are lost in digital translation. At one point, a son is talking to his mother. "He broke off, and she fancied that he looked sad," Forster writes. "She could not be sure, for the Machine did not transmit nuances of expression. It only gave a general idea of people—an idea that was good enough for all practical purposes." The son implores his mother to visit him in person, reflecting the spirit of Forster's most iconic phrase, his call for us to get closer to one another: "Only connect!"

This insight, that real-life interpersonal relations are the source of happiness and meaning, comes to us not just from visions of the future, but also from the distant past. One of the first works of political science, Aristotle's *Politics*, written around 350 BC, declares on its first pages that man is by nature a "social animal." The phrase is sometimes translated as "political animal." Both touch on a key part of the meaning, and the original Greek is instructive. It's *zoon politikon*, from the same transliterated root for animal as zoonosis—and from the concept of a polis, an ancient Greek city-state and its human community.

Aristotle goes on to explain that human beings cannot be fulfilled except in a city, comparing them to bees that can only truly thrive in beehives. For him, humans are unusual animals in that they are not fully formed at birth. They must be shaped by their environment, and the surroundings that are best at molding them into fully formed adults is the city. In fact, the core purpose of the city is to make us into model human beings and, crucially, citizens. For Aristotle, cities are not fundamentally about monuments and parks; they are about people and their character.

Humans create cities and cities make humans—these are two sides of the same coin. The reason our cities grow and endure, even when faced with calamities, is because most of us are naturally drawn to participation, collaboration, and competition. Rationalizations for city living vary—work, companionship, entertainment, culture, or all of the above. But beneath those outward reasons lie deep urges toward social interaction. Covid-19 will not short-circuit this hardwiring. In fact, the isolation of the lockdowns might have the opposite effect, reminding humans of that simple but profound insight—by nature, we are social animals.

Aristotle was right.

LESSON SEVEN

Inequality Will Get Worse

PANDEMICS SHOULD BE the great equalizer. Infectious diseases often seem blind to nationality, race, class, and creed. Humanity has turned to artists to convey this idea, from the plague years to the time of cholera. "Death is democratic," remarked the Mexican artist José Guadalupe Posada. "At the end, regardless of whether you are white, dark, rich or poor, we all end up as skeletons." Drawing on this morbid idea, Posada's most famous creation, an etching titled *La Catrina*, depicts an elegant female skeleton in a large plumed hat, a macabre figure in Victorian finery that has become associated with Mexico's Day of the Dead. He first crafted this indelible image around 1910, when cholera remained rampant. Indeed, another of Posada's works from the same year is called *The Skull of Morbid Cholera*. But for all of its equalizing impulses, the Catrina image is also very much about inequality. By dolling up a skeleton in high-society fashion, *La Catrina* serves as a sendup of the class and wealth gaps not only within Mexico, but also between Mexico and much richer Western European nations—between what we have come to think of as the developing world and the developed world.

Inequality may always be with us, it seems, joining death and taxes as the only certain things in this world. But we have come to regard the phenomenon as especially pernicious in recent years. Scholars have devoted shelves of books to the subject—journalists have written hundreds of columns on it. A Pew survey found that in thirty-one of thirty-nine countries, a majority believe it is "a very big problem." So you might be surprised to learn that, by some important measures, inequality has been going down. Global inequality, that is, the gap in income between the richest and poorest countries in the world, has been declining for several decades. The gap in income between richer and poorer people everywhere— say, between Americans and Malaysians—has also been narrowing over the same period. The shift in that latter metric is significant, because it had been widening since 1820, when the Industrial Revolution pushed the West decisively ahead of the rest of the world. In the post-World War II era, a few non-Western countries like Singapore and South Korea joined the club of industrialized nations. But despite these exceptions, the overall gap between the world's rich and poor had kept growing—until recently.

What we often mean by income inequality is the gap between rich and poor *within* countries. Here the data is more mixed. That kind of inequality rose for several decades but recently began to stabilize. Between 1993 and 2008, of the ninety-one countries analyzed by the World Bank, forty-two saw rises in inequality while thirty-nine saw declines. And between 2008 and 2013, in those same countries the news got even better: for every country in which inequality rose, there were two where it fell. In Latin America, legendary for its hierarchical societies, over this period, twelve of the sixteen countries studied showed more widely shared prosperity.

How to measure inequality is a matter of spirited debate. I have opted for the standard measure, the so-called Gini coefficient, which has been used by the World Bank, the IMF, and most scholars for decades. It is a measure of relative inequality. So if I was earning $100 and you were earning $1,000, and then our incomes both went up by 10%, our relative inequality would be unchanged. But since 10% of $1,000 is a lot more than 10% of $100, in absolute terms, you would have gained more. That is of course also true for countries. If America grows at 3.5% a year and China at 5%, the United States, which has a bigger economy to start with, would see its economic output rise more in absolute terms than China, even though China would be narrowing the gap in relative terms. Some use another lens, focusing on the gains to the top 10% or 1% of earners. Viewed that way, the gap has widened dramatically, because these groups have done much better than the rest of society. In other words, there are legitimate ways of looking at inequality that show that it has increased, but using the traditional, historical measure, we can see that after a long unbroken climb upward, *global* inequality has recently declined.

The richest and most successful countries in the world are an exception to this trend; inequality has risen sharply in many of them. That is especially true of the United States, where the Gini coefficient has climbed to its highest level since 1928, when it had soared from years of unchecked capitalism that led to the Great Depression and then the reforms of the New Deal. In 2013, President Obama called the relentless rise in inequality in America "the defining challenge of our time." But the American challenge should not obscure the progress in much of the rest of the world. We devote most of our attention to crises, tragedy, and failure, but we should also acknowledge this remarkable and broad success.

The decline in global inequality was in large part caused by sustained economic progress in China, India, and other developing countries, which grew much faster than developed countries over the last quarter century, narrowing the gap and lifting hundreds of millions of people out of poverty. I have seen the change in places in India that I have visited regularly since I was a child in the 1960s. The villages have turned into towns and the towns into cities. Homes have grown larger, with more permanent structures and a makeshift bathroom or two. Bicycles, scooters, and cars have proliferated, giving people much-needed mobility. All this has caused many problems, from toxic air and dirty water to overcrowded roads and trains. But at the same time, it has slashed the kind of poverty that caused so many children to die of malnutrition. In September 2000, the United Nations established its Millennium Development Goals. One of them was to cut in half the share of people living in extreme poverty (defined as living on less than $1.25 a day) by 2015. That goal was met five years ahead of schedule. Worldwide, the total number of people who live in extreme poverty dropped from 1.9 billion in 1990 to 650 million in 2018. On one crucial metric, the progress has been immense: the mortality rate for young children dropped 59% over the same period.

THE GREAT UNEQUALIZER

With Covid-19, much of this progress could be reversed. The pandemic might erase many of the gains made by developing countries over the last quarter century and return us to a world of great and widening global inequality. Initially, it didn't look like that would be the case. The first wave of the virus missed most of the developing world. In fact, the map of the outbreaks posed a puzzle: Why were there so few infections in poorer places? At the end of April 2020, low-income and middle-income countries, which have 84% of the world's population, were home to just 14% of the world's known deaths from Covid-19. Some of the developing world's low death tolls could be explained by a lack of testing and a failure to attribute deaths to the disease. There may be other factors. In wealthy countries, the disease ripped through densely packed nursing homes, which accounted for a large share of deaths; these are rare in the developing world. Heat may have some effect in reducing the spread of the virus, though this remains unproven. Some medical experts have privately speculated that it's possible that people in developing countries have stronger immune systems since they have been exposed to many more diseases over their lifetimes (though there are few good studies on this).

Some of these explanations may be valid—after all, we are still learning more about the disease. But the developing world appeared to have been spared the disease in the early months in large measure because it was less connected, by travel and trade, to the initial hotspots. The virus moved from China to Europe to America because that's where people were going back and forth. (China sends out the largest numbers of tourists and travelers on the planet—almost 170 million in 2019.) But in the pandemic's next phase, the coronavirus moved slowly but steadily across South Asia and Latin America and then Africa. The density of work and living quarters and the poor sanitary conditions in these places are a combustible mixture. In India, the early epicenter was in Mumbai, where one slum, Dharavi, houses about a million people and has a population density that is nearly thirty times that of New York City. In Africa's largest city, Lagos, Nigeria, two-thirds of people live in congested slums, with many taking crowded buses to work. Hospitals in lower-income countries are sparse. In Bangladesh, there are fewer than eight hospital beds for every 10,000 people, a quarter the capacity in the United States and an eighth the capacity in the European Union. At the start of the pandemic, there were fewer than 2,000 ventilators across forty-one African countries, compared with 170,000 in the US alone. The *New York Times* drily noted that South Sudan, population 11 million, had more vice presidents than ventilators.

In many developing countries, large segments of the population make just enough each day to feed themselves and their families. So governments faced a dilemma: If they shut down the economy, people would starve. If they kept it open, the virus would spread. Given that these governments don't have the money to pay people to stay home or subsidize shuttered businesses, the wisest course, in retrospect, was probably not to impose full-scale lockdowns. India, for example, partly as a result of the lockdown, is on track to see its economy shrink by 5% in 2020, rivaling the worst performance in its history. And yet, as of July 2020, the number of people confirmed to have died from Covid-19 in the country was about 28,000, fewer than the 60,000 children who die of malnutrition there *each month*. Even supposing, as seems plausible, that deaths from the disease are being vastly undercounted, this horrifying figure puts Covid-19 in perspective for the developing world. Though intended to save lives, the shutdown of nearly all activity led to economic collapse. This has caused untold hardship and ironically, exacerbated many health problems, from hunger to depression. Was it worth it? These are difficult decisions, but one cannot but think that in many developing countries, not enough thought was given to the calamities that would follow a lockdown. This is probably why, when cases spiked after quarantines were lifted, few developing countries even considered reimposing them.

After the paralysis comes the inevitable debt crisis. In the United States, Europe, Japan, and China, the economic damage is brutal, but it will be ameliorated by massive government spending to soften the blow. These countries, America above all, can borrow trillions of dollars at low interest rates with relative ease. That's not the case for poor countries that are already deeply indebted. Capital is a coward, as the saying goes, and in the first months of the pandemic, over $100 billion fled from emerging markets. To keep their economies afloat, these countries will have to take out loans in dollars and at high interest rates, which they must pay back in their own rapidly depreciating currencies. Down the line, without massive debt forgiveness programs, they will face the real prospect of hyperinflation or default.

Over the last few decades, as global trade accelerated, the developing world grew faster than the developed world, and standards of living rose accordingly. Even after the global financial crisis, poor countries recovered faster than rich ones did. Less exposed to complex financial products, they weathered the downturn relatively well. After the pandemic, the work of decades was undone in months. Various studies estimate that somewhere between 70 million and 430 million people will be pushed back into extreme poverty over the next few years. The most essential inequality—between the very richest and the poorest humans on the planet—is now growing again and at a rapid rate.

The differences between rich and poor countries will likely be accentuated as the world divides in two: places with good health-care systems and places without them. Nations have begun opening their borders more readily to people from countries where the coronavirus is under control and banning travel from places where infection is more likely—the latter category includes countries that have failed to control the virus, like Brazil, Russia, and (sadly and stunningly) the

United States. New Zealand's prime minister, Jacinda Ardern, raised the possibility that her country and Australia, both of which handled Covid-19 well, would create a "trans-Tasman bubble" in which residents of each could travel freely to the other. But, she added, "We will not have open borders with the rest of the world for a long time to come." Poor Pacific Island nations, extremely dependent on these countries for tourism dollars, responded by frantically lobbying to join the new travel zone.

But alas for Tonga and Tuvalu, going forward, travelers and businesspeople will be reluctant to visit places where they could find themselves without good medical care, and exotic destinations will lose their appeal. The economies of many developing countries will face particular hardship. For example, Thailand, the Philippines, and Mexico get between 15% and 25% of their GDP from travel and tourism. For the smaller countries of Barbados and the Bahamas, that number exceeds 30%. Fear is a great divider—and fears of disease in particular have divided the world in the past. In the nineteenth century, when the bubonic plague had long disappeared from Europe but lingered in some parts of Asia, it reinforced the divide between the industrial and nonindustrial world, between colonizers and colonized.

THE BIG GET BIGGER

The story of inequality is not just about nations but about companies as well. The retreat to safety and security will manifest itself in corporate life, where the big will get bigger. This is, again, the acceleration of an ongoing trend. Over the last few years, scholars have noted that in sector after sector, in the West and beyond, large companies have been gaining profits and market share, leaving their smaller competitors in the dust. Think of Amazon, Google, Walmart, CVS, and Home Depot in America—or Volkswagen, Carrefour, and Siemens in Europe. In China, most of the largest companies are state-owned and thus have built-in advantages, but even the private-sector behemoths like Alibaba and Tencent gain ground every year.

Usually innovation is a great leveler, as start-ups and entrepreneurs find new ways to solve problems and raise productivity while large legacy companies lumber along established paths. No more. A study by the Organisation for Economic Co-operation and Development shows that between 2001 and 2013, across the industrialized world, the most productive 5% of manufacturers boosted their productivity by 33%. The top 5% of service firms boosted theirs by 44%. All other manufacturers gained just 7% in productivity and all other service firms saw a 5% increase. Other research shows this trend growing in recent decades. Why? In today's economy, big is beautiful. Size allows companies to take advantage of the two dominant economic trends of our times—globalization and the Information Revolution. It is easier for Volkswagen and Ikea to enter the Chinese and Indonesian markets than it is for smaller firms. Large banks can find new customers across the globe, while regional ones cannot.

The Internet was meant to be the ultimate equalizer, providing small start-ups access to customers everywhere. And there is some truth to this idea. But the larger truth is that far from being a platform that has enabled competition, the Internet by nature encourages the creation of monopolies on a scale rarely seen in history. One example: the Internet enables instant price comparisons, so customers can always buy at the cheapest possible price. Thus big firms, with fixed costs spread across vast revenues, are advantaged over small ones. Today, the leading company in a given sector routinely has around 50% of the market share. Indeed, in e-commerce and social networking, people often cannot quickly bring to mind the number two player to, say, Amazon or Facebook. In search, many know the name of Google's nearest rival, Bing, because it is the pet project of another tech giant, Microsoft. But Google's global market share is close to 90% and Bing's is around 5%. Peter Thiel, the provocative tech entrepreneur and investor, admits with startling honesty that "competition is for losers." The goal of every company, he notes, should be to create a monopoly. In the tech world, the winners have succeeded beyond any historical standard.

The new force reshaping information technology is big data—which multiplies the advantages of size. Most big companies can invest heavily in technology, often creating customized programs that harness data to make operations more efficient. Walmart is famous for using technology to maintain tight supply chains, knowing in real time what is selling fast and where to resupply. Computers can now handle almost infinite amounts of data, which gives the front-runners even more advantages. In 2018, JPMorgan Chase processed 49 million credit and debit card transactions every day, totaling more than $1 trillion. That data, properly analyzed, is a gold mine, except that unlike gold, which is finite in supply, data mines just keep getting bigger.

Covid-19 will make bigger even better. Between the pandemic and the lockdown, large digital companies have become vital and seen business boom. They will continue to flourish as people get more comfortable living a digital life. But the advantages of size go beyond Internet companies. Large firms tend to have stronger lines of credit and can weather storms. They have regional or global brands and wider networks of supply and demand. If some economies recover fast while others stay stagnant, big companies can take advantage by concentrating on areas of growth in a way that a small local business cannot. Megacorporations have armies of lobbyists to ensure that when government money is spent on subsidies or stimulus, they will get the largest infusions of cash. The gains from Federal Reserve support, and from America's major pandemic relief bill, the 2020 CARES Act, went disproportionately to larger and better-connected businesses.

Those historically disadvantaged are even more vulnerable now. A McKinsey report found that minority-owned small businesses may be particularly endangered—small businesses owned by Blacks and Hispanics were twice as likely to be classified as "at risk" or "distressed" pre-Covid. These firms were disproportionately clustered in sectors hit hard by the pandemic, such as food and retail. (No wonder the report found that minorities made up 37% of the US labor force in February 2020 but accounted for 58% of the newly unemployed by mid-March.) This is, of course, another way that the pandemic will deepen existing divides, which then makes tackling them even harder.

In general, in times of turmoil and change, people will gravitate toward the security of established brands. For years now, the stock market has favored the biggest firms, whose share prices have kept soaring. The Federal Reserve's action to guarantee a vast swath of assets—so as to provide the economy with a "floor" after the Covid crisis—has served to benefit established players, even those who have taken wild risks. The Fed is offering investors the upside of a range of risky investments, including junk bonds, while guaranteeing that there will be virtually no downside. It is a fundamental remaking of capitalism—one with no punishment for failure, no dangers of collapse, and no real mechanism for valuation of assets.* And because the people most likely to own and trade stocks also tend to be the wealthiest, the policy serves to hypercharge wealth inequality. It is a textbook example of what some economists have called "the Matthew Effect," which takes its name from a verse in the Gospel according to Matthew: "For to every one who has will more be given, and he will have abundance; but from him who has not, even what he has will be taken away." The Fed's action is, as the saying goes, socialism for the rich and capitalism for the poor.

---

*As Frank Borman, the CEO of Eastern Airlines, once quipped, "Capitalism without bankruptcy is like Christianity without hell." (Eastern Airlines filed for bankruptcy in 1989.)

And it could hardly have come at a worse moment in American history.

TWO AMERICAS

Many scholars have shown that high levels of inequality make for bad economics and politics. It means lower economic growth—fewer people who can spend—and lower levels of trust in each other and in political institutions. As we have seen, historical estimates put American inequality at the highest since the Great Depression—and government studies back this up for more recent decades. The US Census Bureau has collected data on inequality since 1967. America's Gini coefficient has risen by 22% since then. If we focus on the top 10%, or even worse, the top 1%, the gap has grown even more sharply. These groups have seen their share of national income rise almost everywhere in the world—but among developed nations, nowhere has it spiked more than in America. In 1970, the top 1% of income earners captured less than 10% of all national income. In 2019, that number passed 20%. By contrast, the bottom 50% of earners have seen their share of income go in the opposite direction, from 22% in 1970 to 15% today. And finally, when you calculate inequality by wealth, rather than by income, the results are almost unimaginable. The top 10% of America owns almost 70% of the total wealth of the country—from houses and cars to stocks and bonds—while the bottom 50% own just 1.5% of assets. Back in the 1980s, Reagan's heady vision seemed to promise that America could grow its way out of addressing poverty and inequity. In 2020, growth—at least in developed countries like the US—looks likely to stay sluggish, as it has for two decades. Inequality in America looms worse than ever, the worst in the Western world, even after accounting for taxes and government transfers. By its Gini coefficient, America is closer to Brazil than to a European country like Denmark.

Covid-19 heightens all these divides. It will cut America in half. In many ways, the virus has produced a vivid picture of America's existing inequalities. Silent, unseen, the disease travels through society, oblivious—in theory—to a person's wealth or race. But look at the results. Poor areas have much higher rates of infection than rich ones and worse health outcomes. In New York City, certain poor neighborhoods in the Bronx, Queens, and Brooklyn have seen four to six times the fatality rates of the Upper East Side and the Upper West Side, even though the latter are far more densely populated. This is a window into American inequality, where poor people have more preexisting conditions like heart disease and diabetes, receive inferior care, and fear getting tested for Covid-19 as the costs of treatment could mean bankruptcy. If not infected yet, they are more likely to get infected because they have to work—and not from a distance in the comfort of their homes.

In a sad reminder of America's greatest inequity, Blacks are more than twice as likely to get Covid as Whites. Moreover, nationwide, Blacks have an overall Covid fatality rate 2.3 times higher than Whites, and in some states up to four times higher. (America is not alone in this—non-Whites in the UK are suffering similarly disproportionate death tolls.) Most striking of all might be the emotional and psychological impact of this disparity: one-third of African Americans say they personally know someone who has died of Covid-19, compared to only 9% of Whites. Grief, despair, and growing awareness of the pandemic's disproportionately harsh impact on Black America may have contributed to the upswell of activism after George Floyd's killing.

Racism's contribution to inequality goes back centuries, but recent structural shifts are also fueling it. For one thing, the financial benefits of a college education have risen steadily as the economies of the industrial world become more digital and service-oriented. America has simply not found ways to move poor bright children up the educational ladder. A study looking at college admissions from 1999 to 2013 found a staggering result—the top 1% of earners are *seventy-seven times more likely* to have a child attend Ivy League or other elite schools, compared to poorer children from families in the bottom 20% of earners. Meanwhile, as the economist Thomas Piketty and others have noted, investment income is growing faster than wages. And as we have seen, routine work—at first blue-collar and now increasingly white-collar—can be done by someone in a low-wage country or a computer. The premium that labor could once command simply does not exist in a postindustrial world. Capital moves freely around the planet, rewarding the most efficient enterprises. Technology increasingly performs tasks faster, cheaper, and better than humans can—and artificial intelligence will only accelerate the changes.

But these structural changes are not the only contributors to inequality's rise. Government policy has also supported the rich. The tax codes in many Western countries favor capital over labor in myriad ways. With many policy roadblocks like "right to work" laws in many US states, unions find it increasingly hard to gain traction. College loans and home ownership are subsidized while high school graduates and renters struggle. Since elections cost money, the rich can buy political influence, shaping the rules, regulations, and taxes in their countries. Nowhere is this more true than in the United States, where in the face of the greatest levels of inequality in the industrialized world, Congress passed trillions of dollars' worth of tax cuts in 2001, 2003, and 2017, the benefits of which have gone disproportionately to the top 10% of the country. Donald Trump, elected in part as an economic populist who railed against Wall Street, still implemented these regressive policies. The political scientists Jacob Hacker and Paul Pierson call this two-faced ideology "plutocratic populism."

There must be a better way. With structural pressures pushing inequality up and up, we need to be more creative and ambitious in tackling it. We need, for example, policies for training and retraining of workers on a scale like the GI Bill, which educated millions of veterans after World War II. Other broader measures like the Earned Income Tax Credit, which I have touched on earlier, should be greatly expanded. These are expensive ideas—but the costs of inaction may be even higher. Historically the lesson is clear: if growing inequalities are not addressed by reforms, revolution might follow.

MONEY AND MORALITY

In a democratic society, we want significant aspects of life to be shared ones that everyone experiences as equals. These have become much rarer in a monetized world. Most countries have embraced markets, which undoubtedly produce economic efficiency. But as Michael Sandel, a Harvard philosopher, explained in his 2012 book, *What Money Can't Buy: The Moral Limits of Markets*, we have moved from accepting a market economy to creating a market society, one in which everything is seen through the prism of price. Goods and services once considered above being turned into commodities can now all be bought for the right price. Want your doctor's cell phone number? Some physicians will give it to you for $1,500 a year. Want a nicer dorm room for your child with access to a fancier cafeteria? Easily done, for a few thousand dollars. There are prisons where an inmate can upgrade his cell for $90 a night. Are you a lobbyist who would like someone to stand in line for you to get a seat at a congressional hearing? That's cheap, just $20 an hour. Even a country's most sacred asset, citizenship, is up for sale in many places. Passports from certain Caribbean islands go for $100,000, while an American green card will set you back $900,000 to $1.8 million, and the UK's Tier 1 investor visa about $2.5 million. Cyprus, Malta, and Bulgaria—all EU members with few travel restrictions within the bloc—sell citizenship, too.

When everything can be bought, every aspect of life becomes unequal. Take a simple example. Watching sports live in a stadium used to be one of the great communal events. It will not be communal anymore. Historically, sports stadiums were built with seats that were all the same, the only differences being in their location. Today, they reflect our tiered society, with elaborate hierarchies from the cheap seats for the masses to better ones for the middle class to air-conditioned boxes with bars and gourmet food for the 1%. What once brought us together now reminds us how much we are growing apart. If money can buy a better house or car or even a yacht, that's one thing. But if it can buy citizenship, special access to public spaces, preferential treatment at colleges, and favors from politicians, it becomes a corrupting and corroding force.

Perhaps the most vivid example of how inequality affects societies in the wake of the Covid-19 pandemic can be seen by studying the places that handled the disease the best. Almost all have high levels of trust, both among people and between people and larger institutions. Surveys that ask whether "most people can be trusted" reveal that societies where a large share say yes—Northern Europe and East Asia generally—have been able to tackle the pandemic well. And while there are many reasons for high levels of trust, it is clear that low levels of inequality help immensely. We have seen that countries with less inequality, like Denmark, have more "social capital," of which trust is a key ingredient. As America has become more unequal over the past five decades, its levels of trust have declined sharply. African Americans feel, with great justification, that they live in a separate and unequal world, one that is subject to different laws, standards, and attitudes than the world of White Americans. Poor Americans, too, feel the system is rigged against them. If people feel a shared sense of purpose with their fellow citizens, they will have greater trust in them. But if we lead lives that are increasingly worlds apart, separated by partitions physical and invisible, we will think of ourselves as sharing little. There is then no common good.

The most glaring inequality that infectious disease creates is between the healthy and the ill, what the writer Susan Sontag called the border between the "kingdom of the well" and the "kingdom of the sick." So great is the divide that one's worldview can change permanently when crossing it—as Franklin Roosevelt did when he contracted polio. But while disease can sometimes erase inequalities, most of the time it exacerbates them. If we face another pandemic, as is highly likely, we must recognize that we will need to keep everyone safe and healthy, whether rich or poor. That should be an essential form of equality that we strive for. Perhaps the novel coronavirus is forcing us to live up to a piece of wisdom that is very old, contained in so many sacred texts and works of philosophy, declared boldly in the American and French revolutions. Inequality may be inevitable. But in the most fundamental, moral sense, all human beings are equal.

LESSON EIGHT

Globalization Is Not Dead

L ILIANA DEL CARMEN RUIZ died from Covid-19 in the early morning of March 31, 2020. She was a pediatrician in northwestern Argentina, fifty-two years old, with underlying medical conditions that might have made her more susceptible. She had not traveled abroad, and before the test confirmed that she had the novel coronavirus, she was thought to be suffering from dengue fever. The daughter of a baker and a domestic worker, she had survived cancer, earned a medical degree in the city of Córdoba, and returned to work in her home province of La Rioja. Ruiz contracted the first known case of Covid-19 in that province and was the first to die from it.

During the pandemic there have been hundreds of thousands of tragic deaths across the globe, but I've chosen to highlight this one for a simple reason. In the province of La Rioja, not far from where Ruiz died, lies the antipode (the point on the exact opposite side of the planet) of the location where the virus first emerged, just a few months earlier—Wuhan, China. A remote, landlocked corner of Argentina was affected by something that happened in a wildlife market twelve thousand miles away. We are all connected and no one is in control.

There is a paradoxical feature of pandemics: even though they have come to be named for specific locations, they are decidedly *not* contained by borders. That has been true for centuries, since the Silk Road caravans and merchant galleys of the medieval world, and especially over the past 150 years since the age of steamships and trains. There was the "Russian flu" of 1889–90, the "Spanish flu" of 1918–19, the "Asian flu" of 1957–58, the "Hong Kong flu" of 1968–69, the "Middle East Respiratory Syndrome" (MERS) of 2012, and now the "Wuhan virus" of 2019–20. By revealing an obsession with foreign labels, these names—even when incorrect as to the origin of the virus—betray the diseases' much wider reach. The urge to view a pathogen as coming from abroad is strong, but of course, those diseases have rarely been known by those monikers in the places they're named for. In Spain, the "Spanish flu" was just the flu.

It has also been the case that for over a hundred years, people have worried about the link between disease and the flattening of the world that we now call globalization. Following the influenza as it worked its way across continental Europe and then through the United Kingdom, the journalist Florence Fenwick Miller wrote in a London newspaper in 1890, "The enterprising microbe has travelled with speed. . . . We must pay the price of our advantages, and the trains which carry us and our letters so rapidly about serve also, apparently, for the quick conveyance of the destructive microbes of disease." As that pandemic ravaged Europe, a fifteen-year-old Winston Churchill was moved to compose a poem for his high-school newspaper describing the disease's relentless march west from Asia: "The Ural peaks by it were scaled / And every bar and barrier failed / To turn it from its way; / Slowly and surely on it came, / Heralded by its awful fame, / Increasing day by day."

Today, concerns about disease and globalization have rapidly congealed into the notion that the pandemic will unravel this interconnected world—that, as one columnist grimly predicted, Covid-19 is "the final nail in the coffin of globalization." But is it really? People have been protesting globalization and warning of its demise for decades. Books have been written decrying it. Political movements have based much of their appeal on the idea of turning back this supposedly terrible tide. But has anyone done that? *Can* anyone do that? Writing in the early weeks of the pandemic, the author Zachary Karabell concluded that once we examine the data more closely, "we are likely to find fresh confirmation of what we already know about globalization: that it's easy to hate, convenient to target and impossible to stop."

The current anti-globalization argument is that we are all too intertwined, our lives and economies so entangled that we have lost control over our own destiny. One particular element of this concern is that in an emergency like Covid-19, global supply chains make us vulnerable to critical shortages in medical goods. The new conventional wisdom is that some things must be manufactured locally. It is hardly the first time we have seen renewed anxiety about the loss of control that accompanies a bewildering global economy. In the late 1960s, Harold Wilson, as prime minister of Great Britain, faced pressures from international markets and vowed to resist the "gnomes of Zurich." Throughout the 1990s, we watched economic crises unfold, from Mexico to East Asia to Russia, and in each one people claimed that their countries were being immiserated because financiers in places like New York and London were callously betting against them. When markets shower you with cash, you consider it your just rewards, but when they withdraw their blessings, you holler that the game is rigged.

In 1999, as trade was expanding rapidly and the Internet was roaring, another kind of blowback began—this time taking the form of popular backlash. That year, a farmer named José Bové organized a group of activists who destroyed a McDonald's franchise being built in the small French town of Millau—for Bové, the Golden Arches embodied homogenous, American-style capitalism sweeping the globe. In December 1999, tens of thousands of angry demonstrators descended on a meeting of the World Trade Organization in Seattle. The September 11, 2001, attacks were, in a sense, also a backlash against an open world. But these crises did little to slow the onward march of global trade. In response to 9/11, countries did put in place a series of checks and barriers to travel and immigration, but, after a brief setback, people resumed traveling in ever-growing numbers. From 2001 to 2018, air travel more than doubled, from 1.7 billion annual passengers to 4.2 billion.

The financial crisis of 2008 dealt a more lasting blow. The shocks to the American and European markets reverberated globally, with the flow of capital, goods, and services falling sharply around the world, by 9% or more. As economies recovered, these flows grew very slowly. Trade, capital flows, and foreign direct investment never recovered to their 2008 levels. People began attributing the crisis to an overly complex and connected global economy, one that benefited capital at the expense of labor—bankers and investors over everyday workers. Then came the recovery, fueled by historically low interest rates and other active monetary policies, which caused stocks and other financial assets to rise in value, further deepening the divide between capital and labor. Populist politicians who railed against "globalism" were elected in major countries, including the United Kingdom and the United States. People began to speak of "deglobalization." And then came the pandemic.

THE DRIVE FOR INDEPENDENCE

Covid-19 and the ensuing national lockdowns caused economic indicators to slump more dramatically than at any time on record. In April 2020, compared to a year earlier, global air traffic fell by 94%, new car registrations in the European Union were down 76%, and the United States had 20 million fewer jobs. By May, the US unemployment rate peaked at 14.7%—the figures were literally off the charts. Alongside these economic shocks came the imposition of border controls and travel restrictions, even between countries famous for their openness to one other. Europe's Schengen zone, within which EU citizens normally travel without any visas or restrictions, barred almost all foreign visitors, and for a while, even stopped internal freedom of movement.

In addition, people became deeply concerned about their reliance on overseas producers for key medical supplies. One in every three pills taken by Americans, for example, are generics produced in India, which itself gets two-thirds of pharmaceutical ingredients from China. At the height of the pandemic in mid-March 2020, the arteries of world trade narrowed and clogged up. With far fewer flights, the per-pound cost of transporting goods across the Pacific tripled. Seeking security, many governments—from the EU to Japan to India—announced their resolve to pursue greater self-sufficiency, or at least make the system of global supply chains more resilient. Even previously committed globalists suddenly began talking about "reshoring." In a national address, French president Emmanuel Macron lamented his country's "dependence on other continents," and announced his new post-pandemic goal would be to achieve the "independence of France" in technology and industry. Weeks later, lifelong internationalist Joe Biden released a $400-billion "Buy American" plan. A constellation of forces seems to be coming together to reverse the free flow of goods, services, money, and people that has transformed the world in these last four decades.

Will it work? Let's take a look at a few measures, which

mostly tell us what the situation looked like before the pandemic. (More recent figures are not yet available.) One common metric of globalization is exports as a percentage of the global economy. It went down sharply after 2008, and while it has recovered somewhat, it stood at 30.1% in 2018, just below its high in 2008 of 30.8%. But where was this measure just twenty years ago, in 2000? At 26%. Thirty years ago, in 1990? At 19%. Or consider foreign direct investment. In 2016, these flows amounted to $2.7 trillion. That figure had ballooned from 2000, when it stood at $1.6 trillion. In 1990, it was $240 billion. Air travel and related tourism in 1998 contributed $1.4 trillion to global GDP, a figure that had almost doubled by 2016. In other words, by almost all measures since the 1990s, globalization has galloped forward

SEVEN DECADES OF GLOBALIZATION

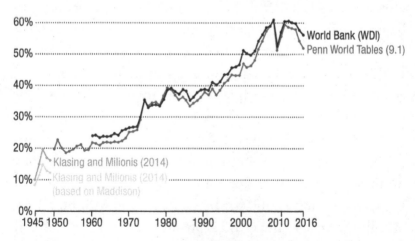

The "trade openness index" looks at all exports and imports as a share of the total world economy, expressed on the y-axis as a percentage of GDP.

and in the last few years it has taken one or two steps back. That's not deglobalization—that's a pause.

Overall, the global economy remains deeply interconnected. The broadest measure, the "trade openness index," which looks at all exports and imports as a share of the total world economy, was down to 54% in 2016 from 61% in 2007. But look at the chart historically, and since 1945, when trade openness stood at about 10%, you see an almost unbroken upward path of increasing globalization. The fallback since 2008 is real but small, a blip on the long-term trend.

The short-term effect of the pandemic and lockdowns, of course, has been to curtail all economic activity, domestic and international. This reversal will probably grow into a phase of real but modest deglobalization. But economic indicators could improve just as rapidly as they have deteriorated, especially once a treatment or vaccine is at hand. The longer-term effects are unclear, but the melodramatic rhetoric against globalization has yet to translate into equally extreme policy. Almost no country has enacted major new tariffs in response to the virus, nor does any have plans to do so. Erecting barriers wouldn't make much sense, since most countries will be searching for the strongest ways to boost growth, and placing obstacles in front of trade is a sure way to impede the recovery.

The Trump administration has bucked America's long tradition of promoting free trade, at great cost to American taxpayers—some $1,300 per household—and with little benefit. But the rest of the world is pressing onward. The last few years have seen the revised Trans-Pacific Partnership (minus America), the EU-Canada deal, the EU-Japan deal, and the

African Continental Free Trade Area. True, since 2008, countries have put in place hundreds of small new protectionist measures or tariffs. But their net effect is modest. The average tariff rate in the industrialized world in the 1960s, before a round of liberalization that culminated in 1967, stood at 15%. In 2017, the global average—even including traditionally trade-skeptical developing countries—was under 3%. Perhaps it will rise to 4%. Again, great strides forward and a step or two back.

As they were tackling the Covid-19 outbreak, several countries, including the US, India, and France, spoke out about the dangers of dependence on foreign suppliers for vital medical products. But at least in the West, many of the goods that were in short supply were not complicated machinery or drugs; they were simple equipment like face masks and cotton swabs, which naturally tend to be produced in lower-income countries. Bringing back the mass manufacturing of basic consumer products like these would be enormously expensive. And the next emergency might be a climate catastrophe, requiring entirely different emergency supplies. Even the next pandemic could be something totally different from a respiratory virus and need its own set of critical equipment. Is the government supposed to anticipate every imaginable scenario and subsidize dozens of industries to insure against all possible shortages during the next shock? That would truly reshape the face of capitalism.

The supply problem could be solved far more easily if governments simply bought large quantities of a variety of medical supplies and stored them, periodically replenishing those that expired. The shortages are usually short-term, right when the crisis hits—after which the private sector ramps up to fulfill demand. This is exactly what happened during the Covid-19 pandemic. For a few months, face masks were running desperately low worldwide, prompting many governments to ban exports of protective equipment. India did so, and over the following months, Indian manufacturers boosted production capacity of N95 masks to fifty-seven times their pre-pandemic level. By July, many places faced massive oversupply. In China, wholesale mask prices fell 90%.

Instead of reshoring, the goal should be to create a kind of strategic medical reserve akin to the strategic petroleum reserve. The United States does have such a stockpile but it is limited and often neglected. Its medical supplies were never significantly replenished after the H1N1 outbreak in 2009. Many of the Asian countries that handled Covid-19 well had in fact created large reserves of crucial equipment, a lesson they learned from the SARS and MERS outbreaks. It would not be hard for countries to think through potential disasters, study what critical goods and equipment would be essential, and create reserves. Companies should also think about staying resilient in such emergencies, perhaps maintaining their own reserve stockpiles of some inputs and materials. All this would be much cheaper than keeping entire industries afloat in perpetuity, for the possibility that once in a decade products we need might be in short supply for a few months.

For many countries, however they might couch it, the fear is less a general unease with dependence on foreign countries; it is specifically a fear of dependence on China. This concern, which predates the pandemic, is rooted in the legitimate worry about the massive concentration of supply from that one country—70% to 80% of global production for some consumer products. In fact, the Trump administration is taking advantage of Covid-19 to move forward in a direction it has long favored: decoupling from China. Some European governments are doing the same. These efforts are motivated not only by a desire to diversify supply chains but also by concerns about China using its market power for geopolitical purposes. But the easiest way to diversify away from Chinese suppliers is to move factories to places where companies can still keep production costs low without worrying about great-power politics, such as Vietnam or Bangladesh or Romania. This transition was already under way, as China becomes a middle-income country and its labor costs rise. In fact, the greatest long-term beneficiary of this Covid-related concern might well be Mexico, as American firms move Chinese facilities closer to home while still taking advantage of cheap labor. Whatever the virtue of these moves—and some are justified—they do not herald the end of globalization. They merely represent a reorganizing within the world of trade and cross-border investment.

Some factories will come home. Governments from Japan to the European Union have created incentives for firms to onshore production. The Trump administration has encouraged its largest companies to make more in the USA, in part by giving tax breaks to American exporters. But even with such incentives, rebuilding domestic production will be a slow process. The efforts run up against one of the most powerful forces on the planet: comparative advantage. Globalization has flourished because of the simple economic fact that it is easier for different countries to specialize in certain areas. Advanced countries are not well suited to making basic consumer goods, which is why most of them have seen manufacturing's share of employment decline sharply since the 1950s and '60s. Levi's selvedge jeans cost around $130, while their "Made in the USA" version of the same pants costs about $350.

Despite Donald Trump's promises to America's blue-collar workers and his imposition of the most extensive duties since the infamous Smoot-Hawley Tariff of 1930, the percentage of American jobs that are in manufacturing has stayed flat under his watch, still down more than half from 1980. This stagnation will likely persist. During the pandemic, Brooks Brothers announced that it was closing its three American factories. The CEO explained that these facilities had never been financially viable—they were part of the brand's "Made in America" marketing effort—but in light of the economic downturn, the company could no longer afford to run them at a loss. (In fact, the company soon filed for bankruptcy, and as of this writing was searching for a new owner.)

Apple faced a similar dilemma. In 2012, the company's CEO, Tim Cook, proudly announced on prime-time television that its new computer would be manufactured in the United States. It was to be the first Apple product in many years bearing the words, "Assembled in USA." But the plan to make Macs in Austin, Texas, turned out to be far more difficult than imagined, and sales of the computer were delayed by several months. The main obstacle ended up being something tiny, a custom screw that American manufacturers couldn't produce enough of and that Apple ended up having to order from China. The broader problem is that China has specialized in manufacturing for technical products like computers while the United States has not. As Cook said in 2017, "In the U.S., you could have a meeting of tooling engineers and I'm not sure we could fill the room. In China, you could fill multiple football fields." Now, amid the US-China trade war and the pandemic, Apple is again exploring moving some of its production out of China—to Vietnam and India.

This entire discussion has focused on material goods, an important part of many advanced economies, for sure, but a declining one. Most modern economies have more jobs devoted to services than ones making physical products. Seventy percent of US GDP is produced by the service sector. Four out of every five American jobs are in services. One hears paeans to Germans' extraordinary prowess at making things, but the reality is that even in Germany, the numbers are similar: around 70% of its economic output and its jobs are in services. In France, manufacturing makes up less than 10% of GDP. Advanced economies are today, almost by definition, service economies. (Ironically, we have continued to call the world's most advanced economies "industrialized countries," when really they are all *post*industrial.) Services are hard to export because many, like hospitality, are inherently local, and others, like law and accounting, are regulated in a way that favors domestic firms. The fastest-growing service in many places is health care, which is both local and highly regulated.

And yet, there are service industries from banking to consulting that are finding ways to globalize and grow.

But the biggest shift in global economics in recent years has been the rise of the digital economy, which is by nature global. Video streaming, email, and file sharing are all growing relentlessly. As software continues to "eat" hardware, it might become difficult to distinguish between a digital and a physical product. How would you describe an X-ray that is taken in New York but analyzed by a combination of computers in Singapore and people in Mumbai? If you're in Paris and an Uber driver picks you up in a Prius, are you paying for the Japanese car, the French labor, or the Californian smart network that routes you to your destination? Companies around the world are selling their products on platforms like Amazon, Facebook, and Alibaba and using digital tools to enhance production, marketing, and delivery. As a result, the digital economy is booming. From 2005 to 2016, Cisco calculates, the use of cross-border bandwidth grew ninetyfold, and it is expected to grow an additional thirteenfold by 2023. While starting from low bases, digital products now dominate many industries. Most online services traverse borders continually and invisibly.* That's why the economists Susan Lund and

---

* There is one large exception to this borderless digital world and that is China, which has walled its Internet off to outside companies. But China's example has not been followed by other countries—few have the scale to do it anyway—and so we have, in some areas, two digital worlds, China and the rest.

Laura Tyson make the case that globalization is not in fact retreating; it's just changing forms.

Even as globalization goes digital, its traditional form is making new inroads in emerging markets, especially in Asia. As Lund and Tyson write, "more than half of all international trade in goods involves at least one developing country, and trade in goods between developing countries—so-called South-South trade—grew from seven percent of the global total in 2000 to 18 percent in 2016." These emerging markets are opening up rather than closing down to trade. Asia increased its share of world trade between 1990 and 2016, from 24% to 34%, while over the same period trade went from comprising less than 35% of Asia's GDP to over 55%. China's Belt and Road Initiative—a vast infrastructure investment program offered to countries in Asia, Africa, Latin America, and even Europe—has mercantilist, perhaps even imperial motivations. But it is still a massive expansion of foreign trade and investment. From 2014 to 2017 alone, China lent some $120 billion for infrastructure projects in Belt and Road countries.

Since 1945, America has led the world toward more open and freer trade. Trump marks a sharp break with this tradition. But even in the absence of American leadership, countries around the world, from East Asia to Africa, keep searching for more ways to trade and connect. If you want to raise the living standards of your people, you have to find ways to buy and sell from the rest of humanity. Consider the Trans-Pacific Partnership, which Trump abandoned in January 2017. Every other country involved forged ahead, and a successor trade pact is now in force, covering 495 million people and 15% of the world economy. For now, America has a large enough internal market that it can wall itself off from the world—though it will pay a price in higher costs and lower efficiency. But for most of the rest of the world, there is no alternative to more trade.

GLOBALIZATION EVER AFTER?

Human beings don't want to stand still. Movement has been the way of the world for tens of thousands of years. If we think of globalization as the increasing movement of people, goods, and capital, it has been at work ever since the first humans began migrating out of Africa sometime between 60,000 and 90,000 years ago—most likely as increasing droughts and famines (and perhaps disease) forced them to search for new pastures. In the intervening millennia, the long process of globalization has continued apace, through wars and plagues. As empires rose—Persian, Roman, Incan, Mali, Mongol, and Ottoman—they all expanded trade routes, discovered new frontiers, and caused the intermingling of peoples.

The point at which modern globalization was born can be dated more precisely. No less a luminary than Adam Smith suggested two years—1492 and 1498. In the former, Columbus "discovered" the Americas; in the latter, Vasco da Gama found a new route to Asia by going around Africa. Smith called these "the two greatest and most important events recorded in the history of mankind." Why? They meant that the global economy had massively expanded, adding millions of new consumers and producers. "The commercial towns of Europe, instead of being the manufacturers and carriers for but a very small part of the world (that part of Europe which is washed by the Atlantic ocean, and the countries which lie round the Baltic and Mediterranean seas)," he explained, "have now become the manufacturers for the numerous and thriving cultivators of America, and the carriers, and in some respects the manufacturers too, for almost all the different nations of Asia, Africa, and America." Smith was writing at a time when agriculture still dominated almost every nation's economy, but he foresaw how this expanded global market would cause trade and manufacturing to grow steadily at the expense of farming. Cities and towns, he predicted, would replace the countryside as creators of greatest economic value.

After the Industrial Revolution, trade took off like never before. Sugar, wine, tobacco, and cod were shipped across the world in ever-increasing quantities. (Globalization also involved the brutal, horrific trade in enslaved people who for centuries provided free labor for industries like sugar and tobacco.) But the brisk trade in goods did not fundamentally improve overall living standards until the early nineteenth century. The historians Kevin O'Rourke and Jeffrey Williamson argue that globalization's "big bang" began in the 1820s and proceeded throughout the nineteenth century. It was triggered by the collapsing price of transportation. Between 1882 and 1914, they note, the cost of shipping rice from Rangoon (modern-day Yangon in Myanmar) to Europe fell by three-quarters. So too did the freight rate on coal between Shanghai and Nagasaki. In just three decades, the tonnage of world shipping almost tripled. Prices for products began to converge globally. And alongside this globalization came a broad rise in incomes in those countries that were participating in this new and much larger market.

Equally dramatic transformations can be found in our own age, particularly in the collapse of the cost of communication that took place with the rise of fast Internet connections. When I was in college, a three-minute call to my mother in India was so expensive that I had to budget the call and watch the clock. Today my daughter can spend five hours on Face-Time with a friend in Singapore and it costs nothing. And while we can describe this drop as a fall in the cost of communication, it is really a fall to zero in the cost of transport for many goods and services that are digital. It has powered the second big bang of globalization, one in which we are still living.

The deep currents of today's globalization make it very different from previous versions. Investments flow around the world. Goods are manufactured in one set of countries, and then marketed, sold, and serviced in another. Sometimes a product moves five or six times back and forth across countries. Information zips instantly around the world. Underneath all this is the ceaseless movement of people—5 million international students, 270 million migrants, 1.5 billion tourist trips each year. Can this all be reversed? Perhaps the rates of increase will slow or pull back modestly, but there are so many structural forces pushing globalization forward that a full-scale reversal would require a massive unwinding with huge consequences. It is worth remembering, however, that it did unwind once before in modern history—and it can happen again.

The last great era of global integration was in the early years of the twentieth century. The world was largely at peace. The technological revolutions that drove the era were stunning—telegraphs, telephones, radio, trains, steamships, automobiles, and electric lighting. Trade had swelled to unprecedented levels. Describing that heady time, the economist John Maynard Keynes observed that people were getting used to previously unimaginable conveniences: "The inhabitant of London could order by telephone, sipping his morning tea in bed, the various products of the whole Earth, in such quantity as he might see fit, and reasonably expect their early delivery upon his doorstep." People traveled abroad without passports and communicated across borders in a way that they never before had. Tens of millions of immigrants had settled in new lands like America, Canada, and Australia. From 1870 to 1914, the total number of workers residing in a foreign country increased fivefold. By 1914, some 15% of the United States' population were immigrants, a figure the country is only now coming close to matching a century later.

Keynes's fellow countryman Lord Bryce, one of the keenest observers of the age, declared in 1902 that "for economic purposes all mankind is fast becoming one people." Later that decade, Norman Angell's best-selling book *The Great Illusion* argued that the major European countries had become so interdependent that starting a war would evidently be self-defeating. Disrupting global commerce and impoverishing your enemy (and trading partner) would be more costly than any possible economic gain from victory. "The warlike nations do not inherit the earth; they represent the decaying human element," he wrote.

Angell was right that war would prove costly and counter-productive, but Europe decided to run the experiment none-theless. Four blood-soaked years later, 20 million people had died and Europe's intertwined economy lay in ruins. Four vast multinational empires—the Russian, Austro-Hungarian, Ottoman, and German—had collapsed. The war set off eco-nomic and political whirlwinds, bringing communism to Russia and fascism to Germany and Italy. Then came the Depression and another, even bloodier world war. By many measures, it took some sixty years for global trade and travel to return to the peaks they reached before World War I. What undermined the last great age of globalization was not economic or technological backlash but politics—of the oldest kind, realpolitik.

History doesn't repeat itself but it rhymes, goes the saying. And while we are living in a new age of globalization and technological change, we are seeing the return of one of the oldest stories in international relations—the rise of a new great power and the unease this creates in the existing hegemon. Hard-edged realpolitik might be back with the rise of China and the intensifying great-power competition between it and the United States—the two largest economies on the planet. One can confidently say that, given the levels of interdepen-dence between the two countries, sustained conflict would be wrenching, costly, and ultimately—for the average citizen of both countries—hugely counterproductive. But as Norman Angell discovered, that does not mean it won't happen.

In short, globalization isn't dead. But we could kill it.

The World
Is Becoming Bipolar

"EVERY MORNING in the endless month of March, Americans woke up to find themselves citizens of a failed state," declared the writer George Packer in the early weeks of the Covid-19 outbreak. The sense of shock prompted by the pandemic and America's hapless response was real, but it came against the backdrop of growing worries about the state of the country. Since the 2008 financial crisis, which soiled America's reputation, many had feared that the country was in deep trouble. Some economists wrote about slowing productivity and growth—"secular stagnation." Others highlighted rising inequality, while still others the striking rise in mortality caused by alcoholism, drug use, and suicide—the so-called deaths of despair. The election of a reality TV star in 2016 was a sign of the collapse of politics. (Even those

who saw Trump as a savior believed that the system was broken; they just thought that he was the solution.) And then
came the pandemic, which shone a harsh light on America's problems—from ineffective government to patchy health
care to vicious polarization. "Over more than two centuries,
the United States has stirred a very wide range of feelings in
the rest of the world: love and hatred, fear and hope, envy
and contempt, awe and anger," the Irish commentator Fintan
O'Toole wrote in April 2020. "But there is one emotion that
has never been directed towards the US until now: pity."

Covid-19 did not just accelerate talk about American
decline; it did so in the context of concerns about the rise
of China. Just as America's decaying infrastructure was often
compared with China's gleaming cities, Washington's inef-
fectual pandemic response was set against Beijing's effective
taming of the disease. Despite being the original epicenter of
the coronavirus, China managed not only to flatten its curve,
but to crush it—at a dramatic speed and scale. At one point
the Chinese government imposed a partial or full lockdown
on 800 million people, and at another point it tested 10 million people in Wuhan in less than three weeks. The Trump
administration tried to deflect attention from its own problems
by shifting the blame to China, which had indeed mishandled
the virus initially and misled the world about it. Many around
the world, distressed at China's deceptions, were nonetheless
struck by its competence. Within China, commentators saw
Washington's rhetoric as the signs of a superpower in decline
trying to hold back its rising rival.

We have been here before. In an essay in *Foreign Affairs*

in 1988, the Harvard scholar Samuel Huntington found so many instances of people talking about American decline that he coined a term for them—"declinists." He argued that America was then witnessing its fifth wave of declinism. The first was triggered by the Soviet launch of Sputnik, the second in the late 1960s by the US quagmire in Vietnam, the third by the oil shock of 1973, the fourth by the hangover from Watergate and the stagflation of the late 1970s, and the fifth by the rise of Japan in the late 1980s (when he was writing). In the years since, America has been so dominant that it has taken a lot to shake its confidence. But the Iraq War, the 2008 financial crisis, and now Covid-19 have produced what is clearly a sixth wave of declinism.

Huntington noted that no matter how eloquent and intense were the predictions of American decline, in each case, they did not come true. His contrarian perspective has over the years created its own conventional wisdom, spawning a cottage industry of scholars and journalists who argue vigorously against "the myth of American decline." Will this sixth wave prove to be yet another mistaken case of doom and gloom? Or are we watching weaknesses accumulate, each one adding to the last, in a way that will eventually lead to downfall? In *The Collapse of British Power*, the historian Correlli Barnett argued that Britain, the superpower of its age, went through a similar pattern. It endured a number of setbacks, but over time, the problems festered, the mistakes compounded, and the international competition grew tougher. After many decades of erosion, by the late 1940s, despite having won World War II, the country was effectively bankrupt. Britain's empire fell apart, and it spent the next half-century adjusting to its diminished global role. Is that what the future has in store for America?

There are reasons to worry. The United States' poor handling of the pandemic highlighted weaknesses in its own domestic system and undermined its image as the world's leader, feeding disenchantment with the American model of capitalism and democracy. Over the last two decades, the Internet has given people across the world broader exposure to the American model—and they have recoiled from some of its more brutal aspects. The United States has far more gun violence, police shootings, and prison inmates than other advanced countries, sometimes an order of magnitude more. Inequality is markedly greater. Large numbers of people lack the basic security of health insurance. The racial divide persists, unhealed. When I was growing up in India, people criticized American foreign policy but still saw the American model as the most advanced and successful in the world. Today, they look at that model with much greater skepticism and, yes, sometimes even pity.

But the reality is that America, for all its flaws, continues to perform extremely well on the most basic measure of global power: economic heft. It remains the largest economy in the world by far, comprising about a quarter of all global output—more than the next two countries, China and Japan, put together. America's share of global GDP has actually expanded over the last decade as the US rebounded from the global financial crisis faster and stronger than most of its economic peers. Its banks, which were at the center of that crisis, emerged from it more dominant globally. In the World Economic Forum's Global Competitiveness Index, the US ranks second (to tiny Singapore). In Deloitte's most recent rankings for Global Manufacturing Competitiveness, it nearly ties China for first place. The United States hosts a majority of the world's largest and most technologically advanced companies. The world's reserve currency remains the US dollar, which has only expanded its reach in recent years, now accounting for almost 90% of all currency transactions. The economist and investor Ruchir Sharma observes that if China and the US "maintained their officially reported 2019 nominal GDP growth rates—around six percent and four percent, respectively—China would not catch up to the United States until around 2050." And of course, Washington has the world's most powerful military by far, spending more on defense than the next ten countries combined—half of which, as US treaty allies, are on its team.

America is a messy, ragged, unequal country with dramatic strengths and weaknesses. It could be better governed and more equitable, but it remains incredibly strong, at least as measured by traditional metrics of power. What has shifted noticeably in recent years is America's "soft power"—often defined as its appeal, example, and capacity to set the agenda. The scholar who invented the concept of soft power, Joseph Nye, and who has generally been skeptical of American decline, has warned in recent years of unmistakable signs of the erosion of America's soft power. Nye notes that global attitudes toward the United States have soured. In a 2018 Pew Survey, only 50% of those polled across twenty-five countries held a favorable view of it, compared with 43% who held an unfavorable view. Only 28% thought that America took into account the interests of other nations. And only 14% believed that it was doing more to help with global problems than it had a few years earlier. Some of this is a direct reflection of the collapse in support for the American president, from 64% for Obama to 29% for Trump. But, beyond personalities, this slide seems to have more to do with what is going on outside America rather than within. It is out there, with the "rise of the rest," that real change has taken place—and fast.

To understand why America's power is waning, focus on the core idea of power: the ability to get others to do what you want. Compare America's ability to influence, say, Turkey, today versus three decades ago. In the 1980s, Washington could get Turkey to do whatever it asked. The country's economy was a basket case, often bailed out with American help. Its military was politically dominant and remained a faithful ally of the United States all through the Cold War. Today, Turkey acts with almost no regard for Washington's views, pushing its own ideas and agenda, staunchly opposing US support for the Kurds in Syria and buying sensitive military equipment from Russia. Turkey's growing lack of deference to Washington dates back to well before the Trump era. In 2003, the Bush administration, accustomed to the old relationship with Turkey, decided that it would use the country as one of its two fronts for the invasion of Iraq. It was stunned when the Turks refused permission.

I use the example of Turkey because it illustrates the central reason for the growing limits on American power, which is not the decline of America but rather the rise of the rest.

In the 1980s, Turkey was a dutiful ally because it depended on Washington for its economic, political, and military survival. But the Cold War has long passed, and Turkey's security concerns are more parochial in nature, having less to do with global threats like Soviet communism and more to do with its neighbors. Meanwhile, since 1990, its economic output has quintupled, and per capita GDP has tripled. Its political system has, relatively speaking, grown much more stable and developed. The country's leader, Recep Tayyip Erdoğan, repeatedly voted into office, rules with increasing confidence. The military has much less influence in politics; in 2016, Erdoğan thwarted an attempted coup, avoiding a fate that had befallen many elected Turkish leaders. Turkey is not unusual. Substitute it with Indonesia, Brazil, or Kenya, and you will find a similar pattern of economic and political growth leading to independence and assertiveness. The best example of that pattern, of course, is China.

ONE WORLD, TWO POWERS

Any discussion of the rise of China begins with the key underlying trend: economic growth. At the start of the post-Cold War era, the country accounted for less than 2% of global GDP. Now it accounts for 16%. For the last decade, China has been the single largest source of global growth. It is now the world's number one trading nation in goods, taking the place of the United States, which had held that position for seven decades. China is the world's largest manufacturer and the second-largest importer, and it holds the world's largest foreign exchange reserves. It is number one in shipbuilding and the production of solar panels and wind turbines. It is the biggest market for cars, computers, and smartphones in the world. It has 226 of the 500 fastest computers in the world, twice as many as America.

In other words, China has arrived. Its rise has been so dramatic that one can now see the outlines of a bipolar international system. The United States remains the number one nation by far, but the distinguishing feature of any bipolar system is that the two top powers are miles ahead of all the others, and that is certainly true of the United States and China. (When the foreign policy theorist Hans Morgenthau described the post-World War II order as bipolar, his reasoning was that, with the collapse of British power, the US and the USSR towered above all other major countries.) In 2020, China's share of global GDP ranks second, but it is almost as large as that of the *next four countries combined*. Its defense budget is now second only to the US—but there too, China's military spending is larger than those of the next four countries put together.

As China has risen in economic power, it is Europe, not America, that has slipped. America's share of global GDP has stayed roughly constant since 1980. Since 1990, the countries that now compose the EU saw their share of the world economy shrink from 30% to below 20%, and geopolitically, the EU is still mostly ineffective as a single power. The richest European nation, Germany, is about a quarter the size of China's economy. Other countries are not even in the same league. India, often cited as a counterweight to China, has an even smaller economy, about a fifth in size. Russia has some of the formal attributes of a major power, such as a UN Security Council veto and a vast nuclear arsenal. But its economy is now one-eighth the size of China's and its military budget a quarter.

No two bipolar systems are the same. The Soviet Union equaled the United States in terms of military power (at least by some metrics) but on every other measure, it lagged far behind. China is in some ways the mirror opposite. Its military remains much weaker than America's, but in many economic and technological arenas, it is a peer competitor. Further down the list, the world's third- and fourth-largest economies—Japan and Germany—are for historical reasons destined to play a somewhat passive role in international affairs. All of this means that there is a growing chasm between the two superpowers and everyone else.

Are we then destined for conflict between these two poles in the emerging international system? Scholars, starting with Thucydides, have long worried about the dangers of "power transitions," when a rising great power bumps up against an established one. Initially, China and America did not look like rivals. By 2006, the economic interdependence between the two countries seemed so deep that the scholars Niall Ferguson and Moritz Schularick came up with the word "Chimerica," arguing that "China and America had effectively fused to become a single economy." But things began to unravel after the global financial crisis, with the rise to power of Xi Jinping in China and then of Donald Trump in America. By 2020, there were many tensions that had built up between the two nations, over trade, technology, and geopolitics. The pandemic allowed them to burst into the open, with Washington ramping up both rhetoric and action against Beijing. Looking back, will future generations say that the most profound consequence of Covid-19 was the start of the Second Cold War?

The shift in Sino-US relations has taken place in both capitals. Under President Xi Jinping, who came to power in 2012, Beijing has become far more assertive internationally, from grabbing Indian territory to asserting maritime claims in the South China Sea. It has imposed greater control over Hong Kong and sought more deference from countries that receive Chinese foreign aid and loans—while pressuring nations, firms, and global organizations to accept China's position on Taiwan and other issues. The Chinese foreign ministry has become more belligerent with its new "Wolf Warrior diplomacy," an approach that gets its name from a Chinese action-movie franchise that shows China's military flexing its muscle around the world.

The Trump administration, for its part, came into office determined to get tough with Beijing. In particular, it sought to decouple the United States from the country economically and technologically, an effort that went into rhetorical overdrive once the pandemic began. China also saw an opportunity. Having largely tamed its outbreak at home and dodged the issue of its initial mishandling of the virus, Beijing pivoted to seeking advantage abroad, sending medical supplies and experts to win goodwill through "mask diplomacy." The contrast between the two countries' approaches to pandemic public relations could not have been starker. China pledged $2 billion to the global response to Covid-19 while the US moved to cut funding for the World Health Organization and withdraw from the agency altogether. In fact, US contributions to the WHO have, until now, far exceeded China's, while American Covid aid to other countries amounts to $2.4 billion. America remains a pillar of the international order, but Trump's inflammatory bluster has overshadowed that reality. Beijing won this round of public diplomacy, which has given it greater confidence in making such efforts in the future.

But in bashing China, Trump reflects a rare bipartisan consensus that has been growing for several years. Washington's ever-tougher line on China is rooted in the belief that its decades-long policy of "engagement" failed—that attempts at cooperation did not turn China into a more liberal and democratic country. Some accounts of the failure of engagement sound like the despondent sighs of an unrequited lover. In fact, however, this grand disappointment is based on a grand misunderstanding. US policy toward China was never purely one of engagement; it has always been a combination of engagement and deterrence. This strategy was sometimes described as "hedging."

Since the 1970s, US officials concluded that inviting China into the global economic and political system was better than having it sit outside it, resentful and disruptive. Washington continued to couple its effort to integrate China with consistent support for other Asian powers, including continued arms sales to Taiwan. In the Clinton years, the US guaranteed it would maintain a significant military presence in East Asia (a plan called the Nye Initiative). In the Bush years, Washington overturned decades-long policies and embraced India as a nuclear power, as one more check on Beijing. The Obama administration made a famous "pivot" to Asia, enhancing military ties with Japan and Australia and nurturing a stronger bond with Vietnam. It also proposed the Trans-Pacific Partnership, a way to counterbalance China's weight in Asia—but Trump pulled out of the pact on his first workday in office.

The hedging strategy worked. Before Nixon reestablished US relations, China was the world's greatest rogue state. Mao Zedong was obsessed with the idea that he stood at the vanguard of a revolutionary movement that would destroy Western capitalism. There was no measure too extreme for the cause—not even nuclear apocalypse. "If the worst came to the worst and half of mankind died," Mao explained in a speech in Moscow in 1957, "the other half would remain while imperialism would be razed to the ground and the whole world would become socialist." Mao's China funded and fomented anti-Western insurgencies and ideological movements around the world, from Latin America to Southeast Asia.

By comparison, today's China is a remarkably restrained nation on the geopolitical and military front. It has not gone to war since 1979, when it briefly invaded Vietnam. Nor has it funded or supported proxies or armed insurgents anywhere in the world since the early 1980s. That record of nonaggression is unique among the world's great powers. All the other permanent members of the UN Security Council have used force many times in many places over the last few decades—a list led, of course, by the United States.

Though it does not bear directly on China's foreign policy, for many in Washington, China's failure to become a liberal democracy was deeply disappointing. Understandably so—but it should not have been a surprise. At the senior level, few US officials ever claimed that fundamentally changing the Chinese political system was the goal. What they believed, rather, was that as China modernized, it would soften its authoritarianism, the Internet would create greater space for freedom in various ways, and the state's role in the economy would shrink. Many Chinese intellectuals and officials hoped this, too. For a while, it even appeared possible, as China experimented with growing economic reform and even local elections. But in recent years, the regime's direction became clear: greater state control and repression. It would be wrong, however, to take this as proof that US policy has failed. China's tighter grip is the result not of anything that happened in Washington but of something that happened in Beijing: the rise of a new leader, Xi Jinping.

CHINA'S THIRD REVOLUTION

So radical are Xi's changes that the scholar Elizabeth Economy argues that his approach represents a "third revolution" in China, comparable to Mao's original Communist revolution and Deng Xiaoping's move toward markets and America in the 1980s. Xi has acted on four fronts: greater power for himself, a larger role for the Communist Party in the economy and society, heightened regulation of information and capital, and a more assertive foreign policy. Veteran China watcher Orville Schell, who has observed the rise and fall of engagement since the 1970s, describes this last tendency in stark terms. For all Xi's rhetorical embrace of multilateralism and talk of national rebirth, there has been, Schell notes, "a darker side to Xi's grand ambitions that grew out of his paranoid fixation on the idea of 'hostile foreign forces' . . . perennially and covertly arrayed against China." Perhaps Xi's moves mark the start of a decades-long shift, just as the first two revolutions did, or maybe they will turn out to be one of the many adjustments in Chinese policy that get reversed in time. For now, the United States and the rest of the world are dealing with a new China in what Xi calls his "new era."

The rising repression is a tragedy for the Chinese people. They are now led by a leader who has slowed economic reforms, tightened the screws of Communist Party control and repression, and angered the country's neighbors. This turn has been especially tragic for the inhabitants of the Muslim-majority Xinjiang region, where the government has interned a million ethnic Uighurs in holding camps for "re-education," and subjected millions more to intrusive surveillance. (As trade negotiations drag on, President Trump has been notably silent on this abuse. Obsessed with his reelection, Trump reportedly begged Xi to have China buy more Midwestern soybeans to help him win—while assuring Xi that repressing China's Muslims was the right thing to do.) Beijing has tightened its grip on Hong Kong, too, imposing a draconian "national security" law on the autonomous territory in July 2020.

China's foreign policy has also become more ambitious under Xi, from its pursuit of leadership roles in UN agencies— where it now outnumbers the US four-to-one—to the vast Belt and Road Initiative, to the construction of islands in the South China Sea. The country's growing belligerence marks a break with its previous passivity, captured by Deng Xiao-ping's adage "Hide your strength, bide your time." The military buildup, in particular, suggests that China is executing a long-term plan.

But what would be an acceptable level of influence for China, given its economic weight in the world? If Washington does not first ask this crucial question, it cannot make serious claims about which uses of Chinese power cross the line. When in 1990 Deng advised fellow Chinese leaders to bide their time, the country was impoverished, with a puny economy. That economy has expanded by 800% and is now a colossus. China bided its time and developed its strength, and today, it is seeking a larger regional and global role as all great powers do as they rise in wealth and strength. How much larger is appropriate and how much constitutes dangerous expansionism? That is the fundamental strategic question that Washington and the world have never seriously examined.

Consider the case of another country that was rising in strength, this one back in the nineteenth century, although not nearly on the scale of China today. The United States in 1823 was what would now be called a developing country—a nation of farmers, with poor infrastructure, not even among the world's top five economies—and yet with the Monroe Doctrine, it declared the entire Western Hemisphere off-limits to the great powers of Europe. Britain reluctantly acquiesced, accepting and sometimes even enforcing US regional hegemony. The American case is an imperfect analogy, but it serves as a reminder that as countries gain economic strength, they seek greater influence abroad. If Washington defines every such effort by China as dangerous, it will be setting itself up against the natural dynamics of international life and creating a self-fulfilling prophecy.

For the United States, dealing with a competitor like China is a new and unique challenge. Since 1945, the major states rising to wealth and prominence have been Washington's closest allies, if not quasi-protectorates: Germany, Japan, and South Korea. A normally disruptive feature of international politics—the rise of new powers—has thus been extraordinarily benign for the United States. The People's Republic of China, however, is not only much larger than the rising powers that came before; it has also always lived outside the United States' alliance structures and sphere of influence.

American foreign policy elites of both parties have grown comfortable with a world in which the United States is the undisputed leader. When she was secretary of state, Madeleine Albright described why America had the moral authority to use military force (in this case, to bomb Iraq in 1998). "We are America; we are the indispensable nation," she said. "We stand tall and we see further than other countries into the future." It is unlikely that many other countries would agree with that proposition today. In 2019, Secretary of State Mike Pompeo asserted—in a patronizing statement that would surely infuriate any Chinese citizen—that the United States and its allies must keep China in "its proper place." China's sin, according to Pompeo, is that it spends more on its military than it needs to for its own defense. The same, of course, could be said of the United States—and of France, Russia, the United Kingdom, and most other large countries.

In fact, one useful definition of a great power is a country that is concerned about more than just its own immediate security. The political climate in Washington always pushes policy-makers toward being "tough" rather than "soft"—which is a dangerous way to frame international affairs. The real question is, can they be smart rather than stupid?

America's new hawkish consensus on China is strangely solipsistic, devoid of discussion of how its target would react. Beijing has its own hawks, who have warned for years that the United States wants to keep China down and even seeks regime change in Beijing. More and more, the Trump administration's posture has vindicated those voices, thereby giving them leverage in China to push exactly the kind of assertive and destabilizing behavior that US policy is trying to prevent. This dynamic, with each side's hawks reinforcing the other's, heightens tensions and raises the risk of conflict. It is crucial to note that Trump's tough tactics have not achieved any of their goals—from ending US trade deficits to gaining Beijing's support in tackling North Korea and Iran. In fact, they have resulted in a China that is more aggressive abroad and repressive at home.

American hawkishness is rooted in the fear that China might at some point take over the globe. This is a dangerous fear, because historically, when the dominant power believes that it is losing ground to a new challenger, it often acts pre-emptively, hoping to take advantage of a perceived "window of vulnerability" after which the challenger's rise becomes unstoppable. It was this sort of rationale that led European statesmen to sleepwalk into war in 1914. A similar strange fatalism about China's inexorable rise animates the Washington establishment. But there is reason to doubt this nightmare scenario. Neither the Soviet Union nor Japan managed to take over the world, despite intense, sometimes paranoid fears in Washington about their rise. And China, for all its achievements and strengths, is beset by a series of internal challenges, from demographic decline to mountains of debt. The Communist Party also faces an uncertain political future. Despite a decade of intensifying political repression on the mainland, it remains true that the rise of a middle class creates aspirations for greater political openness, as is apparent in two Chinese societies watched closely by Beijing—Hong Kong and Taiwan.

Most important, China's rise has triggered great anxiety among almost all its neighbors, from Japan to India to Australia. Xi's foreign policy has dramatically heightened these countries' fears, causing several of them to fundamentally rethink their own foreign policies. Since a June 2020 border skirmish that left dozens dead, India appears to be initiating a long-term strategy to balance China. Despite its deep dependence on the Chinese market, Australia now regards China as its main adversary, particularly in light of Beijing's many cyberattacks on Australian targets, and it has led global calls for an investigation into the way Beijing mishandled the initial outbreak of Covid-19. Japan resurrected the Trans-Pacific Partnership, brought the other nations on board, and ensured the agreement entered into force. Even Vietnam, wary of its giant neighbor, has begun what was once unimaginable:

military partnership, if not alliance, with its old enemy the United States. Horrified at Hong Kong's fate, the population of Taiwan has reelected an anti-China president and is turning more antagonistic toward the mainland, making military options for Beijing more difficult and costly. (Invading a hostile land with millions of people chafing under what they regard as a foreign occupation can quickly turn into a nightmare, as Washington planners could explain to their counterparts in Beijing.) China's fundamental geostrategic weakness has always been an abundance of nearby countries that oppose its rise. Yet far from ameliorating this deficiency, Xi's policies have exacerbated it. China today is still rising—but embedded in a vast continent, encircled by hostile neighbors that are growing more adversarial by the month.

BIPOLARITY WITHOUT WAR

Tensions between the United States and China are inevitable. Conflict is not. We have a picture in our minds of what international politics looks like that is drawn largely from modern European history. It is of great powers jockeying for influence in a great game of realpolitik and frequently descending into war. This international system is often called "multipolar"—characterized by many great powers—and it is inherently unstable. With many countries of roughly equal strength competing, each eyeing the other suspiciously, miscalculation, aggression, and war become highly likely, which is why Europe became an arena of constant conflict for centuries. But a multipolar system describes just one period of world history—roughly the sixteenth century through the mid-twentieth century. More often, there have been unipolar systems, dominated by one power, from the Roman Empire in the West to a series of Chinese empires in the East.

The bipolar order characterized by the rivalry between the Soviet Union and the United States lasted less than fifty years. It ushered in the longest sustained period of peace among the great powers in 150 years, and ended, astonishingly, with one side capitulating and collapsing—without a single shot being fired. If the international system returns to a bipolar order, it does not have to be frightening. You can have bipolarity without war.

You can even have bipolarity without a *cold* war. That's because the original Cold War was triggered by international tensions of a kind difficult to imagine today. The Soviet Union had been invaded from the west by the Nazis in 1941 and lost around 25 million men, women, and children—more than 10% of its entire population. After bearing the brunt of the sacrifices to win World War II, Moscow sought to control all neighbors on its western border in Eastern and Central Europe, to create a ring of buffer states so it would never be invaded again. It then cast its eyes south, on Turkey and Greece, and ventured even farther afield for territory and influence. The Soviet regime was organized around an ideology of global communist revolution that celebrated conflict with the West. America, for its part, considered Soviet communism a dire threat to its very existence, and viewed every Soviet ally anywhere as a danger. (Even neutrals were viewed with deep suspicion.) Consider how the two superpowers acted. Moscow placed nuclear missiles in Cuba, risking a cataclysmic war, to extend its global influence and counter Washington's. For its part, America sent a total of three million troops into the jungles of Vietnam to prevent a poor, minor country on the other side of the globe from becoming communist.

Relations between Washington and Beijing are far less tense in every aspect. Beijing's "Market-Leninism" does not truly represent a viable societal alternative to the West. The China model is an unusual combination of liberal and mercantilist economics and repressive politics, emanating from China's particular history. It is a juggling act more than a coherent ideology and has been copied almost nowhere else in the world. For all its disregard for human rights, China is more fully part of the international order than the Soviet Union ever was. Moscow stood opposed to almost every facet of that order. During the Cold War, US-Soviet trade in goods, when it existed at all, rarely went above $2 billion a year. US-China trade in goods is nearly $2 billion—*every day*. This era's superpowers are deeply intertwined economically, which creates strong incentives for cooperation. That is why even the Trump administration has a hot-and-cold China policy, urging a technological decoupling with China while also seeking deeper interdependence—by asking Beijing to buy more American goods and provide greater access to American firms.

Rather than the original Cold War, a closer parallel to the current situation is the rivalry between an established Britain and a rising Germany that started in the late nineteenth century. In explaining the origins of World War I, President Woodrow Wilson succinctly summarized the dynamic between the two powers: "Britain has the earth, and Germany wants it." Several scholars have explored the parallels between that Anglo-German clash and today's US-China tensions. One historical analysis runs through the similarities:

> Both rivalries take place amidst the emergence of economic globalization and explosive technological innovation. Both feature a rising autocracy with a state-protected economic system challenging an established democracy with a free-market economic system. And both rivalries feature countries enmeshed in profound interdependence wielding tariff threats, standard-setting, technology theft, financial power, and infrastructure investment for advantage.

The mismanagement of that rivalry dragged the world into a war that devastated Europe and set the stage for a second world war.

It is worth remembering, however, that all these analogies come from a very different era. Today, the world is defined by a single global system. That has never really been the case before. As an example of prior systems, look at the world as it was around AD 200. The planet's most populous regions were ruled by empires—Rome in Europe and around the Mediterranean, and the Han in China. These were powerful states, presiding over their own unipolar international systems, but almost entirely disconnected from one another. Today, these regions are deeply intertwined, with people, goods, and ideas moving constantly between them. And today, moreover, global interactions take place within what is known as the "liberal international order." This framework, established by the United States after World War II, is marked by openness in trade and economics, international institutions like the UN, rules and norms that regulate international conduct, and facilitate cooperative solutions to common problems. As the scholar John Ikenberry has noted, despite many changes and challenges, this order has endured because it is in everyone's interest, being in his words "easy to join and hard to overturn." It has also helped produce the longest period of peace among the major powers in modern history and allowed more people to escape poverty than in all history. As tense as US-China bipolarity may become, it remains embedded in this enduring, powerful, *multilateral* world, to which we will turn next.

Looking at the shape of international politics in the future, it's clear—bipolarity is inevitable. A cold war is a choice.

LESSON TEN

Sometimes the Greatest Realists Are the Idealists

COVID-19 IS a global phenomenon that has, paradoxically, caused nations everywhere to turn inward. The pain and suffering, economic hardships, and dislocations have led world leaders to abandon ideas of international cooperation and instead hunker down, shut their borders, and make their own plans for resilience and recovery. By April 2020, Donald Trump's strategy on the pandemic had devolved into little more than an appeal to American nationalism, with the president blaming China for spreading the disease and attacking the World Health Organization as an accomplice. China, for its part, paid lip service to global cooperation while quickly embracing "vaccine nationalism." As the hawkish Communist Party mouthpiece, the *Global Times*, editorialized, "there is no way for China to rely on Europe or the US in vaccine development. China has to be by itself in this crucial field." India's leadership came to the same conclusion as Beijing about the central issue of the hour. New Delhi restricted exports of key medical supplies and invested over $1 billion to reduce its dependence on China for pharmaceutical ingredients. It readied itself to develop drugs and manufacture crucial supplies on its own. Everywhere, even in Europe, self-interest and self-reliance seemed the new watchwords.

From a historical perspective, it is strange to watch this crisis make leaders so narrow-minded and nationalistic. The pain of the pandemic is real and deep, but it doesn't quite compare to the period between 1914 and 1945—a great war that ripped Europe apart, a pandemic far deadlier than Covid, a global depression, the rise of totalitarianism, another world war that destroyed Europe yet again and laid waste to Japanese cities with nuclear weapons—all told, over 150 million dead. And yet, after those hellish crises, leaders pushed for more international cooperation. Having witnessed the costs of unbridled nationalism and narrow self-interest, the warriors and statesmen who survived believed that they had a duty to create a world that did not lapse back into nihilistic competition.

We have enjoyed the fruits of their labor: seventy-five years of relative peace. But as a result, we have become cynics, contemptuous of the idealism that got us to where we are. It is now fashionable to bash "globalism," with little thought to the costs of the alternative. Britons can posture and embrace the petty nationalism of Brexit because they no longer have to worry about real nationalism and geopolitical competition, the kind that killed nearly 20,000 British soldiers on a single day—July 1, 1916—in the Battle of the Somme, to gain just three square miles of muddy ground. The statesmen who led the Allied countries through war and depression knew better and resolved to give idealism a chance.

Franklin Roosevelt was assistant secretary of the navy in Woodrow Wilson's administration and a great admirer of Wilson's vision of a world "made safe for democracy." He watched that idealism collapse in the years after World War I, leading to an even wider war during his own presidency. But the lesson FDR drew from Wilson's experiences was to try international cooperation again, this time with America at the center of the new system—and this time giving the great powers stronger practical incentives to fully commit themselves to the peace. A few months after America entered World War II, when victory was still uncertain and distant, FDR began formulating plans to create international institutions and systems of collective security that made future world wars unlikely. His longtime secretary of state, Cordell Hull, having seen how the trade wars of the 1930s spiraled into hot war, singlemindedly championed a new, international free trade regime. His successors realized this vision in the years after 1945— first through the General Agreement on Tariffs and Trade, which evolved into the World Trade Organization.

Roosevelt was known to be an idealist at heart, but his successor, Harry S. Truman, had no such reputation. Truman is credited as the hard-nosed realist who dropped the atomic bombs on Hiroshima and Nagasaki, created NATO, worked to contain the Soviet Union, and waged war in Korea. But Truman was also a deeply idealistic man, and he too had drunk from the well of Wilsonian internationalism. In his last year of high school in Independence, Missouri, he was enraptured by a lofty poem by Alfred, Lord Tennyson, "Locksley Hall." He copied out the following stanzas on a piece of paper:

> For I dipt into the future, far as human eye could see,
> Saw the Vision of the world, and all the wonder that
>   would be,
> Saw the heavens fill with commerce, argosies of magic
>   sails,
> Pilots of the purple twilight, dropping down with costly
>   bales;
> Heard the heavens fill with shouting, and there rain'd a
>   ghastly dew
> From the nations' airy navies grappling in the central blue;
> Far along the world-wide whisper of the south-wind rush-
>   ing warm,
> With the standards of the peoples plunging thro' the
>   thunder-storm;
> Till the war-drum throbb'd no longer, and the battle-flags
>   were furl'd
> In the Parliament of man, the Federation of the World.
> There the common sense of most shall hold a fretful realm
>   in awe,
> And the kindly earth shall slumber, lapt in universal law.

Decades later, whenever officials or members of Congress asked the president why he so fervently supported the United

Nations, Truman would pull out his wallet and read them Tennyson's lines.

Truman's successor, Dwight D. Eisenhower, had battled the German and Italian armies across Europe as the commander of Allied forces on the continent. He had seen that human nature could be dark and vicious—the Wehrmacht fought ferociously till the bitter end. And the conclusion he drew from his wartime experience was: go the extra mile for peace and cooperation. Twenty years after D-Day, Walter Cronkite interviewed Eisenhower on a bench in the US military cemetery at Colleville-sur-Mer in Normandy, where 9,000 American bodies were buried. Gazing at the gravestones, Eisenhower explained to Cronkite, "These people gave us a chance, and they bought time for us, so that we can do better than we have before. . . . So every time I come back to these beaches, or any day when I think about that day 20 years ago now, I say once more we must find some way to work to peace, and really to gain an eternal peace for this world."

As president, Eisenhower made proposals that would be unthinkable today. In 1953, in the midst of the Cold War and with the Korean War still ongoing, he delivered a speech proposing that all nations adopt strict limits on the numbers and nature of arms, with the disarmament process to be administered by the United Nations. He also called for the abolition of nuclear weapons and offered that all nuclear energy be placed under international control and be used only for peaceful purposes. Eisenhower spoke in language that few left-wing peaceniks would dare to employ today. "Every gun that is made, every warship launched, every rocket fired signifies, in the final sense, a theft from those who hunger and are not fed, those who are cold and are not clothed," he said. "This is not a way of life at all, in any true sense. Under the cloud of threatening war, it is humanity hanging from a cross of iron."

It was not just the Americans preaching idealism. Winston Churchill was the most deeply nationalistic—even racist—and bellicose Allied statesman of that period. And yet just one year after World War II ended, he said in a famous speech, "We must build a kind of United States of Europe," adding, "We cannot aim at anything less than the union of Europe as a whole, and we look forward with confidence to the day when that union will be achieved." This federation would be based, he said, on the same principles that motivated the League of Nations and the idealists of the 1920s and 1930s, who had imagined that greater cooperation could rid the world of war. In the years after Churchill's speech, French statesmen like Jean Monnet and Robert Schuman worked with German leaders like Konrad Adenauer to create what turned into the European Union—an unprecedented pooling of national sovereignty and the most striking example of peaceful cooperation in human history.

It is now common to view these kinds of lofty aspirations with cynicism. Today, many leaders proudly advocate for a narrow vision of their nations' interests. "I will always put America first," Donald Trump declared at the UN General Assembly in 2017, "just like you, as the leaders of your countries, will always, and should always, put your countries first." But the world that we inhabit was built by statesmen who took a broader view—that collective security, and collective endeavors, were in each nation's enlightened self-interest. The United States was the most powerful country in the world when it built the UN and the web of associated international organizations, all of which constrained America's unilateral power. It helped Europe and East Asia recover from the ruins of World War II—in effect, financing its future competitors. It agreed to conventions and organizations in which it had just one vote, the same as the smallest nation. But in doing all this, it built a global system that has kept the peace among the great powers for three quarters of a century, encouraged the growth of democracy and respect for human rights, and allowed for the largest reduction in poverty in human history. Europe found a way to overcome centuries of nationalism and war and create a continent of peace, prosperity, and security by sharing power in the European Union and NATO. Southeast Asian countries, after decades of colonialism and war, banded together in the Association of Southeast Asian Nations, and have had peaceful relations for two generations. All these successes, large and small, represent an astonishing track record for idealism and globalism.

THE DEATH OF GLOBALISM?

And yet, faced with Covid-19, many have retreated to selfishness. Trump's America has led the pack. The US president largely dismissed international warnings about the disease, and when he finally acted, did so unilaterally, not even bothering to inform his closest European allies before announcing travel bans on those countries. Predictably, Brazil's Jair Bolsonaro and India's Narendra Modi—populist nationalists like

Trump—approached the pandemic with a similar distrust of any kind of global efforts or multilateral solutions. Modi reminded Indians of the dangers of global supply chains and urged that they be "vocal for local," buying and promoting all things Made in India. But the pandemic seems to have brought out nationalism even in places where one would least expect it, like Europe.

Nationalists like to point out that multilateral cooperation didn't stop the pandemic. They assert that the global institution that many trusted to handle disease outbreaks across borders, the World Health Organization, performed badly. As late as January 14, 2020, with the announcement of the first coronavirus case outside China, the WHO still credulously accepted Beijing's claim that there was no evidence to support human-to-human transmission. It delayed declaring the virus as a pandemic until March 11, when much of the world had already realized the severity of the crisis and was scrambling to lock down. Such failures have led people to argue for greater national control and resiliency.

But the problems with the WHO prove the need for more multilateralism, not less. The organization has a tiny budget and relies on voluntary cooperation from its member states. It has no authority to force them to do anything, and often cannot even shame its more powerful funders into action. These rules were written with the full support of the United States, which has always been allergic to the idea that an international organization could interfere with its domestic affairs. And yet, in this pandemic, global cooperation has offered powerful advantages. The ability for money and medical equipment to move quickly across the world to those in need has proved vital. That scientific ideas and best practices can flow freely has been even more important. Thousands of lives have been saved thanks to the openness and speed of the international system. Even the United States, the richest country in the world, eagerly accepted supplies from China to bridge temporary shortfalls in some equipment. The WHO, for all its faults, had by late April provided 1.5 million test kits and sent protective equipment to 133 nations—a godsend for the world's poorest countries.

In addition, most things that went wrong actually went wrong inside countries, not between them. The places that performed the best, like Taiwan and South Korea, faced the same international problems as others—and indeed, had far more travelers from China per capita than Western countries did. Those that did not manage to quickly flatten the curve, like Britain and America, failed largely because of their parochial problems and poor national leadership, not some defect in the international system. And still, somehow, global multilateralism takes the blame. This myopic finger-pointing is just as obtuse as arguing that individual failures of US or UK governance somehow prove that nation-states themselves are defunct. A dysfunctional dynamic has set in, whereby many people use multilateral institutions for their benefit but then turn on them whenever problems emerge. When hundreds of miles of highways are built in a European country using EU funds, local leaders take the credit and no one thanks Brussels—but when budgets need to be cut, they point the finger at some EU rule and say, "those evil Eurocrats in Brussels made me do it."

At a global level, the idealism of the post-World War II era lives on in the form of its signal creation, the liberal international order. There are many who acknowledge the past achievements of this US-led framework for cooperation, but who argue that it is now doomed. Covid-19 might prove to be the immediate cause of the order's demise. But, they say, it was already crumbling in an unruly world and was destined to collapse.

A SHOCK TO THE SYSTEM

Voltaire famously noted that the Holy Roman Empire "was in no way holy, nor Roman, nor an empire." The same can be said of the liberal international order, which was never as liberal, as international, or as orderly as it is now nostalgically described. It has been a messy reality, with idealism mixed in with self-serving nationalism from the start. Its beginnings can be traced to thinkers like Hugo Grotius and Immanuel Kant, but the first time they were articulated by a major world statesman was in the late nineteenth century, when another liberal superpower, Great Britain, enabled the first great burst of cooperation and globalization. In 1879, William Gladstone, the four-time prime minister of Britain and a giant of nineteenth-century liberalism, gave a series of speeches on foreign policy. In them, he advocated a new kind of diplomacy to ensure peace among the great powers, a novel approach based on restraint, the "equal rights of all nations," and "the love of freedom." It wasn't just words. Britain played a crucial role protecting global sea-lanes, while the British pound sterling served as the global reserve currency. The UK's naval hegemony preserved a modicum of international stability.

To be sure, this era still saw intense economic competition, rising powers, domestic revolutions at home, and aggressive imperialism abroad. Gladstone's "love of freedom" was selectively applied: Britain itself was enthusiastically imperialistic, crushing rebellions from India to Ireland. At times, it was deeply mercantilist as well. But, relatively speaking, compared to any prior period of human history, this was an age marked by unprecedented peace, the expansion of trade, and the seedlings of international cooperation like the first modern arms control agreements. In short, it was a nascent liberal international order. It came to a crashing end with World War I, a rupture that endured through the fractious interwar years and then through World War II.

After 1945, when America took the baton of global leadership from Britain, Washington started building a more formal set of international norms and institutions. But the emerging system faced vociferous opposition from the Soviet Union, followed by a series of breakdowns of cooperation among allies (most painfully, over the Suez Canal in 1956 and over Vietnam a decade later). It even suffered the partial defection of the United States under Richard Nixon, who in 1971 ended Washington's practice of underwriting the international monetary system using US gold reserves. So a more realistic picture of the era after 1945 is that of a weak order, marred from the start by exceptions, discord, and fragility. Within it, the great powers often bucked its rules—none more so than the United

States. Between 1947 and 1989, when America was on the one hand building up the liberal international order, it attempted regime change around the world seventy-two times, by one scholar's count, almost every time without UN approval.

But still the order grew, despite many countervailing tendencies and setbacks. More and more countries joined in, and after the Soviet Union collapsed in 1991, nearly every nation on earth became, in some sense, part of the open world economy, embracing at least in theory the norms around international conduct. Even now, the liberal international order accommodates a variety of regimes—from Cuba to Saudi Arabia to Vietnam—and still provides a rules-based framework that encourages greater peace, stability, and more civilized conduct among states. Now many in Washington and beyond argue that it faces a new and maybe fatal threat. They charge that China's rise has broken the system because Beijing has abused the open international economy to bolster its own statist and mercantilist system. They point out that China has sought to water down the UN's commitment to human rights. And they allege that it is seeking to establish its own parallel international system, a framework that is incompatible with the existing, Western-sponsored one. So what does the rise of China mean for the international order?

Consider China's abuse of the open world economy. Almost all economists agree that the country owes most of its economic success to three fundamental factors: the switch from communist economics to a more market-based approach, a high savings rate that enables large capital investments, and rising productivity. The embrace of markets has also included opening itself up substantially to foreign investment, more so than most other large emerging markets. China is the only developing country to have ranked in the top twenty-five markets for foreign direct investment every year since 1998.

China today presents some new challenges, especially given President Xi's fondness for using state power to give the country economic dominance in crucial sectors. But its greatest advantage in the global trading system has come not from its willingness to violate the rules, but from its sheer size. Countries and companies want access to China and are willing to make concessions to get it. This hardly makes it unusual. Other countries with equal clout often get away with similar behavior or worse—the United States chief among them. A 2015 report by the financial services giant Credit Suisse tallied nontariff barriers against foreign goods put in place by major countries between 1990 and 2013. With a total count of almost 450, the United States is in a league of its own. Next is India, with some 350, then Russia, with around 250. China comes in at number five, with fewer than 150. Trump's trade wars with China and Europe are the latest and most egregious examples of America's own mercantilism.

Government support for state-owned enterprises is greater than it was a few years ago, but Beijing has abandoned what was once a central part of its mercantilist strategy: using an undervalued currency to boost exports. The economist Nicholas Lardy has calculated that the end of currency mercantilism, and the resulting drop in China's trade surplus, accounts for "about half of China's growth slowdown since the global financial crisis." Of course, reforms such as these are often undertaken only in the face of Western pressure and, even then, because they serve China's own competitive interests. But it is also true that Beijing faces increasing pressure to undertake even more reforms. Many Chinese economists and senior policymakers have argued that doing so is the only way for the country to modernize and grow its economy. Avoiding reform, they have warned, will leave the country floundering in the "middle-income trap"—a common fate in which countries escape poverty, only to hit a wall at a per capita GDP somewhere around $10,000, having refused to modernize their economic, regulatory, and legal systems any further. China passed the $10,000 milestone in 2019, but it could still get stuck. Even before the pandemic slashed its growth, China was resisting further reforms. Other countries that have done the same eventually find themselves obliged to continue on the reformist path or get mired on a sluggish track. The pandemic may provide an impetus for further opening—or lead Beijing to double down on its inward-looking nationalist agenda. Even if it chooses the latter, it is still far from seeking to topple the multilateral order and replace it with a China-based one.

The truth about the liberal international order is that there never really was a golden age, nor has the order decayed as much as is often claimed. The core attributes of this order—peace and stability among major countries—are still firmly in place, with a marked decline in war and annexation since 1945. (Russia's invasion of Ukraine is an exception that proves the rule.) China's economic mercantilism must be addressed, and the Trump administration deserves some credit for high-

lighting it. But Trump deserves strong criticism for approach-
ing the issue unilaterally, not least because it would be far more
effective to present Beijing with a set of demands made by the
US and its allies—say, the EU, UK, Canada, Japan, South
Korea, and Australia, a grouping that would, with America,
together comprise 58% of the global economy. The interconnected world gives Washington leverage against China.
Decoupling from it reduces that leverage. Yes, it's true the
United States has never faced an adversary as formidable as
China. But China has its own hurdles: no rising power in history has tried to emerge into a world so intricately crisscrossed
with multilateral channels of cooperation and defense. Any
Chinese attempt at a full "breakout" from all global rules and
norms would draw strong opposition from its neighborhood
and beyond. Perhaps most important, the best way to deter
China is to strengthen the system that constrains it. That
would, of course, require that the United States join and support bodies like the Convention on the Law of the Sea and
the International Criminal Court. If America flouts the rules
and norms it has little standing to criticize China for doing
the same.

America's most significant contribution to international
life has been that, unlike every other victorious great power in
history, after decisively triumphing—in the world's bloodiest
conflict—it chose to forgive, rebuild, and rehabilitate the van-
quished. It imagined a new way for the nations of the world.
It often acted in ways that were inspired by the common good
and not just narrow national interest. Those who look at the
challenges of the moment—China's rise, and now the Covid-

19 pandemic—and conclude that America should abandon this rich legacy and simply behave like any other great power, becoming an English-speaking version of Imperial Germany, are blind to the history and achievements of the United States.

That raises the most serious threat to the liberal international order—which is not China's expansionism but America's abdication. The architect of this system is rapidly losing interest in its own creation. As the scholar Walter Russell Mead has pointed out, Trump's instincts are Jacksonian, in that he is largely uninterested in the world except insofar as he believes that most countries are always swindling the United States, including and especially its allies. Trump is a nationalist, a protectionist, and a populist, determined to put "America first." But truthfully, more than anything else, he is an isolationist who has abandoned the field. Trump has withdrawn the United States from more organizations, treaties, and accords than any president in American history. Not only has he slow-rolled a trade deal with the European Union but he has also started a trade war against the bloc and moved to pull troops from European bases—seemingly heralding the end of a seventy-year Atlantic partnership. Trump has dealt with Latin America through the prism of either keeping immigrants out or winning votes in Florida. He has even managed to alienate Canadians (no mean feat). And he has subcontracted Middle East policy to Israel and Saudi Arabia, largely so the US can retreat. With a few impulsive exceptions—such as the narcissistic desire to win a Nobel Prize by trying to make peace with North Korea—what is most notable about Trump's foreign policy is its absence.

The pandemic has accelerated America's selfish turn—its abandonment of its role as leader of the free world and provider of public goods within the multilateral system. Perhaps the most striking example came with its vaccine strategy. Far from coordinating a global effort, or even encouraging its allies to pool resources, the Trump administration was simply looking to "win," edging out other countries in a race to get the vaccine first. The German press reported that the American government offered "large sums of money" to secure a German company's vaccine "for the U.S. only." Meanwhile, partners like France, Brazil, and Canada accused the US of swooping in on deals to acquire critical medical equipment and outbidding them, or even blocking shipments.

The US has long been secure on the home front, guarded by two oceanic moats from instability and war. This position has given American leaders since 1945 the farsightedness to use a portion of their power and resources for the common good. Consider Washington's leadership in fighting twenty-first-century diseases. The George W. Bush administration launched an initiative to fight AIDS in Africa that has brought $85 billion to bear on the epidemic, saving up to 18 million lives; the Obama administration led the charge on Ebola, marshaling the funds and expertise to successfully contain that virus. Other nations donate, but no other country has played that central, organizing role in the world.

By the middle of 2020, tragically, with the pandemic raging across most of its fifty states—long after Europe and East Asia contained their outbreaks—America had no attention for anything or anyone but itself, except to bash Beijing. The Trump administration is not wrong to critique China's handling of Covid-19. But coming from such a messenger, the message lands with a thud. A lifelong friend of America, the former Australian prime minister Kevin Rudd wrote in *Foreign Affairs* of his horror and disappointment over how far America has fallen: "Once there was the United States of the Berlin airlift. Now there is the image of the USS *Theodore Roosevelt* crippled by the virus, reports of the administration trying to take exclusive control of a vaccine being developed in Germany, and federal intervention to stop the commercial sale of personal protective equipment to Canada. The world has been turned on its head."

TIME TO REBUILD

At this point, the restoration of an American-dominated international order is not possible. Too many new powers are rising, too many new forces have been unleashed that cannot be tamed, even if the American president were a dedicated multilateralist. China has become a rival and, in many realms, a peer, unlikely to accept a reboot of American hegemony. The rise of the rest continues. The world is now filled with new groupings and institutions, many of them regional in nature. China has established the Asian Infrastructure Investment Bank and helped fund the New Development Bank. Beijing has set up a series of multilateral groups in Latin America and Eastern Europe that revolve around it, as well as its much larger endeavor, the Belt and Road Initiative, that is spinning a web of supply chains, infrastructure, and transit networks across Eurasia and Africa, with China at its center. Russia has tried to organize its own sphere of influence, bringing together former Soviet republics in a defense treaty and a stillborn "Eurasian Economic Union" (Putin's aggression in Crimea understandably made Russia's neighbor states wary of tying themselves to Moscow). Older regional blocs like the Association of Southeast Asian Nations and the African Union have grown more active in recent years.

Despite all the predictions of its demise, Europe might well come out of this crisis stronger and more unified, determined to play its own independent role in the world. Even French president Emmanuel Macron, who made verbal concessions to nationalism in his speech calling for France's "independence," signaled that he wants his country ever more firmly embedded within the multilateralism of a federal Europe that is strong enough to stand up and "face China, the United States, and global disorder." The rhetoric may be of independence, but the reality is of interdependence. None of these blocs is as strong as a nation-state superpower; but collectively, they reflect the new constellation of more distributed, diverse actors on the world stage. It's not a multipolar world, but it is a multilateral one—because wise leaders know that little can be accomplished internationally by any one country alone, even if that country is the US or China. America could play a pivotal role in this new era: as the leading power, the US could still set the agenda, form coalitions, and organize collective action. But it would be a different role from its hegemonic one—and

Washington's imperial class might resist the need for genuine consultation and diplomacy.

There could be advantages to this new multilateralism. It is based on greater participation for other countries, large and small. It recognizes the genuinely global character of the international system, stretching from Brazil to South Africa to India and Indonesia. If it works, an international system that gives greater voice to more countries would result in a more vibrant democratic system. Let's be clear. It all rests on a wager: that the ideas underlying the American-led international order can survive the end of American hegemony. The alternative, a restoration of that hegemony, will not happen. But there is reason for rational hope. The drive for multilateralism is not purely idealistic. The United States, Europe, Japan, South Korea, and especially China have gained immeasurably from being part of an open, rules-based system. All of them—even Beijing— would have every incentive to uphold that system rather than bring the house down. Russia is more of a spoiler, sometimes seeking to sow chaos—yet the country decreases in strength every year and will find itself more isolated over time. India and most other emerging powers should welcome a system in which China is constrained by a web of institutions and rules, even if it also constrains them. They will find greater stability and prosperity in such a world.

Above all, a functional multilateral system offers a chance to solve common problems. The pandemic illustrates perfectly the risks and opportunities of an interconnected world. The crisis is by nature global, affecting all countries, rich and poor.

None is secure unless all can have some measure of security. Environmental problems likewise require collective action. Cyberspace is an arena that knows no borders. Climate change is, of course, the most dramatic example of a global challenge because it could threaten human survival itself and cannot be solved without sustained cooperation among all, but especially between the biggest polluters, the United States and China.

Climate scientists who warn of the dangers of our current path are unconsciously mirroring Nobel laureate Joshua Lederberg's warnings to us about viruses, back in 1989. Like him, they are urging us not to assume that nature is a benign force that has any particular interest in the survival of life on this earth. The climate doesn't care about us; it is simply an accumulation of chemical reactions that could easily get out of control and destroy the planet and all who live on it. Millions of other planets in other celestial systems may have suffered the same fate. In our own solar neighborhood, NASA's recent computer modeling suggests that Venus might have been habitable for around 2 billion years, after which a "runaway greenhouse gas effect" led to the scorched and sterile conditions on the Venus of today. We can mitigate the forces that are pushing the earth in a similar direction. If that is not a sound reason for cooperation, then we will not find another.

If we do not find a way to have some framework of cooperation, we will face a world of unrestricted nationalist competition. Its perils are harrowing, yet vastly underrated. The perils of a world of unrestricted nationalist competition are harrowing—and vastly underrated. If the United States and China, the world's two most dynamic and technologically advanced countries, were to descend into a no-holds-barred conflict—from the militarization of space to the weaponizing of cyberspace, fueled by an arms race in artificial intelligence—the results could be catastrophic. It would certainly mean the end of the kind of world that we have been building—an open world of global trade, travel, and communication, with common efforts to alleviate poverty and fight disease. Cold War II can be avoided but only through some sustained process of diplomacy and cooperation, ideally involving other major powers like the European Union and India. America and China are very different societies, but both are proud and patriotic. The domestic political incentives both in Washington and Beijing are to sound and act hawkish. The risks of belligerence are vague and seemingly far in the future. We are sleepwalking into conflict once again, just as in 1914.

Despite these difficulties, despite the current tensions and setbacks, I don't despair. We have faced tougher challenges in the past and managed to tackle them. We have made huge progress, whether we look back decades or centuries. When Tennyson wrote "Locksley Hall" in the 1830s, the first great global conflict, the Napoleonic Wars, had ended and given way to a fragile new era of peace in Europe. Feudalism was being replaced by industrialism, and revolutions in trade and technology were connecting the world. With a new queen ascending the British throne, the poem was a symbol of early Victorian idealism. Yet near the end of his life, Tennyson decided that he had been foolishly naïve and wrote another poem, "Locksley Hall Sixty Years After." He concluded that the nineteenth century had ended up being filled with war, revolution, urban poverty, and a loss of faith. "When was age so crammed with menace? Madness? Written, spoken lies," he wrote angrily.

Soon after the poem's publication, its pessimism was rebutted. An extraordinary essay appeared in the periodical *The Nineteenth Century*, defending the accomplishments of the age. The great liberal lion William Gladstone—in between two of his four terms as prime minister—acknowledged that while some of the grandest dreams of the idealists had not come to pass, consider what had been achieved. He ran through the inventory. In the historian Paul Kennedy's words, "The list is numbing, boring, and impressive at the same time. The percentage of children in school had shot up . . . the rights of women had been enlarged . . . the disgusting criminal code . . . had been cast aside . . . and commerce had increased fivefold, while crime had greatly diminished."

The same can be said of the liberal international order of our time. It is incomplete and has had many faults. It has seen much conflict, misery, and hypocrisy. But on the whole, it has bettered the lives of more people than any previous system humans have lived with. And it has done so because it is based not on some dreamy delusion of a world in which evil is abolished and virtue reigns. The idealism underlying liberalism is simple and practical. If people cooperate, they will achieve better outcomes and more durable solutions than they could acting alone. If nations can avoid war, their people will lead longer, richer, and more secure lives. If they become inter-twined economically, everyone ends up better off. That is the hope at the heart of Tennyson's earlier poem, the one Truman kept in his wallet. Its visionary lines imagine a world in which "the common sense of most shall hold a fretful realm in awe / And the kindly earth shall slumber, lapt in universal law." It is not a flight of fancy to believe that cooperation can change the world. It is common sense.

CONCLUSION

Nothing Is Written

I T IS ONE OF THE greatest moments in cinema. In the sweeping historical drama *Lawrence of Arabia*, the young British diplomat-adventurer T. E. Lawrence—played unforgettably by Peter O'Toole—has convinced a group of Arab tribes to mount a surprise attack on the Ottoman Empire, from whom they seek independence. Lawrence leads a band of these Bedouin warriors across the desert, approaching the Ottoman port of Aqaba from the rear. They cross the desert in blistering heat, braving swirling sandstorms. At one point, they discover that one of the Arab soldiers, Gasim, has fallen off his camel. Lawrence instantly decides that he must turn around and get the lost man. Sherif Ali, the chief Arab leader, played in the movie by Omar Sharif, objects. One of his aides tells Lawrence, "Gasim's time has come. It is written." Lawrence snaps back, "Nothing is written!" Then he turns around, ventures back, searches amid the sands and cyclones, and finds Gasim staggering about, half-dead. Lawrence brings him back to the camp to a hero's welcome. When Sherif Ali offers water, Lawrence looks at him and before quenching his thirst calmly repeats, "Nothing is written."

This book has described the world that is being ushered in as a consequence of the Covid-19 pandemic. But it is really describing forces that are gathering steam. In order to complete the story, we must add in human agency. People can choose which direction they want to push themselves, their societies, and their world. In fact, we have more leeway now. In most eras, history proceeds along a set path and change is hard. But the novel coronavirus has upended society. People are disoriented. Things are already changing, and in that atmosphere, further change becomes easier than ever.

Think about the changes we have accepted in our own lives in response to the pandemic. We have agreed to isolate ourselves for long stretches. We have worked, attended meetings, and had deeply personal conversations by talking to our laptops. We've taken online courses and seen doctors and therapists using telemedicine. In a month, companies changed policies that would normally have taken them years to revise. Overnight, cities turned avenues into pedestrian walkways and sidewalks into cafes. Attitudes toward people previously ignored or overlooked are shifting, as can been seen in the newly adopted phrase "essential workers." And governments have opened up their coffers in ways that were once unimaginable and could lead to much greater willingness to invest in the future.

These changes could be the start of something new, or momentary blips. We have many futures in front of us. We could turn inward and embrace nationalism and self-interest, or we could view this global pandemic as a spur to global cooperation and action. We have confronted just such a crossroads before. During the 1920s, after a world war and a great pandemic, the world could have gone in either of two different directions. Some of the leaders who came out of the conflict wanted to create structures of peace that might prevent another one. But Congress rejected Woodrow Wilson's plans, and the United States turned its back on the League of Nations and efforts to create a system of collective security in Europe. European leaders imposed harshly punitive terms on Germany, pushing the country toward collapse. These decisions led to a very dark world in the 1930s—hyperinflation, mass unemployment, fascism, and another world war. A different set of choices could have led the world down an entirely different path.

Similarly, in the 1940s, Stalin's Soviet Union chose a strategy of challenge and confrontation, refusing the offer from the United States for Marshall Plan aid, and rejecting any negotiations to place nuclear energy under international authority for peaceful use. Had a different Soviet leader been in power at that time, say Nikita Khrushchev, the Cold War might have been a much less tense and hair-raising period in history. It might even never have happened.

When we look at the world today, it is clear that there are trends pushing forward—and fast. I have tried to describe some of them. Economic development is creating ever-greater climate risks. For demographic and other reasons, countries are growing more slowly. The rich are getting richer; the big are getting bigger. Technology is moving so fast that for the first time in history, human beings might lose control over their own creations. Globalization will persist, but the opposition to it is growing louder and louder. Nations are becoming more parochial. The United States and China are headed toward a bitter and prolonged confrontation. But we can make choices that shape and alter these trends.

We could settle into a world of slow growth, increasing natural dangers, and rising inequality, and continue with business as usual. Or we could choose to act forcefully, using the vast capacity of government to make massive new investments to equip people with the skills and security they need in an age of bewildering change. We could build a twenty-first-century infrastructure putting to work many of those most threatened by new technologies. We could curb carbon emissions simply by placing a price on them that reflects their true cost. And we could recognize that along with dynamism and growth, we need resilience and security—or else the next crisis could be the last. To some radicals, my proposals might sound like an agenda of reform, not revolution. True. But we do not need an overthrow of the existing order in the hope that something better would take its place. We have made real gains, economically and politically. The world is a better place than it was fifty years ago, by almost any measure. We understand the deficiencies and the ways to address them. The problem has not been to arrive at solutions—it has been to find the political will to implement them. We need reforms in many areas, and were they actually enacted, these reforms would add up to a revolution of sorts. With even some of these ideas implemented, the world could look very different twenty years from now.

Countries can change. In 1930, most nations in the world had tiny governments and did not consider it their job to promote the general welfare of their people. By 1950, every one of the world's major nations had embraced that mandate. It was not easy. On October 20, 1935, Gallup published its first official public opinion poll. It revealed that—in the midst of the Great Depression and the Dust Bowl—60% of Americans believed "expenditures by the Government for relief and recovery" were *too great*. Only 9% said they were too little, while 31% said they were about right. That did not deter Franklin Roosevelt from steaming ahead with the New Deal—and continuing his efforts to educate the American public about the need for government as a stabilizing force in the economy and society. Great leaders like FDR read polls to understand the nature of their challenge, not as an excuse for inaction.

Consider the European Union. At first, the pandemic made its members close up. They shut down borders, competed for medical supplies, and accused one another of malice and venality. Public sentiment was running strongly against the EU in hard-hit countries like Italy. But after the initial shock, Europeans began to consider how to handle the fallout from Covid-19. They recognized that it placed unprecedented stress on the continent, particularly on its weakest members. Thanks to wise leadership from the biggest powers, France and Germany, as well as from the EU's top officials, an accord was struck in July 2020 to issue European bonds that will allow the poorer countries to access funds that are, in effect, guaranteed by the richest. This might sound like a technical matter, but it represents a dramatic step forward in a more deeply interconnected Europe. European leaders saw the direction in which Covid-19 was pushing them and pushed back. A pandemic that initially drove countries apart could prove to be the catalyst for a long-sought closer union.

The same tension between integration and isolation can be seen across the world. The pandemic is leading countries to look inward. But enlightened leaders will recognize that the only real solution to problems like pandemics—and climate change and cyberwar—is to look outward, toward more and better cooperation. The solution to a badly funded, weak World Health Organization is not to withdraw from it in the hope that it withers away, but rather to fund it better and give it more autonomy so that it could stand up to China— or the United States—if a health emergency required it. No single country can organize the entire world anymore. None wants to. That leaves only the possibilities of chaos, cold war, or cooperation.

It is true, as the critics charge, that real international collaboration requires some element of collective decision-making. While it sounds sinister to some ears, it is in fact what countries do all the time. It is the mechanism by which we regulate everything from international telephone calls to air travel to trade and intellectual property to the emission of chlorofluorocarbons. There is no global "one world government," and there never will be—it is just a phrase designed to scare people into imagining a secret army descending on them in black helicopters. What actually exists, and what we need more of, is global *governance*, agreements among sovereign nations to work together to solve common problems. It shouldn't be so hard. Cooperation is one of the most fundamental traits in human beings, one that many biologists believe is at the root of our survival over the millennia. If we are to survive well into the future, cooperation will surely help us more than conflict.

Of course, trends matter. Technological forces, economic realities, and biological imperatives all determine the parameters of what one can do. "Men make their own history," Karl Marx wrote, "but they do not make it as they please; they do not make it under self-selected circumstances, but under circumstances existing already, given and transmitted from the past." That is why the wisest leaders try to understand history, evaluate the larger forces at work, and determine how much room there is for human action. The man who almost single-handedly unified Germany, Otto von Bismarck, described his role in these terms: "The statesman's task is to hear God's footsteps marching through history, and to try and catch on to His coattails as He marches past."

Sometimes, even in the midst of great structural forces moving in one direction, countries can make decisions that reshape our path. In May 1958, at the height of the Cold War, there was a moment of choosing, in Minneapolis, Minnesota. The deputy minister of health of the Soviet Union, Dr. Viktor Zhdanov, attended the annual meeting of the WHO's governing body, the World Health Assembly. It was the first time a Soviet delegation had attended since the WHO's founding a decade earlier. Zhdanov urged the organization to mount a global campaign to eradicate smallpox once and for all. In a nod to the United States, he quoted in his speech a letter Thomas Jefferson had written to Edward Jenner, who had pioneered the smallpox vaccine. "Future nations will know by history only that the loathsome small-pox has existed," Jefferson wrote. It was an early attempt to put into action Nikita Khrushchev's post-Stalin plan of "peaceful coexistence" with the West.

The United States was resistant at first, not least for thinking the Soviet proposal would pull attention away from American-led efforts to eradicate malaria. Yet once Washington threw its support behind the project, this cooperation ramped up during the Johnson administration and became a central focus of the WHO. The two superpowers facilitated not only the mass production of vaccines, but also a program to vaccinate people throughout the Third World. By 1980, smallpox had been officially eradicated. The Harvard historian Erez Manela says it "was arguably the single most successful instance of superpower collaboration in Cold War history." And it's a lesson that Beijing and Washington should learn in the post-Covid, bipolar world to come.

In *Lawrence of Arabia*, the lesson about fate versus human agency gets more complicated. The night before the attack on Aqaba, the Arab tribes start quarreling bitterly over a murder committed by one tribesman against a member of another tribe. As an outsider, Lawrence offers to execute the murderer so that justice could be done by an impartial hand—only to realize that the murderer is Gasim, the man whose life he had saved in the desert. And yet he walks up and calmly shoots six bullets into his chest. The lesson perhaps is that Gasim was destined to die. Lawrence had been able to save him in the desert, and in doing so, gave him a reprieve. But, by his actions, Gasim threw away that chance for a different future.

In his own way, Dwight Eisenhower was making a similar point to Walter Cronkite as they sat overlooking the rows of graves in Normandy. The soldiers who died during World War II gave us all a chance to build a better and more peaceful world. So, too, in our times, this ugly pandemic has created the possibility for change and reform. It has opened up a path to a new world. It's ours to take that opportunity or squander it. Nothing is written.

Acknowledgments

THE PANDEMIC HAS accelerated much in our lives and it did the same to the writing and production of this book. It all began with a list on a piece of paper. Once Covid-19 hit, I realized that it was going to have broad and long-term effects. I began to write down the ways that it might change the world and that original list is pretty close to the ten lessons in this book. Then began the process of research, reading, and writing, which was all-consuming but also all-absorbing. In a sense I found my own way to deal with the pandemic—think, read, and write about it.

I asked three brilliant young associates to help me by critiquing and fact-checking each draft. Jonathan Esty, Jonah Bader, and John Cookson dived into the project—working long hours and late nights—and the result was a wonderfully stimulating, fast-paced digital seminar of sorts. They corrected my errors, made excellent suggestions, and caught logical lapses. Jonathan, who took the lead and organized the effort, works with me on projects at Schmidt Futures, the innovative philanthropic venture set up by Eric and Wendy Schmidt. Jonah works on my show at CNN, producing and editing my opening commentary, among other tasks. And John worked on the show some years ago and has moved on to other places, including the Chicago Council on Foreign Relations.

Stuart Reid, a managing editor at *Foreign Affairs*, took time off from his own book project and read the entire manuscript and greatly improved it with his judicious suggestions. Zachary Karabell read the first chapters and steered me in a better direction at the start. Eric Schmidt and Jared Cohen patiently heard me test out several versions of these ideas. Needless to say, none of these associates and friends bear responsibility for any of my mistakes, nor do I mean to imply that they agree with everything I have written.

Drake McFeely, my editor at Norton, was instantly enthusiastic about this book, even though I actually owe him another book on a different subject. (Next up, Drake, I promise!) He has been my editor for eighteen years, through four books, and is now my indispensable coconspirator, friend, and guide in these efforts. I was fortunate to have worked with Stuart Proffitt of Penguin Press once before and was thrilled that he signed up again to publish the book in Great Britain and the Commonwealth. His erudition and elegance greatly improved the manuscript. This is the first time I have worked with Andrew Wylie. It did not take me long to understand why he is a legend in the industry.

My thanks to the Norton team. Drake's assistant, Bee Holekamp, has kept the project on track and on schedule. Avery Hudson copyedited the manuscript in record time. Becky Homiski, Julia Druskin, and Joe Lops put in long hours to speed up the production of the book. Rachel Salzman and Meredith McGinnis have handled the marketing and publicity with great skill and enthusiasm.

I am grateful to Jeff Zucker for giving me the independence and support to do my show and a series of documentaries for CNN. In these last few years, I have watched Jeff do his job—and do it superbly—under extraordinary pressure. I've learned a lot from him, as my boss but also as a friend. I have been fortunate to write for Fred Hiatt at *The Washington Post*, who runs the finest editorial page in the country—one that continues to showcase diversity of all kinds and simultaneously set high standards for excellence.

I'd like to thank my team at CNN. I am genuinely grateful to each one of you: Tom Goldstone, who runs the *GPS* show, Melanie Galvin, who handles all my various projects, Jessica Gutteridge, Dana Sherne, Caroline Richenberg, Nida Najar, Matthew Kendrick, Kiara Bhagwanjee, Chris Good, Simon Bouvier, Katrina Kaufman, Dan Logan, Jennifer Dargan, Peter Stevenson, Liza McGuirk, Diane Beasley, Tal Trachtman Alroy, Jenny Friedland, Zac Leja, Nicholas Paolo Accinelli, and Ingrid Holmquist. At *The Washington Post*, my sincere thanks to Mike Larabee, Ruth Marcus, Christian Caryl, Mili Mitra, Josh Alvarez, and Sophie Yarborough.

Working on a tight schedule makes demands on one's family and friends. My mother's boundless love has always been my ballast, even now when she is unable to express it. For their support and affection, I am grateful to my children, Omar, Lila, and Sofia, and to my ex-wife, Paula. My brother Arshad and I have talked about the issues in the book often and his wife, Ann, a brilliant scientist, educated me on some of them as well. My brother Mansoor and his wife, Rachel, and my sister Tasneem and her husband, Vikram, have always been supportive. Finally, many thanks to Julian, who put up with me as I put in long hours and obsessed over small things to get the book right and done.

I've dedicated this book to Dan, Joanna, and Gideon Rose. I met Gideon when I was a freshman in college and he was a sophomore. Ever since then, for thirty-eight years now, we have been in touch at least weekly, often more frequently. His parents, Dan and Joanna, are my unofficial godparents and have given me and my family love, support, and encouragement for almost four decades as well. As Dan often says when we are parting company after a wonderful evening of food and wine and conversation, *to be continued* . . .

Notes

Epigraph

vii   **"The Future never spoke—":** Emily Dickinson, *The Poems of Emily Dickinson: Reading Edition*, edited by Ralph W. Franklin (Cambridge, MA: Belknap Press, 1999).

Introduction: The Bat Effect

1   **"spiky blob":** Cara Giaimo, "The Spiky Blob Seen Around the World," *New York Times*, April 1, 2020, https://www.nytimes.com/2020/04/01/health/coronavirus-illustration-cdc.html.

2   **1/10,000th the size of the period:** SARS-CoV-2 virion is 0.1 micrometers in diameter (100 nanometers): Yinon M. Bar-On, Avi Flamholz, Rob Phillips, and Ron Milo, "SARS-CoV-2 (COVID-19) by the Numbers," *eLife* 9 (April 2, 2020): e57309, https://www.ncbi.nlm.nih.gov/pmc/articles/PMC7224694/; a period is approximately 100,000,000 nanometers across: Shige Abe, "How Small Can Life Be?," Astrobiology at NASA, July 9, 2001, https://astrobiology.nasa.gov/news/how-small-can-life-be/.

2   **three-quarters of a trillion dollars:** US defense spending = $732 billion in 2019: Stockholm International Peace Research Institute, "Global Military Expenditure Sees Largest Annual Increase in a Decade," April 27, 2020, https://www.sipri.org/media/press-release/2020/global-military-expenditure-sees-largest-annual-increase-decade-says-sipri-reaching-1917-billion.

3   **the hinge event:** Lawrence Summers, "Covid-19 Looks Like a Hinge in History," *Financial Times*, May 14, 2020, https://www.ft.com/content/de643ae8-9527-11ea-899a-f62a20d54625.

3   **return to business as usual:** Micah Zenko, "The United States Will Learn Nothing from the Pandemic," *Foreign Policy*, June 5, 2020, https:// foreignpolicy.com/2020/06/05/coronavirus-pandemic-covid-lessons -united-states-9-11/.

3   **accelerate it:** Richard Haass, "The Pandemic Will Accelerate History Rather Than Reshape It," *Foreign Affairs*, April 7, 2020.

4   **"wonder clinging to him":** William Maxwell, *They Came Like Swallows* (1937, reprint Vintage International, 1997), 174.

4   **"time for everything":** Katherine Anne Porter, *Pale Horse, Pale Rider* (1939, reprint Houghton Mifflin Harcourt, 1990), 208.

4   **We should have seen it coming:** Uri Friedman, "We Were Warned," *Atlantic*, March 18, 2020.

5   **One medieval chronicler accused:** The Genoese writer Gabriele de' Mussi. See: Mark Wheelis, "Biological Warfare at the 1346 Siege of Caffa," *Emerging Infectious Diseases* 8, no. 9 (2002): 971–75, https://dx.doi .org/10.3201/eid0809.010536.

5   **launching plague-ridden corpses:** Walter Scheidel, *The Great Leveler: Violence and the History of Inequality from the Stone Age to the Twenty-First Century* (Princeton, NJ: Princeton University Press, 2015), 293.

5   **up to half:** 30%–50% of Europe's population dying: James W. Wood et al., "The Temporal Dynamics of the 14th Century Black Death," *Human Biology* (2003), cited in Sharon N. DeWitte, "Age Patterns of Mortality During the Black Death in London, A.D. 1349–1350," *Journal of Archaeological Science* 37, no. 12 (December 2010), https://www.sciencedirect.com/science/ article/pii/S0305440310002803.

5   **a few hundred cases:** World Health Organization, "Plague," https://www .who.int/news-room/fact-sheets/detail/plague.

5   **wages rose and rents fell:** Scheidel, *Great Leveler*, Chapter 10, "The Black Death," 291–313.

6   **questioned entrenched hierarchies:** Barbara W. Tuchman, *A Distant Mirror: The Calamitous Fourteenth Century* (New York: Alfred A. Knopf, 1978). See, for example:

> Survivors of the plague, finding themselves neither destroyed nor improved, could discover no Divine purpose in the pain they had suffered. God's purposes were usually mysterious, but this scourge had been too terrible to be accepted without questioning. If a disaster of such magnitude, the most lethal ever known, was a mere wanton act of God or perhaps not God's work at all, then the absolutes of a fixed order were loosed from their moorings. Minds that opened to admit these questions could never again be shut. Once people envisioned the possibility of change in a fixed order, the end of an age

of submission came in sight; the turn to individual conscience lay ahead. To that extent the Black Death may have been the unrecognized beginning of modern man. (153–54)

6 **setting in motion the Renaissance:** Though this narrative, and the notion of "medieval malaise," is hotly disputed by Renaissance scholars and medievalists. See: Ada Palmer, "Black Death, COVID, and Why We Keep Telling the Myth of a Renaissance Golden Age and Bad Middle Ages," *Ex Urbe*, June 4, 2020, https://www.exurbe.com/black-death-covid-and-why-we-keep-telling-the-myth-of-a-renaissance-golden-age-and-bad-middle-ages/.

6 **tens of millions of people:** *The Native Population of the Americas in 1492*, 2nd ed., edited by William M. Denevan (Madison: University of Wisconsin Press, 1992), cited in Alexander Koch et al., "Earth System Impacts of the European Arrival and Great Dying in the Americas After 1492," *Quaternary Science Reviews* 207 (March 1, 2019): 13–36, https://www.sciencedirect.com/science/article/pii/S0277379118307261.

6 **600 men facing an Aztec Empire . . . "the psychological implications":** William H. McNeill, *Plagues and Peoples* (Garden City, NY: Anchor Press, 1976), Introduction, 23–24; see also Jared Diamond, *Guns, Germs, and Steel: The Fate of Human Societies* (New York: W. W. Norton, 1999).

7 **killed some 50 million people:** Centers for Disease Control and Prevention, National Center for Immunization and Respiratory Diseases, "Partner Key Messages on the 1918 Influenza Pandemic Commemoration," August 10, 2018, https://www.cdc.gov/flu/pandemic-resources/1918-commemoration/key-messages.htm.

7 **the number that died in the fighting:** 20 million deaths in World War I: Nadège Mougel, "World War I Casualties," trans. Julie Gratz (Scy-Chazelles, France: Centre européen Robert Schuman, 2011), http://www.centre-robert-schuman.org/userfiles/files/REPERES%20%E2%80%93%20module%201-1%20-%20explanatory%20notes%20%E2%80%93%20World%20War%20I%20casualties%20%E2%80%93%20EN.pdf.

7 **called the Spanish flu not because it began in Spain:** see John M. Barry, *The Great Influenza: The Story of the Deadliest Plague in History* (New York: Viking, 2004), 171.

7 **how to treat this new infection:** For more on the Spanish flu, see Barry, *The Great Influenza*, especially 353–58.

7 **TED Talk warning:** Bill Gates, "The Next Outbreak? We're Not Ready," TED2015, https://www.ted.com/talks/bill_gates_the_next_outbreak_we_re_not_ready/transcript?language=en.

8 **a speech at the Munich Security Conference:** Bill Gates, Bill & Melinda Gates Foundation, February 17, 2017, https://www.gatesfoundation

.org/Media-Center/Speeches/2017/05/Bill-Gates-Munich-Security
-Conference.

8   **a segment of my CNN show:** Fareed Zakaria, "Global Pandemic Possibility," *Fareed Zakaria GPS: Global Public Square,* CNN, June 25, 2017, http://
transcripts.cnn.com/TRANSCRIPTS/1706/25/fzgps.01.html.

9   *asymmetric* **shocks:** For a treatment of historical pandemics as asymmetric shocks, see: Guido Alfani, "Pandemics and Asymmetric Shocks:
Lessons from the History of Plagues," *VoxEU,* Center for Economic Policy Research, April 9, 2020, https://voxeu.org/article/pandemics-and
-asymmetric-shocks.

9   **$5.4 trillion:** Neta C. Crawford, "United States Budgetary Costs and
Obligations of Post-9/11 Wars Through FY2020," Brown University,
November 3, 2019, https://watson.brown.edu/costsofwar/files/cow/
imce/papers/2019/US%20Budgetary%20Costs%20of%20Wars%20
November%202019.pdf.

10 **Right-wing populism:** Jon Henley, "How Populism Emerged as an
Electoral Force in Europe," *Guardian,* November 20, 2018, https://www
.theguardian.com/world/ng-interactive/2018/nov/20/how-populism
-emerged-as-electoral-force-in-europe.

10 **By some measures:** Charles Riley, "The UK Economy Is Heading for Its
Worst Crash in 300 Years," CNN Business, May 7, 2020, https://www.cnn
.com/2020/05/07/economy/uk-economy-bank-of-england/index.html.

10 **already rivals that of the Great Depression:** The US unemployment rate
hit 14.7%, a record high since the 1930s, per US Bureau of Labor Statistics, "The Employment Situation—June 2020," https://www.bls.gov/
news.release/pdf/empsit.pdf. (All-time record for US unemployment was
24.9% in 1933, per US Census, *Bicentennial Edition: Historical Statistics of
the United States, Colonial Times to 1970,* Chapter D: Labor, cited in Gene
Smiley, "Recent Unemployment Rate Estimates for the 1920s and 1930s,"
Journal of Economic History 43, no. 2 [June 1983]: 487–93, http://www.jstor
.org/stable/2120839.)

11 **$45 trillion market:** Janet Morrissey, "Credit Default Swaps: The Next
Crisis?," *Time,* March 17, 2008, http://content.time.com/time/business/
article/0,8599,1723152,00.html.

11 **three-quarters the size:** Global GDP = $63.6 trillion in 2008, World
Bank DataBank, https://data.worldbank.org/indicator/NY.GDP.MKTP
.CD?locations=1W.

11 **flapping of a butterfly's wing:** This idea is most prominently developed in
Edward N. Lorenz, *The Essence of Chaos* (Seattle: University of Washington
Press, 1995).

12 **influence of the stars:** "Influenza at a Glance," Nieman Foundation
for Journalism at Harvard, https://nieman.harvard.edu/wp-content/

uploads/pod-assets/microsites/NiemanGuideToCoveringPandemicFlu/
AnIntroduction/InfluenzaAtAGlance.aspx.html.

12 *grippe*: "grippe (n.)," Etymology Online, https://www.etymonline.com/
word/grippe.

Lesson One: Buckle Up

13 **no supreme authority, no world government:** There are dozens of books
on this subject. The modern classic is Kenneth N. Waltz, *Man, the State,
and War* (New York: Columbia University Press, revised 2001, originally
published 1959).

14 **"the state and posture of Gladiators":** Thomas Hobbes, *Leviathan*, Chapter XIII, "Of The Naturall Condition Of Mankind," "The Incommodites
Of Such A War."

14 **trade booming:** Esteban Ortiz-Ospina and Diana Beltekian, "Trade and
Globalization," Our World in Data, October 2018, https://ourworldindata
.org/trade-and-globalization.

15 **"policy trilemma":** "Two Out of Three Ain't Bad," *Economist*, August 27,
2016. For another formulation, see also Dani Rodrik, *The Globalization Paradox: Democracy and the Future of the World Economy* (New York: W. W. Norton, 2012).

16 **"nature is declining globally":** United Nations, Sustainable Development
Report: "Nature's Dangerous Decline," May 6, 2019, https://www.un.org/
sustainabledevelopment/blog/2019/05/nature-decline-unprecedented-report/.

16 **"weapon of the weak":** James C. Scott, *Weapons of the Weak: Everyday
Forms of Peasant Resistance* (New Haven, CT: Yale University Press, 1985).

17 **three-quarters of new human diseases:** Centers for Disease Control and
Prevention, "Zoonotic Diseases," https://www.cdc.gov/onehealth/basics/
zoonotic-diseases.html.

17 **at a faster pace:** Jon Hilsenrath, "Global Viral Outbreaks Like Coronavirus, Once Rare, Will Become More Common," *Wall Street Journal*, March
6, 2020.

17 **"perfect cauldron":** Christian Walzer, "COVID-19: Where It Starts and
Stops," Wildlife Conservation Society, Wildlife Health Program, https://
youtu.be/_D_6a56zI_U?t=129.

17 **increasing the odds:** Nita Madhav et al., "Pandemics: Risks, Impacts, and
Mitigation," Chapter 17 in *Disease Control Priorities: Improving Health and
Reducing Poverty*, 3rd ed., National Center for Biotechnology Information
(National Institutes of Health), November 27, 2017, https://www.ncbi.nlm
.nih.gov/books/NBK525302/#pt5.ch17.sec3.

18   **Bats can endure viruses:** Lena H. Sun, "On a Bat's Wing and a Prayer: Scientists' Plan to Track Deadly Marburg Virus Is Literally Held Together with Glue," *Washington Post*, December 13, 2018.

18   **escaped from a UK lab:** Toby Ord, *The Precipice: Existential Risk and the Future of Humanity* (New York: Hachette, 2020), 130–31.

18   **perfect breeding grounds:** See, for instance, bat caves in Uganda as incubators for the Marburg virus, in ibid.

18   **"batnado":** Carolyn Kormann, "The Changing Climate Inside the World's Largest Bat Colony," *New Yorker*, August 5, 2019.

18   **Nipah, hosted in bats:** Robert Kessler, "Nipah: The Very Model of a Pandemic," EcoHealth Alliance, March 2018, https://www.ecohealthalliance .org/2018/03/nipah.

19   **an intermediate host:** "Typically, coronaviruses found in bats have or require an intermediate host before spilling over into humans, like what is observed with MERS-CoV . . ." in Arinjay Banerjee, "Bats and Coronaviruses," *Viruses*, January 9, 2019, 11(1): 41, https://www.ncbi.nlm.nih.gov/ pmc/articles/PMC6356540/.

19   **used in traditional Chinese medicine:** Joel Achenbach, "Coronavirus Came from Bats or Possibly Pangolins amid 'Acceleration' of New Zoonotic Infections," *Washington Post*, February 7, 2020.

19   **"this is not just nature":** Peter Daszak, in conversation with Fareed Zakaria, *Fareed Zakaria GPS: Global Public Square*, CNN, April 22, 2020, https:// www.cnn.com/videos/tv/2020/04/26/exp-gps-0426-daszak-int.cnn.

19   **80 billion animals slaughtered for meat *every year*:** "Meat Production," Our World in Data, https://ourworldindata.org/meat-production. See also estimates of 77 billion: Food and Agriculture Organization of the United Nations, http://www.fao.org/faostat/en/#data/QL.

19   **18% of calories:** World Economic Forum, "New Nature Economy Report II: The Future of Nature and Business," 39, http://www3.weforum.org/ docs/WEF_The_Future_Of_Nature_And_Business_2020.pdf.

19   **99% in America:** Jacy Reese, "US Factory Farming Estimates," April 11, 2019, Sentience Institute, https://www.sentienceinstitute.org/us-factory -farming-estimates.

19   **74% around the world:** Kelly Witwicki, "Global Farmed & Factory Farmed Animals Estimates," Sentience Institute, February 21, 2019, https://www .sentienceinstitute.org/global-animal-farming-estimates.

20   **"even more virulent":** Sigal Samuel, "The Meat We Eat Is a Pandemic Risk, Too," *Vox*, April 22, 2020, updated June 10, 2020.

20   **"most dangerous pathogens possible":** Rob Wallace, quoted in ibid.

20   **North American pig farms:** Charles W. Schmidt, "Swine CAFOs & Novel H1N1 Flu: Separating Facts from Fears," *Environmental Health Per-*

spectives 117, no. 9 (September 2009): A394–A401, https://www.ncbi.nlm
.nih.gov/pmc/articles/PMC2737041/.

20 **factory farms in East Asia:** Fiona Harvey, "Factory Farming in Asia Creating Global Health Risks, Report Warns," *Guardian*, August 13, 201.

20 **"biggest human health risk":** Robert Lawrence, quoted in Samuel, "The
Meat We Eat."

20 **2.8 million Americans fall ill:** Centers for Disease Control and Prevention, "Antibiotic/Antimicrobial Resistance (AR/AMR)," https://www.cdc
.gov/drugresistance/index.html.

20 **one person every fifteen minutes:** Sigal Samuel, "The Post-Antibiotic Era
Is Here," *Vox*, November 14, 2019.

20 **death toll is 700,000 a year:** World Bank Group, "Pulling Together to
Beat Superbugs," October 2019, http://documents.worldbank.org/curated/
en/430051570735014540/pdf/Pulling-Together-to-Beat-Superbugs
-Knowledge-and-Implementation-Gaps-in-Addressing-Antimicrobial
-Resistance.pdf.

21 **tilled the prairies:** Jonathan Coppess, "The Conservation Question, Part
2: Lessons Written in Dust," Gardner Policy Series, Department of Agri-
cultural and Consumer Economics, University of Illinois, October 24,
2019, https://farmdocdaily.illinois.edu/2019/10/the-conservation-question
-part-2-lessons-written-in-dust.html.

21 **blown away:** Ibid.

21 **hottest year on record until 1998:** "National Climate Report—Annual
2014," National Oceanic and Atmospheric Administration, https://www
.ncdc.noaa.gov/sotc/national/201413.

21 **Thousands died:** "Drought of 2012 Conjures Up Dust Bowl Memories,
Raises Questions for Tomorrow," CNN, September 15, 2012.

22 **twenty-three hectares every minute:** United Nations, Sustainable
Development Goals, 2020, https://www.un.org/sustainabledevelopment/
biodiversity/.

22 **"greatest environmental challenge":** Damian Carrington, "Desertification
Is Greatest Threat to Planet, Expert Warns," *Guardian*, December 16, 2010.

22 **Thirty-eight percent of the earth's surface:** Montserrat Núñez et al.,
"Assessing Potential Desertification Environmental Impact in Life Cycle
Assessment," *International Journal of Life Cycle Assessment* 15, no. 1 (Jan-
uary 2010): 67–78, https://www.researchgate.net/publication/226955880_
Assessing_potential_desertification_environmental_impact_in_life_
cycle_assessment_Part_1_Methodological_aspects.

22 **about a third of the groundwater:** Jeremy Frankel, "Crisis on the High
Plains: The Loss of America's Largest Aquifer—the Ogallala," *University
of Denver Water Law Review*, May 17, 2018.

22   **shrivel by 70%:** Carey Gillam, "Ogallala Aquifer: Could Critical Water Source Run Dry?," *Reuters*, August 27, 2013.

22   **6,000 years for rainwater to refill:** Jane Braxton Little, "The Ogallala Aquifer: Saving a Vital U.S. Water Source," *Scientific American*, March 1, 2009.

23   **"man-made species":** Joshua Lederberg, "Viruses and Humankind: Intracellular Symbiosis and Evolutionary Competition," *Frontline*, 1989, https://www.pbs.org/wgbh/pages/frontline/aids/virus/humankind.html.

23   **killed over 99%:** Ed Yong, "The Next Chapter in a Viral Arms Race," *Atlantic*, August 14, 2017.

23   **sheep infected:** Siro Igino Trevisanato, "The 'Hittite Plague,' an Epidemic of Tularemia and the First Record of Biological Warfare," *Medical Hypotheses* 69, no. 6 (2007): 1, 371–74, https://doi.org/10.1016/j.mehy.2007.03.012, cited in Ord, *The Precipice*, 130.

24   **9,000 scientists:** Jonathan B. Tucker, "Bioweapons from Russia: Stemming the Flow," *Issues in Science and Technology* 15, no. 3 (Spring 1999), https://issues.org/p_tucker/, also referenced in Ord, *The Precipice*, 132.

24   **"smaller budget than an average McDonald's":** Ord, *The Precipice*, 132.

24   **our world is terribly fragile:** Thomas L. Friedman, "How We Broke the World," *New York Times*, May 30, 2020.

26   **140 million acres:** Paula vW Dáil, *Hard Living in America's Heartland: Rural Poverty in the 21st Century Midwest* (Jefferson, NC: McFarland, 2015), 80.

26   **"pandemics are optional":** Larry Brilliant, "Outbreaks Are Inevitable, but Pandemics Are Optional," Long Now Foundation, YouTube, March 6, 2020 https://www.youtube.com/watch?v=nVWoHmURDTQ.

27   **73% of all fresh vegetables and meat:** "Will Wet Markets Be Hung Out to Dry After the Pandemic?," *Economist*, May 26, 2020.

27   **exotic trade:** John Vidal, "'Tip of the Iceberg': Is Our Destruction of Nature Responsible for Covid-19?," *Guardian*, March 18, 2020; James Gorman, "Wildlife Trade Spreads Coronaviruses as Animals Get to Market," *New York Times*, June 19, 2020.

Lesson Two: What Matters Is Not the Quantity of Government but the Quality

29   **best prepared to handle an epidemic:** Elizabeth Cameron et al., "Global Health Security Index: Building Collective Action and Accountability," Johns Hopkins Bloomberg School of Public Health, October 2019, https://

www.ghsindex.org/wp-content/uploads/2019/10/2019-Global-Health -Security-Index.pdf.

30 **25% of the world's cumulative confirmed cases:** "Coronavirus Map: Tracking the Global Outbreak," *New York Times,* https://www.nytimes .com/interactive/2020/world/coronavirus-maps.html, accessed July 13, 2020.

30 **death rates…ten times higher than in Europe:** Paul Krugman, Twitter post, July 13, 2020, https://twitter.com/paulkrugman/status/1282 656106762952705/photo/1, citing Our World in Data, "Daily New Confirmed COVID-19 Deaths per Million People," European Union versus United States, July 13, 2020.

30 **the new face of American exceptionalism:** Jeremy Konyndyk, "Exceptionalism Is Killing Americans: An Insular Political Culture Failed the Test of the Pandemic," *Foreign Affairs,* June 8, 2020.

30 **discouraging the public:** Ben Schreckinger, "Mask Mystery: Why Are U.S. Officials Dismissive of Protective Covering?," *Politico,* March 30, 2020, https://www.politico.com/news/2020/03/30/coronavirus-masks-trump -administration-156327.

30 **faulty test kits:** Eric Lipton et al., "The C.D.C. Waited 'Its Entire Existence' for This Moment. What Went Wrong?," *New York Times,* June 3, 2020.

30 **"Not the United States":** Selena Simmons-Duffin, "As States Reopen, Do They Have the Workforce They Need to Stop Coronavirus Outbreaks?," NPR, June 18, 2020.

32 **750 million people:** Raymond Zhong and Paul Mozur, "To Tame Coronavirus, Mao-Style Social Control Blankets China," *New York Times,* February 15, 2020, https://www.nytimes.com/2020/02/15/business/china -coronavirus-lockdown.html.

32 **built two new hospitals:** Lingling Wei, "China's Coronavirus Response Toughens State Control and Weakens the Private Market," *Wall Street Journal,* March 18, 2020.

32 **restricting the publication:** Nectar Gan, Caitlin Hu, and Ivan Watson, "Beijing Tightens Grip over Coronavirus Research, amid US-China Row on Virus Origin," CNN, April 16, 2020, https://www.cnn .com/2020/04/12/asia/china-coronavirus-research-restrictions-intl-hnk/ index.html.

33 **dictatorships often mishandle:** "Diseases Like Covid-19 Are Deadlier in Non-Democracies," *Economist,* February 18, 2020.

33 **respond to famines better:** Amartya Sen, *Development as Freedom* (New York: Anchor, 1999), 16.

33 **over $6 trillion:** Andrew Van Dam, "The U.S. Has Thrown More Than $6 Trillion at the Coronavirus Crisis. That Number Could Grow," *Washington*

Post, April 15, 2020, and Chris Edwards, "Crisis May Add $6 Trillion to Federal Debt," Cato Institute, April 21, 2020, https://www.cato.org/blog/crisis-may-add-6-trillion-federal-debt.

33   **one of the largest per capita:** IMF, "Policy Responses to Covid-19," https://www.imf.org/en/Topics/imf-and-covid19/Policy-Responses-to-COVID-19.

34   **adjusted adroitly:** Faiz Siddiqui and Reed Albergotti, "Ford and General Electric Team Up to Produce Ventilators as Major Manufacturers Shift to Medical Equipment," *Washington Post*, March 30, 2020.

34   **"public squalor":** John Kenneth Galbraith, *The Affluent Society* (Boston: Houghton Mifflin, 1958), 189.

34   **snatched up by big companies and the rich:** Jesse Drucker, "The Tax-Break Bonanza Inside the Economic Rescue Package," *New York Times*, April 24, 2020.

34   **sent money their way:** Brendan Fischer and Kedric Payne, "How Lobbyists Robbed Small Business Relief Loans," *New York Times*, April 30, 2020.

35   **printed with Donald Trump's name:** Lisa Rein, "In Unprecedented Move, Treasury Orders Trump's Name Printed on Stimulus Checks," *Washington Post*, April 14, 2020.

35   **50 million Americans were waiting:** 120 million checks sent by April 30, per US Treasury's Bureau of the Fiscal Service, updated July 6, 2020, https://www.fiscal.treasury.gov/files/news/eip-operational-faqs-for-financial-industry.pdf; House Ways and Means Committee estimates 171 to 190 million payments would need to be made in total, per "Economic Impact Payments Issued to Date," June 5, 2020, https://waysandmeans.house.gov/sites/democrats.waysandmeans.house.gov/files/documents/2020.06.04%20EIPs%20Issued%20as%20of%20June%204%20FINAL.pdf.

35   **a million checks to dead people:** Erica Werner, "Treasury Sent More Than 1 Million Coronavirus Stimulus Payments to Dead People, Congressional Watchdog Finds," *Washington Post*, June 25, 2020.

35   **within the first two weeks of the crisis:** Lauren Vogel, "COVID-19: A Timeline of Canada's First-Wave Response," *Canadian Medical Association Journal News*, June 12, 2020, https://cmajnews.com/2020/06/12/coronavirus-1095847/.

35   **60% of lost wages:** "Germany Offers Cash for Everyone," *Economist*, March 26, 2020.

36   **regularly topping the list:** Heritage Foundation, 2019 Index of Economic Freedom, "Key Findings of the 2019 Index," https://www.heritage.org/index/book/chapter-3.

36   **mere 18%:** Heritage Foundation, 2020 Index of Economic Freedom, "Hong Kong," https://www.heritage.org/index/country/hongkong.

36   **a third of France's figure:** Heritage Foundation, 2020 Index of Economic Freedom, "France," https://www.heritage.org/index/country/france.

36 **eighteen deaths as of late July:** For both Hong Kong and Taiwan, see *New York Times*, "Coronavirus Map: Tracking the Global Outbreak," accessed July 27, 2020, https://www.nytimes.com/interactive/2020/world/coronavirus-maps.html.

36 **6% of its GDP on health care, one-third the American figure:** Tsung-Mei Cheng, "Health Care Spending in the US and Taiwan," *Health Affairs*, February 6, 2019.

37 **"patrimonial":** Max Weber, *Economy and Society* (Berkeley: University of California Press, 1978).

37 **"basic building blocks":** Francis Fukuyama, *Political Order and Political Decay: From the Industrial Revolution to the Globalization of Democracy* (New York: Farrar, Straus and Giroux, 2014), 199.

38 **most of which routinely regulate:** Paul Waldman, "How Our Campaign Finance System Compares to Other Countries," *American Prospect*, April 4, 2014.

39 **"byzantine":** Although the old narrative of a sclerotic, decaying Byzantine Empire has been challenged by recent scholars. See: Judith Herrin, *Byzantium: The Surprising Life of a Medieval Empire* (Princeton, NJ: Princeton University Press, 2007).

40 **"mandarins":** Sarah Zhang, "Why *Mandarin* Doesn't Come from Chinese," *Atlantic*, January 4, 2019.

40 **"war made the state":** Charles Tilly, "Reflections on the History of European State-Making," in *The Formation of National States in Western Europe*, edited by Charles Tilly (Princeton, NJ: Princeton University Press, 1975), 45.

41 **almost three times higher:** John Brewer, *Sinews of Power: War, Money, and the English State, 1688–1783* (London: Unwin Hyman, 1989), 74.

41 **cocktail of state formation:** Frank Snowden, quoted in Jason Willick, "How Epidemics Change Civilizations," *Wall Street Journal*, March 27, 2020.

42 **copied the Prussian bureaucracy:** T. J. Pempel, "Bureaucracy in Japan," *PS: Political Science and Politics* 25, no. 1 (March 1992): 19–24.

44 **"petty barons":** Woodrow Wilson, "The House of Representatives," in *The Collected Works of Woodrow Wilson*, edited by Josephus Daniels.

44 **"one supreme, ultimate head":** Woodrow Wilson, "The Executive," *Congressional Government* (1885), 283, https://archive.org/stream/congressional gov00wilsiala.

45 **its roots in the Roosevelt era:** *Washington Post*, "FDR's Government: The Roots of Today's Federal Bureaucracy," April 12, 1995.

45 **more than 5% of total employment . . . now dropped below 2%:** Data for federal government employees from Federal Reserve Bank of St. Louis, https://fred.stlouisfed.org/series/CES9091000001, total US nonfarm employees, https://fred.stlouisfed.org/series/PAYEMS.

45 **population that is twice as large:** US Census Bureau, "Quickfacts," https://www.census.gov/quickfacts/fact/table/US/AGE775219.

45 **GDP that is seven times as large:** Data from Federal Reserve Bank of St. Louis, https://fred.stlouisfed.org/series/GDPCA.

46 **fewer government officials:** Well below the OECD average, per OECD's "Government at a Glance 2017," https://www.oecd.org/gov/government-at-a-glance-2017-highlights-en.pdf.

46 **only 6% of federal employees:** Fiona Hill, "Public Service and the Federal Government," Brookings Institution, May 27, 2020, https://www.brookings.edu/policy2020/votervital/public-service-and-the-federal-government/.

46 **"drown it in the bathtub":** Jeff Spross, "The GOP Plot to Drown Medicaid in the Bathtub," *Week*, March 9, 2017.

46 **"deconstruction of the administrative state":** Philip Rucker and Robert Costa, "Bannon Vows a Daily Fight for 'Deconstruction of the Administrative State,'" *Washington Post*, February 23, 2017.

46 **2,684 state, local, and tribal health departments:** Polly J. Price, "A Coronavirus Quarantine in America Could Be a Giant Legal Mess," *Atlantic*, February 16, 2020.

46 **90,126 units:** Editorial Board, "Federalism Explains Varied COVID-19 Responses," *Columbus Dispatch*, May 8, 2020, https://www.dispatch.com/opinion/20200508/editorial-federalism-explains-varied-covid-19-responses.

47 **and even fax:** For inadequacies of America's Covid-19 test reporting, see Sarah Kliff and Margot Sanger-Katz, "Choke Point for U.S. Coronavirus Response: The Fax Machine," *New York Times*, July 13, 2020.

47 **"health cards":** On Taiwan's near-real-time "health cards": tracking of Covid-19 patient data, see Jackie Drees, "What the US Can Learn from Taiwan's EHR System and COVID-19 Response," *Becker's Hospital Review*, July 1, 2020, https://www.beckershospitalreview.com/ehrs/what-the-us-can-learn-from-taiwan-s-ehr-system-and-covid-19-response.html; and Ezekiel Emanuel in conversation with Fareed Zakaria, *Fareed Zakaria GPS: Global Public Square*, CNN, July 12, 2020, https://www.cnn.com/videos/tv/2020/07/12/exp-gps-0712-emanuel-on-us-covid-19-response.cnn.

47 **18,000 separate police departments:** Duren Banks et al., "National Sources of Law Enforcement Employment Data," US Department of Justice, October 4, 2016, https://www.bjs.gov/content/pub/pdf/nsleed.pdf.

48 **former British colonies:** Michael Bernhard, Christopher Reenock, and Timothy Nordstrom, "The Legacy of Western Overseas Colonialism on Democratic Survival," *International Studies Quarterly* 48, no. 1 (March 2004): 225–50, https://academic.oup.com/isq/article-abstract/48/1/225/2963246.

49 **seventeen "layers" of appointees:** Paul Light, "People on People on People:

The Continued Thickening of Government," The Volcker Alliance, October 2017, https://www.volckeralliance.org/sites/default/files/attachments/Issue%20Paper_People%20on%20People.pdf.

49 **long blog post:** Marc Andreessen, "It's Time to Build," Andreessen Horowitz, https://a16z.com/2020/04/18/its-time-to-build/.

50 **Pennsylvania Station:** Marc J. Dunkelman, "This Is Why Your Holiday Travel Is Awful," *Politico*, November 11, 2019.

51 **Ezra Klein has observed:** Ezra Klein, *Why We're Polarized* (New York: Simon & Schuster, 2020).

52 **"removed the mark of the devil":** James Traub, "After the Coronavirus, the Era of Small Government Will Be Over," *Foreign Policy*, April 15, 2020.

Lesson Three: Markets Are Not Enough

56 **"the honest financier":** quoted in David Kynaston, *The Financial Times: A Centenary History* (New York: Viking, 1988), 17.

57 **"collective sacrifice":** Editorial Board, "Virus Lays Bare the Fragility of the Social Contract," *Financial Times*, April 3, 2020.

57 **"some form of socialism":** Mohamed Younis, "Four in 10 Americans Embrace Some Form of Socialism," Gallup, May 20, 2019, https://news.gallup.com/poll/257639/four-americans-embrace-form-socialism.aspx.

58 **protectionism:** Pablo D. Fajgelbaum, Pinelopi K. Goldberg, Patrick J. Kennedy, and Amit K. Khandelwal, "The Return to Protectionism," National Bureau of Economic Research, Working Paper No. 25638, issued in March 2019, revised in October 2019, https://www.nber.org/papers/w25638.

58 **higher support for socialism than their elders:** Lydia Saad, "Socialism as Popular as Capitalism Among Young Adults in U.S.," Gallup, November 25, 2019, https://news.gallup.com/poll/268766/socialism-popular-capitalism-among-young-adults.aspx.

60 **"a capitalist to my bones":** In 2018 remarks to the New England Council, as reported by Katie Lannan, Twitter post, July 16, 2018, https://twitter.com/katielannan/status/1018852303212896257?s=20.

60 **less pure:** Donald R. Kinder and Nathan P. Kalmoe, *Neither Liberal nor Conservative: Ideological Innocence in the American Public* (Chicago: University of Chicago Press, 2017).

61 **"market capitalism is not a religion":** Tucker Carlson, "Mitt Romney Supports the Status Quo. But for Everyone Else, It's Infuriating," Fox News Opinion, January 19, 2019.

62 **"the kind of slump":** Paul Krugman, "Saving Asia: It's Time to Get Radical," *Fortune / CNN Money*, September 7, 1998.

62   **wiping out $5 trillion in wealth:** Chris Gaither and Dawn C. Chmielewski, "Fears of Dot-Com Crash, Version 2.0," *Los Angeles Times*, July 16, 2006.

62   **the end of the obsession:** Alex Williams, "2001: When the Internet Was, Um, Over?," *New York Times*, October 8, 2018.

62   **"Another ideological god has failed":** Martin Wolf, "Seeds of Its Own Destruction: The Scope of Government Is Again Widening and the Era of Free-Wheeling Finance Is Over," *Financial Times*, March 8, 2009.

62   **"Capitalism will be different":** Joe Weisenthal, "Geithner Tells Charlie Rose: Capitalism Will Be Different," *Business Insider*, March 11, 2009.

62   **Could we do so again?:** For another observer skeptical that this will mean a break with free market orthodoxy, see: Lane Kenworthy, "The Pandemic Won't Usher In an American Welfare State," *Foreign Affairs*, May 1, 2020.

63   **"end of history":** Francis Fukuyama, *The End of History and the Last Man* (New York: Free Press, 1992).

63   **"We can only harness":** President William J. Clinton, "Remarks on Signing the North American Free Trade Agreement Implementation Act," December 8, 1993, *Public Papers of the Presidents of the United States: William J. Clinton* (1993, Book II), https://www.govinfo.gov/content/pkg/PPP -1993-book2/html/PPP-1993-book2-doc-pg2139-3.htm.

63   **"golden straitjacket":** Thomas L. Friedman, *The Lexus and the Olive Tree: Understanding Globalization* (New York: Farrar, Straus and Giroux, 1999).

64   **fastest-growing major economy in history:** Congressional Research Service, "China's Economic Rise: History, Trends, Challenges, and Implications for the United States," June 25, 2019, https://fas.org/sgp/crs/row/ RL33534.pdf.

64   **"Market-Leninism":** Nicholas Kristof, "China Sees 'Market-Leninism' as Way to Future," *New York Times*, September 6, 1993.

64   **like steel:** World Steel Association, "World Steel in Figures 2019," https://www.worldsteel.org/en/dam/jcr:96d7a585-e6b2-4d63-b943 -4cd9ab621a91/World%2520Steel%2520in%2520Figures%25202019.pdf.

64   **cement:** US Geological Survey, "Mineral Commodity Summaries," https://www.usgs.gov/centers/nmic/mineral-commodity-summaries.

65   **accidentally told the truth:** Attributed to journalist Michael Kinsley. See Jonathan Chait, "The Origins of the Gaffe, Politics' Idiot-Maker," *New York*, Intelligencer, June 14, 2012.

65   **twice as much per capita:** US per capita health-care spending is $10,586, versus an OECD average of $5,287: OECD Health Statistics 2020, https://www.oecd.org/health/health-data.htm, cited in "How Does the U.S. Healthcare System Compare to Other Countries?," Peter G. Peterson Foundation, July 22, 2020, https://www.pgpf.org/blog/2019/07/how-does -the-us-healthcare-system-compare-to-other-countries.

66 **eight NBA teams were tested:** Tim Bontemps, "Adam Silver Lays Out Conditions for NBA's Return, Mulls Charity Game 'Diversion'," ESPN, March 18, 2020.

67 **gatekeepers and mediators in society:** Fareed Zakaria, *The Future of Freedom: Illiberal Democracy at Home and Abroad* (New York: W. W. Norton, 2003), Chapter 6: "The Death of Authority."

67 **a 1993 essay:** Robert A. Dahl, "Why All Democratic Societies Have Mixed Economies," *Nomos* 35 (1993): 259–82, https://www.jstor.org/stable/pdf/24219491.pdf?refreqid=excelsior%3A41633675a96dd0b062c13fd9eaac3053.

70 **"limited upward mobility":** Reihan Salam, "Incarceration and Mobility: One Pretty Big Reason We're Not Denmark," *National Review*, November 23, 2011.

70 **7.5% chance:** Raj Chetty, "Improving Opportunities for Economic Mobility: New Evidence and Policy Lessons," Stanford University/Federal Reserve Bank of St. Louis, https://www.stlouisfed.org/~/media/files/pdfs/community%20development/econmobilitypapers/section1/econmobility_1-1chetty_508.pdf?d=l&s=tw.

70 **percentage of its population that is foreign born—22%:** Éric Grenier, "21.9% of Canadians Are Immigrants, the Highest Share in 85 Years," CBC News, October 25, 2015, https://www.cbc.ca/news/politics/census-2016-immigration-1.4368970.

70 **14% in the United States:** Jynnah Radford, "Key Findings About U.S. Immigrants," Pew Research Center, June 17, 2019, https://www.pewresearch.org/fact-tank/2019/06/17/key-findings-about-u-s-immigrants/.

71 **get to Denmark:** Francis Fukuyama, *Political Order and Political Decay: From the Industrial Revolution to the Globalization of Democracy* (New York: Farrar, Straus and Giroux, 2014), Chapter 1.

70 **alive and well, just not in America:** See, inter alia: Rick Newman, "The American Dream Is Alive and Well—Just Not in America," *U.S. News & World Report*, September 11, 2012, https://www.usnews.com/news/blogs/rick-newman/2012/09/11/the-american-dream-is-alive-and-welljust-not-in-america; Alison Williams, "The American Dream Is Alive and Well, Outside America," *Harvard Business Review*, August 6, 2013, https://hbr.org/2013/08/the-american-dream-is-alive-and-well; and Issie Lapowsky, "Data Reveals the American Dream Is Alive and Well—In Canada," *Wired*, October 13, 2016, https://www.wired.com/2016/10/data-reveals-american-dream-alive-well-canada/.

71 **"Denmark is a market economy":** Lars Løkke Rasmussen, "Nordic Solutions and Challenges—A Danish Perspective," Harvard Kennedy School's Institute of Politics, https://youtu.be/MgrJnXZ_WGo?t=490.

71   **eighth for Denmark, seventh for the US:** 2020 Index of Economic Free-
     dom, Heritage Foundation, https://www.heritage.org/index/ranking.

71   **15%:** "Denmark: Individual—Other Taxes, Inheritance, Estate, and Gift
     Taxes," PwC Denmark, June 2, 2020, https://taxsummaries.pwc.com/
     denmark/individual/other-taxes.

71   **zero in Sweden:** "Taxing Inheritances Is Falling out of Favour," *Economist*,
     November 23, 2017.

71   **zero . . . in Norway:** Norwegian Tax Administration, "Inheritance Tax Is
     Abolished,"   https://www.skatteetaten.no/en/person/taxes/get-the-taxes
     -right/gift-and-inheritance/inheritance-tax-is-abolished/.

72   **45% of its GDP:** "Revenue Statistics—OECD Countries: Comparative
     Tables," Organisation for Economic Co-operation and Development,
     https://stats.oecd.org/Index.aspx?DataSetCode=REV.

72   **European Union's overall average of 20%:** 21% EU average VAT, 25%
     in Denmark: Elle Aksen, "2020 VAT Rates in Europe," Tax Foundation,
     January 9, 2020, https://taxfoundation.org/european-union-value-added
     -tax-2020/.

72   **state sales taxes average just 7%:** Average based on "State Sales Tax
     Rates," Sales Tax Institute, May 1, 2020, https://www.salestaxinstitute
     .com/resources/rates.

72   **beer to eggs to smartphones:** Peter Baldwin, "A U.S. More Like Den-
     mark? Be Careful What You Wish For," *New York Times*, October 20, 2015,
     https://www.nytimes.com/roomfordebate/2015/10/20/can-the-us-become
     -denmark/a-us-more-like-denmark-be-careful-what-you-wish-for.

72   **$15,000 lower:** Mean household adjusted disposable income for Den-
     mark: $29,606. For US: $45,284, per the OECD Better Life Index, http://
     www.oecdbetterlifeindex.org/countries/united-states/ and http://www
     .oecdbetterlifeindex.org/countries/denmark/. Definition of "mean house-
     hold adjusted disposable income" included in "How's Life? 2020: Measur-
     ing Wellbeing," OECD Better Life Index, https://www.oecd-ilibrary.org/
     docserver/9870c393-en.pdf:

        Mean household adjusted disposable income is obtained by summing
        all the (gross) income flows (earnings, self-employment and capi-
        tal income, current transfers received from other sectors) paid to the
        (System of National Accounts) household sector and then subtracting
        current transfers (such as taxes on income and wealth) paid by house-
        holds to other sectors of the economy. The term "adjusted," in National
        Accounts vocabulary, denotes the inclusion of the social transfers
        in-kind (such as education and health care services) that households
        receive from government. The measure used here also takes into

account the amount needed to replace the capital assets of households (i.e., dwellings and equipment of unincorporated enterprises), which is deducted from their income. Household adjusted disposable income is shown in per capita terms and expressed in US dollars (USD) using 2017 purchasing power parities (PPPs) for actual individual consumption. The source is the OECD National Accounts Statistics database.

73   **seventeen times more:** Denmark spends 0.52% of national GDP on worker training; US spends 0.03%. Gary Burtless, "Comments on 'Employment and Training for Mature Adults: The Current System and Moving Forward,' by Paul Osterman," Brookings Institution, November 7, 2019, https://www.brookings.edu/blog/up-front/2019/11/07/employment-and-training-for-mature-adults-the-current-system-and-moving-forward/.

73   **550 more hours of leisure time:** OECD Better Life Index, Denmark and United States.

74   *armed*: Fareed Zakaria, "The Politics of the Future: Be Open and Armed," *Washington Post*, July 7, 2016, https://www.washingtonpost.com/opinions/the-politics-of-the-future-be-open-and-armed/2016/07/07/fd171ce0-447b-11e6-8856-f26de2537a9d_story.html.

Lesson Four: People Should Listen to the Experts— and Experts Should Listen to the People

75   **"very good brain":** Eliza Collins, "Trump: I Consult Myself on Foreign Policy," *Politico*, March 16, 2016.

75   **"experts are terrible":** Nick Gass, "Trump: 'The Experts Are Terrible,'" *Politico*, April 4, 2016.

75   **"enough of experts":** Henry Mance, "Britain Has Had Enough of Experts, Says Gove," *Financial Times*, June 3, 2016.

76   **its vice president:** On Taiwanese vice president Chen Chien-jen, see: Javier C. Hernández and Chris Horton, "Taiwan's Weapon Against Coronavirus: An Epidemiologist as Vice President," *New York Times*, May 9, 2020.

76   **"We listened to the experts":** Greek prime minister Kyriakos Mitsotakis, in conversation with Fareed Zakaria, *Fareed Zakaria GPS: Global Public Square*, CNN, June 14, 2020.

76   **a victim of his own careless attitude:** Ernesto Londoño, Manuela Andreoni, and Letícia Casado, "President Bolsonaro of Brazil Tests Positive for Coronavirus," *New York Times*, July 7, 2020.

77   **move on with their lives:** León Krauze, "Mexico's President Has Given
      Up in the Fight Against the Coronavirus," *Washington Post*, June 18, 2020.

77   **"LIBERATE":** Kevin Liptak, "Trump Tweets Support for Michigan Pro-
      testers, Some of Whom Were Armed, as 2020 Stress Mounts," CNN, May
      1, 2020.

77   **refused to wear a mask publicly:** Until July 13. See: Jonathan Lemire,
      "Trump Wears Mask in Public for First Time During Pandemic," Associ-
      ated Press, July 13, 2020.

77   **warn customers not to drink bleach:** Lysol maker (Reckitt Benckiser)
      cautions customers not to drink or inject bleach: "Improper Use of Dis-
      infectants," https://www.rb.com/media/news/2020/april/improper-use-of
      -disinfectants/.

77   **"game-changer":** Toluse Olorunnipa, Ariana Eunjung Cha, and Laurie
      McGinley, "Drug Promoted by Trump as Coronavirus 'Game Changer'
      Increasingly Linked to Deaths," *Washington Post*, May 15, 2020.

77   **FDA warnings:** US Food and Drug Administration, "FDA Cautions
      Against Use of Hydroxychloroquine or Chloroquine for COVID-19
      Outside of the Hospital Setting or a Clinical Trial Due to Risk of Heart
      Rhythm Problems," updated July 1, 2020, https://www.fda.gov/drugs/drug
      -safety-and-availability/fda-cautions-against-use-hydroxychloroquine-or
      -chloroquine-covid-19-outside-hospital-setting-or.

77   **"Just a feeling":** Donald J. Trump, "Remarks by President Trump, Vice
      President Pence, and Members of the Coronavirus Task Force in Press
      Briefing," White House, March 20, 2020, https://www.whitehouse.gov/
      briefings-statements/remarks-president-trump-vice-president-pence
      -members-c-oronavirus-task-force-press-briefing/.

77   **"truthiness":** Stephen Colbert, "The Word: Truthiness," *Colbert
      Report*, October 17, 2005, Comedy Central, http://www.cc.com/video
      -clips/63ite2/the-colbert-report-the-word---truthiness. Transcript from
      Kurt Andersen, "How America Lost Its Mind," *Atlantic*, September 2017.

78   **"very, very low risk":** J. Edward Moreno, "Government Health Agency
      Official: Coronavirus 'Isn't Something the American Public Need to
      Worry About,'" *Hill*, January 26, 2020.

78   **"remains low":** Alex M. Azar II, "Secretary Azar Delivers Remarks on
      Declaration of Public Health Emergency for 2019 Novel Coronavirus,"
      White House, January 31, 2020, https://www.hhs.gov/about/leadership/
      secretary/speeches/2020-speeches/secretary-azar-delivers-remarks-on
      -declaration-of-public-health-emergency-2019-novel-coronavirus.html.

79   **stop performing non-urgent care:** Alice Park and Jeffrey Kluger, "The
      Coronavirus Pandemic Is Forcing U.S. Doctors to Ration Care for All
      Patients," *Time*, April 22, 2020.

79 **heart attack patients:** S. J. Lange, M. D. Ritchey, A. B. Goodman et al., "Potential Indirect Effects of the COVID-19 Pandemic on Use of Emergency Departments for Acute Life-Threatening Conditions—United States, January–May 2020," Centers for Disease Control and Prevention, *MMWR Morb Mortal Weekly Report* 69 (2020):795–800; and Will Feuer, "Doctors Worry the Coronavirus Is Keeping Patients Away from US Hospitals as ER Visits Drop: 'Heart Attacks Don't Stop,'" CNBC, April 14, 2020.

80 **swine flu could kill 65,000 in Britain … some 450 Britons died:** Jonathan Ford, "The Battle at the Heart of British Science over Coronavirus," *Financial Times*, April 15, 2020; David D. Kirkpatrick, Matt Apuzzo, and Selam Gebrekidan, "Europe Said It Was Pandemic-Ready. Pride Was Its Downfall,' *New York Times*, July 20, 2020.

81 **overblown panic may have contributed:** Ibid.

81 **an April 2020 interview:** Steven Pinker, "Alan Alda & Steven Pinker: Secrets of Great Communication," 92nd Street Y, April 23, 2020.

81 **a science lesson:** Jhag Balla, "This Viral Angela Merkel Clip Explains the Risks of Loosening Social Distancing Too Fast," *Vox*, April 17, 2020; and Katrin Bennhold, "Relying on Science and Politics, Merkel Offers a Cautious Virus Re-entry Plan," *New York Times*, April 15, 2020.

82 **"universal masking":** Lili Pike, "Why 15 US States Suddenly Made Masks Mandatory," *Vox*, May 29, 2020.

82 **fundamentally disingenuous:** For one account of how these missteps could have been avoided, see: Zeynep Tufekci, "Why Telling People They Don't Need Masks Backfired," *New York Times*, March 15, 2020.

82 **US surgeon general admitted:** On *CBS Face the Nation*. See Melissa Quinn, "Surgeon General Says Administration 'Trying to Correct' Earlier Guidance Against Wearing Masks," CBS News, July 12, 2020, https://www.cbsnews.com/news/coronavirus-surgeon-general-jerome-adams-wearing-masks-face-the-nation/.

83 **"Qualification must give way":** Dean Acheson, *Present at the Creation: My Years at the State Department* (New York: W. W. Norton, 1970), 375.

84 **trust in the Conservative government plummeted:** Richard Fletcher, Antonis Kalogeropoulos, and Rasmus Kleis Nielsen, "Trust in UK Government and News Media COVID-19 Information Down, Concerns over Misinformation from Government and Politicians Up," University of Oxford, Reuters Institute, June 1, 2020, https://reutersinstitute.politics.ox.ac.uk/trust-uk-government-and-news-media-covid-19-information-down-concerns-over-misinformation.

84 **lockdown breaches soared:** Chris Curtis, "One in Five Have Started Breaking Lockdown Rules More Following Cummings Saga," YouGov, June 3,

2020, https://yougov.co.uk/topics/health/articles-reports/2020/06/03/one
-five-have-started-breaking-lockdown-rules-more.

84 **Eliot Cohen has shown:** Eliot Cohen, *Supreme Command: Soldiers, States-men, and Leadership in Wartime* (New York: Free Press, 2002).

85 **"too important to be left to the generals":** As the quote is usually rendered in English. The original French: "La guerre! C'est une chose trop grave pour la confier à des militaires" (literally: "War is too serious a matter to entrust to military men"). Note that this quote is variously attributed to several French statesmen of the World War I era.

86 **"Partisanship is a more consistent predictor":** Shana Kushner Gadarian, Sara Wallace Goodman, and Thomas B. Pepinsky, "Partisanship, Health Behavior, and Policy Attitudes in the Early Stages of the COVID-19 Pandemic," *SSRN*, March 30, 2020, https://ssrn.com/abstract=3562796. (Note: This study, and those by Painter and Qiu and Allcott et al. below, has not been peer-reviewed.)

86 **less likely to shelter in place:** Marcus Painter and Tian Qiu, "Political Beliefs Affect Compliance with COVID-19 Social Distancing Orders," *SSRN*, July 3, 2020, https://ssrn.com/abstract=3569098; Hunt Allcott, Levi Boxell, Jacob Conway, Matthew Gentzkow, Michael Thaler, and David Y. Yang, "Polarization and Public Health: Partisan Differences in Social Distancing During the Coronavirus Pandemic," *SSRN*, June 2020, https://ssrn.com/abstract=3574415.

86 **thirty incidents of arson or vandalism:** Adam Satariano and Davey Alba, "Burning Cell Towers, out of Baseless Fear They Spread the Virus," *New York Times*, April 10, 2020.

86 **"motivated reasoning":** Jonathan Haidt, *The Righteous Mind: Why Good People Are Divided by Politics and Religion* (New York: Vintage Books, 2013), 98, 104.

87 **"high-information voters":** Ezra Klein, "Why the Most Informed Voters Are Often the Most Badly Misled," *Vox*, June 8, 2015.

87 **"rationalizing voters":** Christopher H. Achen and Larry M. Bartels, "It Feels Like We're Thinking: The Rationalizing Voter and Electoral Democracy," Annual Meeting of the American Political Science Association, Philadelphia, August 28, 2006, https://web.archive.org/web/20160410201427/http://www.princeton.edu/~bartels/thinking.pdf.

87 **"the slave of the passions":** David Hume, *A Treatise Of Human Nature*, Book III, Part III, Section III, "Of The Influencing Motives Of The Will."

87 **"epistemic crisis":** David Roberts, "Partisanship Is the Strongest Predictor of Coronavirus Response," *Vox*, May 14, 2020.

88 **"'the pure people' and 'the corrupt elite'":** Cas Mudde, "Populism in the Twenty-First Century: An Illiberal Democratic Response to Undemo-

cratic Liberalism," Andrea Mitchell Center for the Study of Democracy, University of Pennsylvania, https://www.sas.upenn.edu/andrea-mitchell -center/cas-mudde-populism-twenty-first-century.

88 **"bold infusion of popular will":** Donald J. Trump, "Let Me Ask America a Question," *Wall Street Journal*, April 14, 2016.

89 *The Fifth Risk*: Michael Lewis, *The Fifth Risk* (New York: W. W. Norton, 2018).

89 **a map that had been altered:** Matthew Cappucci and Andrew Freedman, "President Trump Showed a Doctored Hurricane Chart. Was It to Cover Up for 'Alabama' Twitter Flub?," *Washington Post*, September 5, 2019.

89 **were rebuked:** Christopher Flavelle, "NOAA Chief Violated Ethics Code in Furor over Trump Tweet, Agency Says," *New York Times*, June 15, 2020.

89 **"the issue is power":** Michael Lind, *The New Class War: Saving Democracy from the Managerial Elite* (New York: Portfolio: 2020).

90 **70% of ministers held a postgraduate degree—60% of which were from American universities:** From 1996 to 2000, under President Lee Teng-hui (PhD, Cornell): John Trenhaile, "The New Cabinet," *Taiwan Review*, August 1, 1996, archived at https://web.archive.org/web/20160915152001/ http://www.taiwantoday.tw/ct.asp?xItem=54929&ctNode=2198&mp=9.

90 **around a third of the public:** 33.4% of the US population have college degrees as of 2016: US Census Bureau, "Educational Attainment in the United States: 2016," https://www.census.gov/newsroom/press -releases/2017/cb17-51.html; "31% of 25–64 Year Olds Achieved Tertiary Level Study," European Commission, Eurostat, https://ec.europa.eu/ eurostat/web/products-eurostat-news/-/EDN-20181008-1.

90 **barely 13%:** 13.1% have a master's, professional degree, or doctorate: US Census Bureau, "Educational Attainment in the United States: 2018," https://www.census.gov/library/stories/2019/02/number-of-people-with -masters-and-phd-degrees-double-since-2000.html.

90 **10% of China's population:** As of 2010 Chinese Census, Education at a Glance: OECD Indicators 2016, "People's Republic of China," https:// gpseducation.oecd.org/Content/EAGCountryNotes/EAG2016_CN_ CHN.pdf.

90 **99%:** 99.2% of the Chinese Community Party's 18th Central Committee attended some college as of 2016: Cheng Li, Table 4.1, "Percentage of College-Educated Members on the 8th–18th Central Committees," *Chinese Politics in the Xi Jinping Era: Reassessing Collective Leadership* (Washington, DC: Brookings Institution Press, 2016).

91 **3.7 times as high:** US Census Bureau, "Educational Attainment in the United States: 2018."

91 **Clinton won most of the first group:** Nate Silver, "Education, Not Income,

Predicted Who Would Vote for Trump," FiveThirtyEight, November 22, 2016, https://fivethirtyeight.com/features/education-not-income-predicted-who-would-vote-for-trump/.

91   **two-thirds of rural Americans approve:** Nathaniel Rakich and Dhrumil Mehta, "Trump Is Only Popular in Rural Areas," FiveThirtyEight, December 7, 2018, https://fivethirtyeight.com/features/trump-is-really-popular-in-rural-areas-other-places-not-so-much/.

91   **"no such thing as a Republican city":** Will Wilkinson, "The Density Divide: Urbanization, Polarization, and Populist Backlash," Niskanen Center, June 2019, https://www.niskanencenter.org/wp-content/uploads/2019/09/Wilkinson-Density-Divide-Final.pdf.

91   **those without university degrees:** Anushka Asthana, "People Who Felt Marginalised Drove Brexit Vote, Study Finds," *Guardian*, August 31, 2016.

91   **"yellow vest" protests were powered:** Marie Dupin, "Jeunes, Précaires, Ruraux: Qui Sont Les Gilets Jaunes?," BFM, April 9, 2020, https://www.bfmtv.com/economie/economie-social/france/jeunes-precaires-ruraux-qui-sont-les-gilets-jaunes_AN-201904090053.html.

91   **revolt of car-dependent rural-dwellers:** Feargus O'Sullivan, "Why Drivers Are Leading a Protest Movement Across France," *City Lab*, November 19, 2018, https://www.bloomberg.com/news/articles/2018-11-19/-yellow-vests-why-france-is-protesting-new-gas-taxes.

91   **in German politics as well:** Christian Franz, Marcel Fratzscher, and Alexander S. Kritikos, "German Right-Wing Party AfD Finds More Support in Rural Areas with Aging Populations," *DIW Weekly Report* 8, no. 7/8 (2018): 69–79, http://hdl.handle.net/10419/175453.

92   **warmest support in the ethnic Turkish heartland:** *Daily Sabah*, 2018 presidential election results, https://www.dailysabah.com/election/june-24-2018-election-results.

92   **fewer than 10% worked from home:** "Job Flexibilities and Work Schedules—2017–2018, Data from the American Time Use Survey," Bureau of Labor Statistics, September 24, 2019, https://www.bls.gov/news.release/flex2.nr0.htm.

92   **13% of people in households making over $100,000:** Jeanna Smialek, "Poor Americans Hit Hardest by Job Losses amid Lockdowns, Fed Says," *New York Times*, May 14, 2020, https://www.nytimes.com/2020/05/14/business/economy/coronavirus-jobless-unemployment.html.

93   **"fiercely resented":** Richard Hofstadter, *Anti-Intellectualism in American Life* (New York: Alfred A. Knopf, 1963), 34.

93   **"ultimate aphrodisiac":** Henry Kissinger, "The Sayings of Secretary Henry," compiled by DuPre Jones, *New York Times*, October 28, 1973, cited in Jerry Useem, "Power Causes Brain Damage," *Atlantic*, July/August

2017: "[Power] can even make Henry Kissinger believe that he's sexually magnetic."

93 **Keltner ran studies:** Dacher Keltner, *The Power Paradox: How We Gain and Lose Influence* (New York: Penguin, 2016), 112–13, 116–18.

95 **Jean Edward Smith:** Jean Edward Smith, *FDR* (New York: Random House, 2007).

95 **Doris Kearns Goodwin:** Doris Kearns Goodwin, *No Ordinary Time: Franklin and Eleanor Roosevelt—The Home Front in World War II* (New York: Simon & Schuster, 1994).

95 **"he knew me":** an incident referenced in, for example, Ken Burns, *The Roosevelts: An Intimate History*, PBS, 2014.

Lesson Five: Life Is Digital

97 **killed some 50 million people:** Niall Johnson and Juergen Mueller, "Updating the Accounts: Global Mortality of the 1918–1920 'Spanish' Influenza Pandemic," *Bulletin of the History of Medicine* (Spring 2002), https://www.researchgate.net/publication/11487892_Updating_the_Accounts_Global_Mortality_of_the_1918–1920_Spanish_Influenza_Pandemic.

97 **up to 100,000 speakeasies:** Lisa Bramen, "October 28, 1919: The Day That Launched a Million Speakeasies," *Smithsonian Magazine*, October 28, 2010.

98 **"return to normalcy":** Seen in Harding's 1920 speech: "America's present need is not heroics but healing; not nostrums but normalcy; not revolution but restoration . . . not surgery but serenity": Library of Congress, Presidential Election of 1920, https://www.loc.gov/collections/world-war-i-and-1920-election-recordings/articles-and-essays/from-war-to-normalcy/presidential-election-of-1920/.

98 **the Kenbak-1:** Earliest personal computer as determined by, for instance, the Computer History Museum in Palo Alto, California: Chris Garcia, "In His Own Words: John Blankenbaker," CHM Blog, Curatorial Insights, April 5, 2016, https://computerhistory.org/blog/in-his-own-words-john-blankenbaker/.

99 **"if anyone knew the customer":** Brad Stone, *The Everything Store: Jeff Bezos and the Age of Amazon* (New York: Little, Brown, 2013), Chapter 2.

99 **$10,000 in sales—every second:** In Q1 2020, per calculations from Christopher Rossbach, portfolio manager of the J. Stern & Co. World Stars Global Equity fund: Irina Ivanova, "Amazon Makes $10,000 Per Second

as Shoppers Shelter in Place," CBS News, Moneywatch, May 1, 2020, https://www.cbsnews.com/news/amazon-q1-earnings-75-billion-10000 -per-second/; see also Q1 Amazon net sales of $75.5 billion, $9,709 per second: "Amazon.Com Announces First Quarter Results," https://s2 .q4cdn.com/299287126/files/doc_financials/2020/Q1/Amazon-Q1–2020 -Earnings-Release.pdf.

99   **over 9%:** US Bureau of Labor Statistics, "Unemployment Rate 9.1 Per-cent in August 2011," https://www.bls.gov/opub/ted/2011/ted_20110908 .htm?view_full.

99   **an essay in the *Wall Street Journal*:** Marc Andreessen, "Why Software Is Eating the World," August 20, 2011.

100   **exceeded those of Hollywood and the music business put together:** Video game industry revenues = $78 billion in 2010, $137 billion in 2019, see: Will Partin, "The 2010s Were a Banner Decade for Big Money and Tech—and Esports Reaped the Rewards," *Washington Post*, January 28, 2020; Hollywood revenue = $42.5 billion in 2019, see: Pamela McClin-tock, "2019 Global Box Office Revenue Hit Record $42.5B Despite 4 Percent Dip in U.S.," *Hollywood Reporter*, January 10, 2020, https://www .hollywoodreporter.com/news/2019-global-box-office-hit-record-425b-4 -percent-plunge-us-1268600. US music industry revenue = $11.1 billion in 2019, see: Dan Rys, "US Recorded Music Revenue Reaches $11.1 Billion in 2019, 79% from Streaming: RIAA," *Billboard*, February 25, 2020, https:// www.billboard.com/articles/business/8551881/riaa-music-industry-2019 -revenue-streaming-vinyl-digital-physical.

100   **100,000 brick-and-mortar stores:** Suzanne Kapner and Sarah Nassauer, "Coronavirus Finishes the Retail Reckoning That Amazon Started," *Wall Street Journal*, May 14, 2020.

101   **data as the new oil:** Carl Benedikt Frey, *The Technology Trap: Capital, Labor, and Power in the Age of Automation* (Princeton, NJ: Princeton University Press, 2020), 304.

101   **smartphones now connect the majority:** "Percentage of Mobile Device Website Traffic Worldwide from 1st Quarter 2015 to 1st Quarter 2020," Statista, https://www.statista.com/statistics/277125/share-of-website-traffic -coming-from-mobile-devices.

101   **"only 20 million Indians":** Ravi Agrawal, *India Connected: How the Smart-phone Is Transforming the World's Largest Democracy* (New York: Oxford University Press, 2018), 3.

102   **Over 550 million:** McKinsey Global Institute, "Digital India," 2019, https://www.mckinsey.com/~/media/McKinsey/Business%20Functions/ McKinsey%20Digital/Our%20Insights/Digital%20India%20

Technology%20to%20transform%20a%20connected%20nation/MGI
-Digital-India-Report-April-2019.ashx.

102 **155th in the world:** Mukesh Ambani, in conversation with *India Today*, "India is now world's top mobile data consuming nation: Mukesh Ambani," October 25, 2018, https://www.indiatoday.in/technology/news/story/india -top-mobile-data-consuming-nation-mukesh-ambani-1375253–2018–10–25.

102 **more mobile data:** Ibid.

102 **hundreds of millions more Indians:** McKinsey Global Institute, "Digital India," 6.

102 **staggering $37 billion:** Mobis Philipose, "Why Reliance Jio's Big and Bold 2021 Vision Doesn't Make Sense," *LiveMint*, March 7, 2017.

102 **triggered mob killings:** Geeta Anand and Suhasini Raj, "Rumors on WhatsApp Ignite 2 Mob Attacks in India, Killing 7," *New York Times*, May 25, 2017.

103 **about a third of Americans:** "Of those employed four weeks earlier, 34.1% report they were commuting and are now working from home": Erik Bryn-jolfsson et al., "COVID-19 and Remote Work: An Early Look at US Data," MIT Sloan School of Management, https://mitsloan.mit.edu/shared/ods/ documents/?PublicationDocumentID=6322.

104 **"25% of our workforce":** Sonal Khetarpal, "Post-COVID, 75% of 4.5 Lakh TCS Employees to Permanently Work from Home by '25; from 20%," *Business Today India*, April 30, 2020.

104 **issued a correction:** Saunak Chowdhury, "TCS Refutes Claims of 75% Employees Working from Home Post Lock-Down," *Indian Wire*, April 28, 2020.

104 **450,000 employees:** Tata Consultancy Services, "About Us," https://www .tcs.com/about-us.

106 **up one billion:** Jeff Becker and Arielle Trzcinski, "US Virtual Care Vis-its to Soar to More Than 1 Billion," Forrester Analytics, April 10, 2020, https://go.forrester.com/press-newsroom/us-virtual-care-visits-to-soar-to -more-than-1-billion/.

106 **"greatest contribution to mankind":** Lizzy Gurdus, "Tim Cook: Apple's Greatest Contribution Will Be 'About Health,'" *CNBC Mad Money*, Janu-ary 8, 2019.

107 **97% accuracy:** "Using Artificial Intelligence to Classify Lung Cancer Types, Predict Mutations," National Cancer Institute, October 10, 2018, https://www.cancer.gov/news-events/cancer-currents-blog/2018/artificial -intelligence-lung-cancer-classification.

107 **up to 11% fewer false positives:** D. Ardila, A. P. Kiraly, S. Bharadwaj et al., "End-to-End Lung Cancer Screening with Three-Dimensional Deep

Learning on Low-Dose Chest Computed Tomography," *Nature Medicine* 25 (2019): 954–61, https://doi.org/10.1038/s41591-019-0447-x.

107 **designing proteins to block the virus:** Kim Martineau, "Marshaling Artificial Intelligence in the Fight Against Covid-19," MIT Quest for Intelligence, *MIT News*, May 19, 2020, http://news.mit.edu/2020/mit -marshaling-artificial-intelligence-fight-against-covid-19–0519.

108 **hoped that AI might find solutions . . . The results were mixed:** See, inter alia: Cade Metz, "How A.I. Steered Doctors Toward a Possible Coronavirus Treatment," *New York Times*, April 30, 2020; and O. Kadioglu, M. Saeed, H. Johannes Greten, and T. Efferth, "Identification of Novel Compounds Against Three Targets of SARS CoV-2 Coronavirus by Combined Virtual Screening and Supervised Machine Learning," [preprint], *Bulletin of the World Health Organization*, E-pub: March 21, 2020, http://dx.doi .org/10.2471/BLT.20.255943.

108 **location-tracking app is voluntary:** Salvatore Babones, "Countries Rolling Out Coronavirus Tracking Apps Show Why They Can't Work," *Foreign Policy*, May 12, 2020, https://foreignpolicy.com/2020/05/12/coronavirus -tracking-tracing-apps-cant-work-south-korea-singapore-australia/.

109 **some 30% of the population:** Goh Yu Chong and Nasrath Hassan, "Factsheet: Tracetogether Programme," Smart Nation, Government of Singapore, June 8, 2020, https://www.smartnation.gov.sg/whats-new/press -releases/factsheet--tracetogether-programme.

110 **"between 32 and 50 million US jobs":** "Covid-19 and the Workforce," *MIT Technology Review* and Faethm, 2020, https://mittrinsights.s3.amazonaws .com/AIagenda2020/Covid19workforce.pdf.

110 **cooks:** Rachel Premack, "Robots Are Already Working in Fast-Food Restaurants—Here's Exactly What They're Doing Right Now," *Business Insider*, June 26, 2018, https://www.businessinsider.com/mcdonalds-kfc -panera-robot-employees-2018–6.

111 **Over a million people:** "Road Traffic Injuries and Deaths—a Global Problem," US Centers for Disease Control and Prevention, last updated December 18, 2019, https://www.cdc.gov/injury/features/global-road -safety/index.html.

111 **94% of crashes:** "Critical Reasons for Crashes Investigated in the National Motor Vehicle Crash Causation Survey," US Department of Transportation, February 2015, https://crashstats.nhtsa.dot.gov/Api/Public/ ViewPublication/812115.

111 **almost 4 million Americans:** Jennifer Cheeseman Day and Andrew W. Haidt, "Number of Truckers at All-Time High," US Census, June 6, 2019, https://www.census.gov/library/stories/2019/06/america-keeps-on-trucking .html.

111 **4,000 drivers a week:** Fred Smith, Federal Express CEO, "Transcript: The Path Forward: Business & the Economy," *Washington Post Live*, May 14, 2020.

111 *Machines Like Me*: Ian McEwan, *Machines Like Me: A Novel* (New York: Knopf Doubleday, 2019).

112 **algorithms that can write literature:** Brian Merchant, "When an AI Goes Full Jack Kerouac," *Atlantic*, October 1, 2018.

113 **"spread the bread thin on the butter":** John Maynard Keynes, "Economic Possibilities for Our Grandchildren" (originally written 1930), reprinted in *Essays in Persuasion* (New York: W. W. Norton, 1963), 358–73.

113 **Jetson of the 1960s cartoon:** "works three hours a day, three days a week," per Sarah Ellison, "Reckitt Turns to Jetsons to Launch Detergent Gels," *Wall Street Journal*, January 13, 2003; pushing a button, per Hanna-Barbera Wiki, "The Jetsons," https://hanna-barbera.fandom.com/wiki/The_Jetsons.

113 **four-day workweek:** Zoe Didali, "As PM Finland's Marin Could Renew Call for Shorter Work Week," *New Europe*, January 2, 2020, https://www.neweurope.eu/article/finnish-pm-marin-calls-for-4-day-week-and-6-hours-working-day-in-the-country/.

114 **"bullshit jobs":** David Graeber, *Bullshit Jobs: A Theory* (New York: Simon & Schuster, 2018).

115 **"slaves of time without purpose":** McEwan, *Machines Like Me*.

116 **atoms in the observable universe:** David Silver and Demis Hassabis, "AlphaGo: Mastering the Ancient Game of Go with Machine Learning," Google DeepMind, January 27, 2016, https://ai.googleblog.com/2016/01/alphago-mastering-ancient-game-of-go.html.

116 **all fifty-seven games:** Kyle Wiggers, "DeepMind's Agent57 Beats Humans at 57 Classic Atari Games," *Venture Beat*, March 31, 2020; Rebecca Jacobson, "Artificial Intelligence Program Teaches Itself to Play Atari Games—And It Can Beat Your High Score," *PBS NewsHour*, February 20, 2015.

117 **Stuart Russell:** Stuart Russell, "3 Principles for Creating Safer AI," TED2017, https://www.ted.com/talks/stuart_russell_3_principles_for_creating_safer_ai/transcript?language=en.

117 **if you asked a computer to end cancer:** Stuart Russell, in conversation with Sam Harris, "#53—The Dawn of Artificial Intelligence," *Making Sense*, November 23, 2016, https://samharris.org/podcasts/the-dawn-of-artificial-intelligence1/.

118 **warnings of Oxford philosopher:** Nick Bostrom, *Superintelligence: Paths, Dangers, and Strategies* (New York: Oxford University Press, 2014).

118 **the end of the Enlightenment:** Henry Kissinger, "How the Enlighten-

ment Ends," *Atlantic*, June 2018, https://www.theatlantic.com/magazine/
archive/2018/06/henry-kissinger-ai-could-mean-the-end-of-human
-history/559124/.

118 **"self-imposed immaturity":** Immanuel Kant, "An Answer to the Question: What Is Enlightenment?" (September 30, 1784), trans. Mary C.
Smith.

118 **works in a mysterious way:** Originally rendered "God moves in a mysterious way" in a 1774 hymn by English poet William Cowper, "Light Shining
Out of Darkness," collected in, e.g., *The Columbia Anthology of Poetry*, edited
by Carl R. Woodring and James Shapiro (New York: Columbia University
Press, 1995), 383.

119 **Homo Deus:** Yuval Noah Harari, *Homo Deus: A Brief History of Tomorrow*
(London: Harvill Secker, 2016).

Lesson Six: Aristotle Was Right—We Are Social Animals

122 **hopped species:** From a virus known as SIV, simian immunodeficiency
virus. See: "Where Did HIV Come From?," AIDS Institute, https://www
.theaidsinstitute.org/education/aids-101/where-did-hiv-come-0.

123 **origins of the AIDS epidemic:** Craig Timberg and Daniel Halperin, *Tinderbox: How the West Sparked the AIDS Epidemic and How the World Can
Finally Overcome It* (New York: Penguin, 2012).

123 **scenarios in Asia, with bats, civet cats, and pangolins:** Nicola Decaro and
Alessio Lorusso, "Novel Human Coronavirus (SARS-CoV-2): A Lesson
from Animal Coronaviruses," *Veterinary Microbiology* 244 (May 2020),
https://doi.org/10.1016/j.vetmic.2020.108693.

123 **"that unlucky person":** In conversation with Fareed Zakaria, "On GPS:
Tracing Pandemics Back to Their Source," *Fareed Zakaria GPS: Global Public
Square*, CNN, April 26, 2020, https://www.cnn.com/videos/tv/2020/04/26/
exp-gps-0426-daszak-int.cnn; For more from Daszak, see: Nurith Aizen-
man, "Why the U.S. Government Stopped Funding a Research Project
on Bats and Coronaviruses," NPR, April 29, 2020, https://www.npr.org/
sections/goatsandsoda/2020/04/29/847948272/why-the-u-s-government
-stopped-funding-a-research-project-on-bats-and-coronavirus.

124 **"most lively interest":** Anonymous, *Times*, December 3, 1889, p. 9, quoted
and cited in James Mussell, "Pandemic in Print: The Spread of Influenza in
the Fin de Siècle," https://doi.org/10.1016/j.endeavour.2007.01.008.

124 **just four months:** Alain-Jacques Valleron et al., "Transmissibility and
Geographic Spread of the 1889 Influenza Pandemic," *Proceedings of the*

National Academy of Sciences 107, no. 19 (May 11, 2010): 8778–81, https://doi.org/10.1073/pnas.1000886107.

125 **slashed to 700:** Benoît Morenne and Vivien Ngo, "Train Drain: How Social Distancing Is Transforming Mass Transit," *Wall Street Journal*, June 22, 2020.

125 **bartender took down your name and phone number:** Paul Sandle, "No Name, No Pint: New Rules for England's Pubs After Lockdown," Reuters, June 24, 2020.

125 **Singaporean government's app:** Aaron Holmes, "Singapore Is Using a High-Tech Surveillance App to Track the Coronavirus, Keeping Schools and Businesses Open. Here's How It Works," *Business Insider*, March 24, 2020.

126 **420,000 people left:** Kevin Quealy, "The Richest Neighborhoods Emptied Out Most as Coronavirus Hit New York City," *New York Times*, May 15, 2020.

126 **leaving the Bay area:** Laura Forman, "For Newly Remote Workers, Small Town U.S.A. Will Lose Its Allure Soon Enough," *Wall Street Journal*, June 19, 2020.

126 **decamping to rural regions:** "'Thank You Parisians, Don't Bring the Virus': Plea from Rural France," *Guardian*, March 18, 2020.

127 **Tens of thousands lay dead:** 68,596, according to city records; see John S. Morrill, "Great Plague of London," *Encyclopaedia Britannica*, https://www.britannica.com/event/Great-Plague-of-London.

127 **80% of the city:** That is, of the area of the central, walled city: Matthew Green, "Lost in the Great Fire: Which London Buildings Disappeared in the 1666 Blaze?," *Guardian*, August 30, 2016.

127 **"build back better":** See, for example, "Build Back Better," We Mean Business Coalition, https://www.wemeanbusinesscoalition.org/build-back-better/.

127 **mostly wooden . . . re-created itself in brick and stone:** Andrew Sullivan, "The Very First Pandemic Blogger," *New York*, March 15, 2020.

127 **"discourage the growth of great cities":** Clay Jenkinson, "Thomas Jefferson, Epidemics and His Vision for American Cities," *Governing*, April 1, 2020, https://www.governing.com/context/Thomas-Jefferson-Epidemics-and-His-Vision-for-American-Cities.html.

128 *The World Without Us*: Alan Weisman, *The World Without Us* (New York: St. Martin's Thomas Dunne Books, 2007).

128 **adding a new Chicago:** United Nations, "World Population Prospects 2018," Department of Economic and Social Affairs, Population Dynamics, https://population.un.org/wup/.

128 **just two cities with at least one million:** David Satterthwaite, "The Tran-

sition to a Predominantly Urban World and Its Underpinnings," Human Settlements Discussion Paper Series, "Theme: Urban Change—4" (2007), https://pubs.iied.org/pdfs/10550IIED.pdf.

128–29 **soared to 371; "megacities":** All data in this section drawn from United Nations, *The World's Cities in 2018—Data Booklet*, 2018, https://www.un .org/en/events/citiesday/assets/pdf/the_worlds_cities_in_2018_data_ booklet.pdf.

130 **Glaeser notes:** Edward Glaeser, *Triumph of the City: How Our Greatest Invention Makes Us Richer, Smarter, Greener, Healthier, and Happier* (New York: Penguin, 2011); see also https://www.scientificamerican.com/article/ glaeser-triumph-of-the-city-excerpt/.

130 **half of global GDP:** "The Destiny of Density," *Economist*, June 11, 2020.

131 **94% higher in urban areas:** David M. Cutler and Grant Miller, "The Role of Public Health Improvements in Health Advances: The 20th Century United States," National Bureau of Economic Research, Working Paper No. 10511, May 2004, https://www.nber.org/papers/w10511.

131 **"air is disinfected by sunlight and foliage":** Frederick Law Olmsted, *Public Parks and the Enlargement of Towns* (New York: American Social Science Association, at the Riverside Press, 1870).

131 **"lungs of the city":** Frederick Law Olmsted, "Notes on the plan of Franklin Park and related matters" (1886), in *The Papers of Frederick Law Olmsted*, edited by C. E. Beveridge, C. F. Hoffman, and K. Hawkins, "Supplementary Series 1: Writings on Public Parks, Parkways and Park Systems" (Baltimore: Johns Hopkins University Press, 1997), 460–534.

132 **"rolling disaster":** Steven Johnson, *The Ghost Map: The Story of London's Most Terrifying Epidemic—and How It Changed Science, Cities, and the Modern World* (New York: Penguin Random House, 2006), 25.

132 **blocked a local pump...failed to convince the authorities:** Ibid., 175, 195–96.

132 **typhoid cratered:** David M. Cutler and Grant Miller, "The Role of Public Health Improvements," NBER Working Paper No. 10511, May 2004, https://www.nber.org/papers/w10511.

133 **reduction was higher still:** Ibid.

133 **soda tax:** Note that while Mayor Bloomberg's soda tax proposal was defeated in New York City, it was adopted in other cities, including San Francisco, Seattle, Philadelphia, and Washington, DC. See "State and Local Finance Initiative: Soda Taxes," Urban Institute, 2011–2020, https:// www.urban.org/policy-centers/cross-center-initiatives/state-and-local -finance-initiative/state-and-local-backgrounders/soda-taxes.

133 **two full years higher than the national average...“friends and relatives that you deeply care about":** Michael Howard Saul, "Life Span

in City Exceeds U.S. Average," *Wall Street Journal*, December 28, 2011, https://www.wsj.com/articles/SB100014240529702034791045771251516 28468014.

133 **"If you want to live longer and healthier than the average American":** Stu Loeser, Samantha Levine, Susan Craig, and Alexandra Waldhorn, "Mayor Bloomberg, Deputy Mayor Gibbs, Health Commissioner Farley Announce New Yorkers Living Longer Than Ever, Outpacing National Trend," Official Website of the City of New York, December 7, 2011, https://www1.nyc .gov/office-of-the-mayor/news/453-11/mayor-bloomberg-deputy-mayor -gibbs-health-commissioner-farley-new-yorkers-living-longer#/4.

134 **3% of the earth's surface:** Liu Zhifeng et al., "How Much of the World's Land Has Been Urbanized, Really? A Hierarchical Framework for Avoiding Confusion," *Landscape Ecology* 29 (2014): 763–71.

134 **pollution is sometimes worse in rural areas:** H. E. S. Mestl, K. Aunan, H. M. Seip et al., "Urban and Rural Exposure to Indoor Air Pollution from Domestic Biomass and Coal Burning Across China," *Science of the Total Environment* 377, no. 1 (May 2007): 12–26, https://doi.org/10.1016/j .scitotenv.2007.01.087.

134 **reliance on dirty fossil fuels:** "Country Living, Dirty Air: Oil & Gas Pollution in Rural America," Earthworks and Clean Air Taskforce, https://www .scribd.com/document/383729903/Country-Living-Dirty-Air; see also, for example, Liz Ruskin, "Alaska Remote Diesel Generators Win Exemption from Pollution Rule," Alaska Public Media, September 18, 2019, https:// www.alaskapublic.org/2019/09/18/alaska-remote-diesel-generators-win -exemption-from-pollution-rule/.

134 **"Cancer Alley":** Tristan Baurick, Lylla Younes, and Joan Meiners, "Welcome to 'Cancer Alley,' Where Toxic Air Is About to Get Worse," *ProPublica*, October 30, 2019, https://www.propublica.org/article/welcome-to -cancer-alley-where-toxic-air-is-about-to-get-worse.

134 **mountains of garbage on New York's streets:** New York City's infamous problem of garbage on the sidewalk is an artifact of its dense grid plan. Unlike most other major cities, New York was largely built since the nineteenth century without the alleyways where most other cities stash their trash. See: Gersh Kuntzman, "Will NYC *Finally* Get Garbage out of Pedestrians' Way?," *Streetsblog NYC*, June 4, 2019, https://nyc.streetsblog .org/2019/06/04/will-nyc-finally-get-garbage-out-of-pedestrians-way/.

134 **average urban resident recycles more:** A Pew study found that highly urbanized California (53.4%) and Washington state (50.1%) had among the highest recycling rates in 2011; the lowest were largely rural states like Oklahoma (3.7%), Alaska (4.5%), and Mississippi (4.8%). Drew DeSilver, "Perceptions and Realities of Recycling Vary Widely from Place to Place,"

Pew Research Center, October 7, 2016, https://www.pewresearch.org/fact-tank/2016/10/07/perceptions-and-realities-of-recycling-vary-widely-from-place-to-place/.

134 **consuming less water:** Arumugam Sankarasubramanian et al., "Synthesis of Public Water Supply Use in the U.S.: Spatio-Temporal Patterns and Socio-Economic Controls," *Earth's Future*, May 18, 2017, https://doi.org/10.1002/2016EF000511.

134 **consuming less . . . electricity:** "In almost every metropolitan area, carbon emissions are significantly lower for people who live in central cities than for people who live in suburbs," in Edward Glaeser, "Green Cities, Brown Suburbs," *City Journal*, Winter 2009, https://www.city-journal.org/html/green-cities-brown-suburbs-13143.html.

134 **Major European and Asian cities:** See Arcadis Sustainable Cities Index 2018, https://www.arcadis.com/media/1/D/5/%7B1D5AE7E2-A348-4B6E-B1D7-6D94FA7D7567%7DSustainable_Cities_Index_2018_Arcadis.pdf; and Robert Muggah and Parag Khanna, "These 10 Asian Cities Are the Most Prepared for the Future," World Economic Forum, September 5, 2018, https://www.weforum.org/agenda/2018/09/these-asian-cities-are-best-equipped-for-the-future/.

134 **Many rural areas in the United States:** For instance, reservations like those of the Navajo. See: Ian Lovett, Dan Frosch, and Paul Overberg, "Covid-19 Stalks Large Families in Rural America," *Wall Street Journal*, June 7, 2020.

134 **Many rural areas . . . in Europe:** Ilya Kashnitsky and José Manuel Aburto, "The Pandemic Threatens Aged Rural Regions Most," Center for Open Science, University of Oxford, and Interdisciplinary Centre on Population Dynamics (CPOP) at University of Southern Denmark, https://ideas.repec.org/p/osf/osfxxx/abx7s.html.

134 **Staten Island suffered more than super-dense Manhattan:** "Density & COVID-19 in New York City," Citizens Housing & Planning Council, May 2020, https://chpcny.org/wp-content/uploads/2020/05/CHPC-Density-COVID19-in-NYC.pdf.

135 **just eighteen deaths:** "Coronavirus Map," *New York Times*, accessed July 27, 2020, https://www.nytimes.com/interactive/2020/world/coronavirus-maps.html.

135 **"Private doctors have joined the fever camps":** Soutik Biswas, "How Asia's Biggest Slum Contained the Coronavirus," BBC, June 23, 2020, https://www.bbc.com/news/world-asia-india-53133843.

136 **high risk from natural disasters:** United Nations, *The World's Cities in 2018*, 9.

136 **three decades more:** "A Ride Along Chicago's Red Line: Life Expectancy Varies by 30 Years from One End to the Other," *Economist*, October 10, 2019.

137 **"As a society urbanizes"**: Darrell Bricker and John Ibbitson, *Empty Planet: The Shock of Global Population Decline* (New York: Crown, 2019).

137 **some 80% of the world's megacities**: United Nations, *The World's Cities in 2018*, 5.

137 **89% by 2050**: United Nations, "World Populations Prospects 2019," https://population.un.org/wpp/.

137 **some recent slippage in population**: Sabrina Tavernise and Sarah Mervosh, "America's Biggest Cities Were Already Losing Their Allure. What Happens Next?," *New York Times*, April 23, 2020.

137 **lost 10% of its residents**: Peter W. Colby, "Public Policy in New York State Today," in *New York State Today: Politics, Government, Public Policy* (Albany: State University of New York Press, 1985), Table 17: Change from 1970 to 1980 (-10.4%), 228.

137 **slower growth rates**: William H. Frey, "Even Before Coronavirus, Census Shows U.S. Cities' Growth Was Stagnating," Brookings, April 6, 2020, https://www.brookings.edu/research/even-before-coronavirus-census-shows-u-s-cities-growth-was-stagnating/.

138 **headed for . . . other metros:**: Joel Kotkin, "What the Census Numbers Tell Us," April 5, 2018, http://joelkotkin.com/what-the-census-numbers-tell-us/.

138 **fifteen-minute city**: Natalie Whittle, "Welcome to the 15-Minute City," *Financial Times*, July 17, 2020, https://www.ft.com/content/c1a53744-90d5-4560-9e3f-17ce06aba69a; Jennifer Keesmaat, "The Pandemic Does Not Spell the End for Cities," *Foreign Affairs*, May 28, 2020.

138 **Samuel Kling**: "What Is Paris Mayor Anne Hidalgo's Plan for a '15-Minute City'?," Chicago Council on Global Affairs, February 24, 2020, https://youtu.be/55VkdnzGzhw.

139 **YIMBY**: Alana Semeuls, "From 'Not in My Backyard' to 'Yes in My Backyard,'" *Atlantic*, July 5, 2017.

139 **resoundingly reelected**: "Hidalgo, Mayor since 2014, beat conservative candidate Rachida Dati in France's municipal elections, winning 50.2% of the ballot compared to Dati's 32%. Agnes Buzyn trailed in with just 16%": Carlton Reid, "Anne Hidalgo Reelected as Mayor of Paris Vowing to Remove Cars and Boost Bicycling and Walking," *Forbes*, June 28, 2020.

139 **remain car-free**: Feargus O'Sullivan, "What Happens to Public Space When Everything Moves Outside," *City Lab*, May 29, 2020, https://www.bloomberg.com/news/features/2020-06-29/what-happens-to-public-space-when-everything-moves-outside.

140 **"United City-States of America"**: Parag Khanna, "A New Map for America," April 15, 2016, citing Joel Kotkin's "mega-regions." See map in the digital version: https://www.nytimes.com/2016/04/17/opinion/sunday/a-new-map-for-america.html.

140 **pushed ahead with the agreement:** Ivo Daalder, "Why Cities Need Their Own Foreign Policies," *Politico*, May 6, 2017.

141 **stay in Columbus:** Alina Dizik, "New Residents Are Spending Big in Columbus," *Wall Street Journal*, November 7, 2019.

141 **"Death and Life of Great Cities":** Drawn from the title of Jane Jacobs's masterwork, *The Death and Life of Great American Cities* (New York: Random House, 1961).

141 **"This City now doth":** William Wordsworth, "Composed Upon Westminster Bridge, September 3, 1802."

142 *"Here is New York"*: Elwyn Brooks White, *Here Is New York* (1949), 21.

142 **"Genuine, rich diversity":** Jane Jacobs, "Can Big Plans Solve the Problem of Renewal?," in *Vital Little Plans: The Short Works of Jane Jacobs*, edited by Samuel Zipp and Nathan Storring (New York: Random House, 2016).

143 **"each piece of the mosaic":** Jane Jacobs, quoted in Jared Greed, "The Case for Diversity," *Dirt: Uniting the Built and Natural Environments*, September 30, 2016, https://dirt.asla.org/2016/09/30/jane-jacobs-the-case-for-diversity/.

143 **watercooler conversations:** Tom Simonite, "Remote Work Has Its Perks, Until You Want a Promotion," *Wired*, May 28, 2020.

144 **"Men seldom moved their bodies":** E. M. Forster, "The Machine Stops," *Oxford and Cambridge Review* (November 1909). Note: Forster's original text has the archaic "Pekin" for "Peking" (i.e., Beijing).

145 **"Only connect!":** E. M. Forster, *Howards End* (London: Edward Arnold, 1910).

Lesson Seven: Inequality Will Get Worse

147 **"death is democratic":** Adriana Gomez Licon, "Mexican Day of Dead 'Skeleton Lady' Spreads Look," Associated Press, October 31, 2013.

147 *La Catrina*: Simon Ingram, "La Catrina: The Dark History of Day of the Dead's Immortal Icon," *National Geographic*, October 18, 2019.

147 *The Skull of Morbid Cholera*: José Guadalupe Posada, *La calavera del cólera morbo* (1910), accessed via Library of Congress, https://www.loc.gov/pictures/item/99615954/.

148 **"a very big problem":** Richard Wike, "The Global Consensus: Inequality Is a Major Problem," Pew Research, November 15, 2013, https://www.pewresearch.org/fact-tank/2013/11/15/the-global-consensus-inequality-is-a-major-problem/.

148 **narrowing over the same period:** *Taking on Inequality: Poverty and Shared Prosperity 2016*, The World Bank Group, 9, 81, https://openknowledge.worldbank.org/bitstream/handle/10986/25078/9781464809583.pdf.

149   **forty two saw rises:** "Table 4.1: Trends in the Within-Country Gini Index, 1993–2013," *Taking on Inequality: Poverty and Shared Prosperity 2016*, The World Bank Group, 86, https://openknowledge.worldbank.org/bitstream/handle/10986/25078/9781464809583.pdf.

149   **two where it fell:** Ibid, 88.

149   **twelve of the sixteen:** Ibid.

149   **gap has widened dramatically:** Facundo Alvaredo, Lucas Chancel, Thomas Piketty, Emmanuel Saez, and Gabriel Zucman, "World Inequality Report 2018," 46, https://wir2018.wid.world/files/download/wir2018-full-report-english.pdf.

150   **highest level since 1928:** Markus P. A. Schneider and Daniele Tavani, "Tale of Two Ginis in the United States, 1921–2012," Levy Institute Working Paper (January 2015), http://www.levyinstitute.org/pubs/wp_826.pdf; see also Thomas Piketty, Paris School of Economics, excerpted figures and tables, Table 1.1, http://piketty.pse.ens.fr/files/capital21c/en/Piketty2014FiguresTables.pdf.

150   **"defining challenge":** Barack Obama, "Remarks by the President on Economic Mobility," White House, Office of the Press Secretary, December 4, 2013, https://obamawhitehouse.archives.gov/the-press-office/2013/12/04/remarks-president-economic-mobility.

151   **five years ahead of schedule:** United Nations, "Millennium Development Goals Report 2015," 15, https://www.un.org/millenniumgoals/2015_MDG_Report/pdf/MDG%202015%20rev%20(July%201).pdf.

151   **to 650 million:** Max Roser and Esteban Ortiz-Ospina, "Global Extreme Poverty," Our World in Data, 2019, https://ourworldindata.org/extreme-poverty.

151   **mortality rate for young children dropped 59%:** "Under-Five Mortality," Global Health Observatory (GHO) data, WHO, https://www.who.int/gho/child_health/mortality/mortality_under_five_text/en/#:~:text=Trends,1%20in%2026%20in%202018.

151   **just 14% of the world's known deaths from Covid-19:** Philip Schellekens and Diego Sourrouille, "Tracking COVID-19 as Cause of Death: Global Estimates of Relative Severity," Brookings Institution, May 2020, https://www.brookings.edu/wp-content/uploads/2020/05/Tracking_COVID-19_as_-Cause_of_Death-Global_Estimates_of_Severity.pdf.

151   **Heat may have some effect:** Islam et al., "Temperature, Humidity, and Wind Speed Are Associated with Lower COVID-19 Incidence," 2020, https://doi.org/10.1101/2020.03.27.20045658, cited in: Rapid Expert Consultation on SARS-CoV-2 Survival in Relation to Temperature and Humidity and Potential for Seasonality for the COVID-19 Pandemic (April 7, 2020), National Academies of Science, Engineering, and Medicine, https://www.nap.edu/read/25771/chapter/1.

152 **170 million in 2019:** "Chinese Tourists Made 169 Million Outbound Trips in 2019: Report," China Global Television Network, February 29, 2020, citing China's National Bureau of Statistics, https://news.cgtn.com/news/2020–02–29/Chinese-tourists-made-169-million-outbound-trips-in-2019-report-OtIYWsZmOQ/index.html.

152 **thirty times:** "Dharavi slum has a population density almost 30 times greater than New York—about 280,000 people per square kilometer": Vedika Sud, Helen Regen, and Esha Mitra, *Mercury News,* citing CNN, April 4, 2020, https://www.mercurynews.com/2020/04/03/doctors-india-must-prepare-for-onslaught-of-coronavirus/.

152 **two-thirds of people live in congested slums:** According to Leilani Farha, the United Nations Special Rapporteur on housing, as of 2019: Paul Wallace and Tope Alake, "Lagos Building Luxury Homes in Face of Affordable Housing Crisis," Bloomberg, December 20, 2019.

152 **eight hospital beds for every 10,000 people:** World Bank DataBank, "Hospital Beds (Per 1,000 People)—Bangladesh, European Union, United States," https://data.worldbank.org/indicator/SH.MED.BEDS.ZS?locations=BD-EU-us.

152 **fewer than 2,000 ventilators:** Ruth Maclean and Simon Marks, "10 African Countries Have No Ventilators. That's Only Part of the Problem," *New York Times,* April 18, 2020.

152 **more vice presidents:** Ibid.

153 **shrink by 5%:** "Economy to shrink 5% this year, fiscal stimulus not enough to support growth," *Economic Times,* June 8, 2020.

153 **rivaling the worst performance:** World Bank DataBank, https://data.worldbank.org/indicator/NY.GDP.MKTP.KD.ZG?locations=IN.

153 **60,000 children:** 706,000 annual deaths from under-five malnutrition in 2017: Aastha Ahuja, "68 Per Cent of Child Deaths Under Five Years in India Caused by Malnutrition in 2017: Study," Banega Swasth India, citing India State-Level Disease Burden Initiative Study, https://swachhindia.ndtv.com/68-per-cent-of-child-deaths-under-five-years-in-india-caused-by-malnutrition-in-2017-study-39470.

154 **over $100 billion fled:** IMF Chief Kristalina Georgieva: "in the flight to safety a lot of capital has left the emerging economies, the developing world; nearly $90 billion has flown out. This is way more than during the global financial crisis": World Health Organization, COVID-19 virtual press conference, April 3, 2020, https://www.who.int/docs/default-source/documents/covid-19-virtual-press-conference-transcript-3-april-2020.pdf?sfvrsn=43e2f2f3_6.

154 **poor countries recovered faster:** "Slowly Emerging," *Economist,* April 7, 2015.

154 **between 70 million and 430 million people:** see Daniel Gerszon et al.,

World Bank, June 8, 2020, https://blogs.worldbank.org/opendata/updated -estimates-impact-covid-19-global-poverty; Andy Sumner, Chris Hoy, and Eduardo Ortiz-Juarez, "Estimates of the Impact of COVID-19 on Global Poverty," WIDER Working Paper 2020/43. Helsinki: UNU-WIDER, https://www.wider.unu.edu/publication/estimates-impact-covid -19-global-poverty.

155 **"trans-Tasman bubble":** "New Zealand PM: No Open Borders for 'a Long Time,'" BBC, May 5, 2020.

155 **"not have open borders":** Ibid.

155 **frantically lobbying:** Jamie Smith, "Pacific Islands Plead to Join Australia-New Zealand Travel Bubble," *Financial Times*, June 7, 2020.

155 **15% and 25% of their GDP . . . For the smaller countries of Barbados and the Bahamas, that number exceeds 30%:** World Travel & Tourism Council, "Economic Impact Reports," https://wttc.org/Research/ Economic-Impact.

156 **boosted their productivity by 33%:** Jason Douglas, Jon Sindreu, and Georgi Kantchev, "The Problem with Innovation: The Biggest Companies Are Hogging All the Gains," *Wall Street Journal*, July 15, 2018.

156 **Other research shows this trend growing:** Morgan Stanley Wealth Management, "The Capex Conundrum and Productivity Paradox," Global Investment Committee, November 2017, https://advisor.morganstanley .com/sandra-smith-allison-butler/documents/home-office/investing/The -Capex-Conundrum-and-Productivity-Paradox.pdf.

157 **Google's global market share:** J. Clement, "Global Market Share of Search Engines 2010–2020," Statista, June 18, 2020, https://www.statista .com/statistics/216573/worldwide-market-share-of-search-engines/.

157 **"competition is for losers":** Peter Thiel, "Competition Is for Losers," *Wall Street Journal*, September 12, 2014.

157 **totaling more than $1 trillion:** JP Morgan Chase 2018 Annual Report, https://www.jpmorganchase.com/corporate/investor-relations/document/ line-of-business-ceo-letters-to-shareholders-2018.pdf.

158 **disproportionately to larger and better-connected companies:** See an infographic from the Committee for a Responsible Budget, indicating that even though the CARES Act was trumpeted as a lifeline for Main Street, the act would roughly benefit large businesses and the airline industry as much as small businesses (http://www.crfb.org/blogs/visualization-cares -act). Note: Small business loans (PPP) were later expanded to almost $700 billion, but it should be noted that not all of those small businesses receiving PPP loans were truly "mom-and-pop stores." Recipients include the Shake Shacks of the world—as well as Kanye West's clothing company, Soho House, private jet companies, and Jeff Koons.

158 **twice as likely to be classified as "at risk":** André Dua, Deepa Mahajan,

Ingrid Millan, and Shelley Stewart, "COVID-19's Effect on Minority-Owned Small Businesses in the United States," McKinsey & Company, Social Sector Practice, May 27, 2020, https://www.mckinsey.com/industries/social-sector/our-insights/covid-19s-effect-on-minority-owned-small-businesses-in-the-united-states.

159 **upside of a range of risky investments:** Gene Ludwig and Sarah Bloom Raskin, "How the Fed's Rescue Program Is Worsening Inequality," *Politico,* May 28, 2020.

159 **"Capitalism without bankruptcy":** Attributed to Frank Borman, quoted in Thomas G. Donlan, "The Benefits of Failure," Barrons, April 12, 2010.

160 **inequality . . . means lower economic growth:** Joseph Stiglitz, *The Price of Inequality: How Today's Divided Society Endangers Our Future* (New York: W. W. Norton, 2012).

160 **lower levels of trust:** Richard G. Wilkinson and Kate Pickett, *The Spirit Level: Why More Equal Societies Almost Always Do Better* (London: Allen Lane, 2009).

160 **risen by 22%:** Taylor Telford, "Income Inequality in America Is the Highest It's Been Since Census Bureau Started Tracking It, Data Shows," *Washington Post,* September 26, 2019.

160 **nowhere has it spiked more:** Alvaredo et al., "World Inequality Report 2018," 6, 8.

160 **captured less than 10%:** "The Unequal States of America: Income Inequality in the United States," Economic Policy Institute infographic, adapted from Estelle Sommeiller and Mark Price, "The New Gilded Age: Income Inequality in the U.S. by State, Metropolitan Area, and County," an Economic Policy Institute report published July 2018, https://www.epi.org/multimedia/unequal-states-of-america/#/United%20States.

160 **from 22% in 1970 to 15% today:** Moritz Kuhn, Moritz Schularick, and Ulrike I. Steins, "Income and Wealth Inequality in America, 1949–2016," Federal Reserve Bank of Minneapolis, Institute Working Paper 9, June 2018, 21, https://www.minneapolisfed.org/institute/working-papers-institute/iwp9.pdf.

160 **bottom 50% own just 1.5% of assets:** US Federal Reserve, "Distribution of Household Wealth in the U.S. Since 1989," https://www.federalreserve.gov/releases/z1/dataviz/dfa/distribute/table/.

161 **even after accounting for taxes and government transfers:** Drew Desilver, "Global Inequality: How the U.S. Compares," FactBank, Pew Research Center, https://www.pewresearch.org/fact-tank/2013/12/19/global-inequality-how-the-u-s-compares/; and "Income Distribution Database," OECD, https://stats.oecd.org/Index.aspx?DataSetCode=IDD (choose measure "Gini (disposable income)").

161 **closer to Brazil than ... Denmark:** World Bank DataBank, https://data
.worldbank.org/indicator/SI.POV.GINI?locations=US-DK-BR.

161 **cut America in half:** see, e.g., Joe Pinsker, "The Pandemic Will Cleave
America in Two," *Atlantic*, April 2020.

161 **certain poor neighborhoods:** Larry Buchanan, Jugal K. Patel, Brian M.
Rosenthal, and Anjali Singhvi, "A Month of Coronavirus in New York
City: See the Hardest-Hit Areas," *New York Times*, April 1, 2020.

161 **Blacks are more than twice as likely to get Covid:** "Double Jeopardy:
COVID-19 and Behavioral Health Disparities for Black and Latino
Communities in the U.S.," Office of Behavioral Health Equity, Substance
Abuse and Mental Health Services Administration, US Department of
Health and Human Services, https://www.samhsa.gov/sites/default/
files/covid19-behavioral-health-disparities-black-latino-communities
.pdf.

161 **overall Covid fatality rate 2.3 times higher than Whites:** "The Color of
Coronavirus: Covid-19 Deaths by Race and Ethnicity in the U.S.," APM
Research Lab, July 8, 2020, https://www.apmresearchlab.org/covid/deaths
-by-race.

161 **non-Whites in the UK:** Shaun Treweek, Nita G. Forouhi, K. M. Venkat
Narayan, and Kamlesh Khunti, "COVID-19 and Ethnicity: Who Will
Research Results Apply To?" *Lancet* 395, no. 10242 (June 27–July 3, 2020):
1955–57, https://www.ncbi.nlm.nih.gov/pmc/articles/PMC7292594/; and
Lucinda Platt and Ross Warwick, "Are Some Ethnic Groups More Vulnerable to COVID-19 Than Others?," *VI Inequality*, May 1, 2020, https://www
.ifs.org.uk/inequality/chapter/are-some-ethnic-groups-more-vulnerable-to
-covid-19-than-others/.

161 **one third of African Americans:** Amy Goldstein and Emily Guskin,
"Almost One-Third of Black Americans Know Someone Who Died of
Covid-19, Survey Shows," *Washington Post*, June 26, 2020.

162 *seventy-seven times more likely*: Raj Chetty, John N. Friedman, Emmanuel Saez, Nicholas Turner, and Danny Yagan, "Income Segregation and
Intergenerational Mobility Across Colleges in the United States," *Quarterly
Journal of Economics* 135, no. 3 (August 2020): 1567–633, https://doi.org/10
.1093/qje/qjaa005.

163 **"plutocratic populism":** Jacob Hacker and Paul Pierson, *Let Them Eat
Tweets: How the Right Rules in an Age of Extreme Inequality* (New York: Liv-
eright, 2020).

164 **passports from certain Caribbean islands go for $100,000:** See, for
example, Antigua and Barbuda (https://cbiu.gov.dm/investment-options/),
or Dominica (http://www.antiguabarbuda-citizenship.com/).

164 **$900,000 to $1.8 million:** US Department of State, "Immigrant Inves-

tor Visas," https://travel.state.gov/content/travel/en/us-visas/immigrate/
immigrant-investor-visas.html.

164 **$2.5 million:** "Investor visa (Tier 1)," UK Government, https://www.gov
.uk/tier-1-investor.

164 **Cyprus, Malta, and Bulgaria:** Francesco Guarascio, "EU Sees Crime
Risks from Malta, Cyprus Passport-for-Sale Schemes: Report," Reuters,
January 21, 2019.

165 **"most people can be trusted":** "Can People Be Trusted," General Social
Survey, 2018, https://gssdataexplorer.norc.org/variables/441/vshow.

165 **many reasons for high levels of trust:** Esteban Ortiz-Ospina and Max
Roser, "Trust," 2016, https://ourworldindata.org/trust; see also Paul R.
Ward, Loreen Mamerow, and Samantha B. Meyer, "Interpersonal Trust
Across Six Asia-Pacific Countries: Testing and Extending the 'High Trust
Society' and 'Low Trust Society' Theory," *PLoS ONE* 9, no. 4 (April 23,
2014), ttps://doi.org/10.1371/journal.pone.0095555; and Soo Jiuan Tan
and Siok Kuan Tambyah, "Generalized Trust and Trust in Institutions in
Confucian Asia," *Social Indicators Research* 103, no. 3 (September 2011):
357–77, https://www.jstor.org/stable/41476527?seq=1.

165 **countries with less inequality...have more "social capital":** Fabio
Pisani and Maria Cristina Scarafile, "Income Inequality and Social Capital: An Empirical Analysis for European Regions," University of Rome
Tor Vergata, Società Italiana degli Economisti (Italian Society of Economists), https://siecon3-607788.c.cdn77.org/sites/siecon.org/files/media_
wysiwyg/160-pisani-scarafile.pdf.

166 **the "kingdom of the well" and the "kingdom of the sick":** Susan Sontag,
"Illness as Metaphor," *New York Review of Books*, January 26, 1978, https://
www.nybooks.com/articles/1978/01/26/illness-as-metaphor/.

Lesson Eight: Globalization Is Not Dead

167 **Liliana del Carmen Ruiz:** "The Story of the Pediatrician Who Died
of Coronavirus in La Rioja," Web24 News, April 1, 2020, https://
www.web24.news/u/2020/04/the-story-of-the-pediatrician-who-died
-of-coronavirus-in-la-rioja.html; and Ministerio de la Salud de La
Rioja, Twitter post, March 31, 2020, https://twitter.com/Minsaludlrj/
status/1244962594496143366.

168 **the antipode:** Antipode Map, https://www.antipodesmap.com/#about
-antipodes, "Wuhan, China," accessed July 10, 2020.

169 **"enterprising microbe":** Florence Fenwick Miller, 'The Ladies Column,'
Illustrated London News 96 (1890), 154–55, quoted in J. Mussell, "Writing

the 'Great Proteus of Disease': Influenza, Informatics, and the Body in the Late Nineteenth Century," in *Minds, Bodies, Machines, 1790–1920*, edited by D. Coleman and H. Fraser (Basingstoke, UK: Palgrave Macmillan, 2011), 161–78, https://core.ac.uk/download/pdf/267268737.pdf.

169 **fifteen-year-old Winston Churchill was moved to compose a poem:** Winston Churchill, "The Influenza, 1890," National Churchill Museum, https://www.nationalchurchillmuseum.org/winston-churchill-the -influenza-poem.html; published in the Harrow School newspaper, *The Harrovian*, in 1890, per the Winston Churchill archive: https://www -archives.chu.cam.ac.uk/perl/node?a=a;reference=CHUR%202%2F336.

169 **"final nail in the coffin":** Garry White, "Coronavirus Is the Canary in Globalisation's Coal Mine," *Telegraph*, March 6, 2020.

169 **"impossible to stop":** Zachary Karabell, "Will the Coronavirus Bring the End of Globalization? Don't Count on It," *Wall Street Journal*, March 20, 2020.

170 **hardly the first time:** Adam Tooze, "The Death of Globalisation Has Been Announced Many Times. But This Is a Perfect Storm," *Guardian*, June 2, 2020.

170 **"gnomes of Zurich":** Phrase originally coined by Harold Wilson in a 1956 speech, gaining currency in the UK's inflation struggles of the 1960s: "Why Are Swiss Bankers Called Gnomes?", BBC News, February 25, 2010, http://news.bbc.co.uk/2/hi/uk_news/magazine/8534936.stm.

170 **you holler that the game is rigged:** See, e.g., Jagdish Bhagwati, in a BBC radio debate with a French mayor who was upset that a local factory was moving to England: "When it came to your town, you applauded. Now that they have traveled on, you are agitated. You cannot have it both ways." Quoted in Jagdish Bhagwati, *In Defense of Globalization* (Oxford: Oxford University Press, 2007), afterword.

171 **air travel more than doubled:** 1.674 billion air passengers in 2000, 1.655 billion in 2001, 1.889 billion in 2004, 4.233 billion in 2018: "Air Transport, Passengers Carried," International Civil Aviation Organization, Civil Aviation Statistics, World Bank DataBank, https://data.worldbank.org/ indicator/IS.AIR.PSGR.

171 **falling sharply:** 9.9% decline in global trade, 9% decline in investment in 2009: World Bank Report, "A Decade After the Global Recession: Lessons and Challenges for Emerging and Developed Economies," ed. M. Ayhan Kose and Franziska Ohnsorge, Chapter 3, "Macroeconomic Analysis," http://pubdocs.worldbank.org/en/799211574200483232/Recession -Chapter-3.pdf.

171 **grew very slowly:** Global trade growth slowed to 4.1% annually after 2011, versus 76% from 2002 to 2007: Ibid.

171 **Trade . . . never recovered:** Trade = 30.7% of global GDP in 2008, 30.1%

in 2018: "Exports of Goods and Services (% of GDP)," World Bank Data-Bank, https://data.worldbank.org/indicator/NE.EXP.GNFS.ZS.

171 **capital flows . . . never recovered:** Global capital flows = 22% of world GDP in 2007, 6.9% in 2017: United Nations Conference on Trade and Development, Global Investment Report 2018, Figure 1.1, "Global Capital Flows, 2002–2017 (Per cent of GDP)," 11, https://unctad.org/en/PublicationsLibrary/wir2018_en.pdf.

171 **foreign direct investment never recovered:** World FDI: $3.7 trillion in 2007, $2.2 trillion in 2015, $970 billion in 2018: "Foreign Direct Investment, Net Outflows," World Bank DataBank, https://data.worldbank.org/indicator/BM.KLT.DINV.CD.WD.

171 **benefited capital:** See, for example, Lawrence H. Summers, "The Inequality Puzzle," *Democracy: A Journal of Ideas*, no. 3 (Summer 2014).

171 **"deglobalization":** See Ruchir Sharma, "Our Irrational Anxiety About 'Slow' Growth," *New York Times*, August 17, 2019.

171 **were down by 94%:** Comparing April 2020 air traffic to April 2019: "After April Passenger Demand Trough, First Signals of Uptick," IATA (International Air Transport Association, trade group representing 290 airlines and 82% of global air traffic), Press Release #49, June 3, 2020, https://www.iata.org/en/pressroom/pr/2020–06–03–01/.

171 **were down 76%:** "Passenger Car Registrations," European Automobile Manufacturers' Association, May 19, 2020, https://www.acea.be/press-releases/article/passenger-car-registrations-38.5-four-months-into-2020–76.3-in-april.

172 **literally off the charts:** Quote and 14.7% unemployment figure from Nelson D. Schwartz, Ben Casselman, and Ella Koeze, "How Bad Is Unemployment? 'Literally off the Charts,'" *New York Times*, May 8, 2020.

172 **one in every three pills:** Priyali Sur, "The Coronavirus Exposed the US' Reliance on India for Generic Drugs. But That Supply Chain Is Ultimately Controlled by China," CNN Business, May 16, 2020, https://www.cnn.com/2020/05/16/business-india/india-pharma-us-china-supply-china-intl-hnk/index.html.

172 **cost of transporting goods across the Pacific tripled:** Keith Bradsher and Ana Swanson, "The U.S. Needs China's Masks, as Acrimony Grows," *New York Times*, March 23, 2020.

172 **supply chains more resilient:** See, for example, European Commission, "Coronavirus: Commission Issues Guidelines to Protect Critical European Assets and Technology in Current Crisis," March 25, 2020, https://trade.ec.europa.eu/doclib/press/index.cfm?id=2124; Japan: Walter Sim, "Coronavirus: Japan PM Shinzo Abe Calls on Firms to Cut Supply Chain Reliance on China," *Straits Times*, April 16, 2020; and India: Bill Spindle and Rajesh Roy, "India's Coronavirus Crisis Spurs a New Look at Self-Reliance," *Wall Street Journal*, May 17, 2020.

172 **"independence of France":** Emmanuel Macron, "Addresse aux Français," June 14, 2020, https://www.elysee.fr/emmanuel-macron/2020/06/14/adresse -aux-francais-14-juin-2020.

172 **$400-billion "Buy American" plan:** "The Biden Plan to Ensure the Future Is "Made in All of America" by All of America's Workers," Joe Biden for President, https://joebiden.com/madeinamerica/.

173 **below its high in 2008 of 30.8%:** "Exports of Goods and Services (% of GDP)," World Bank DataBank, https://data.worldbank.org/indicator/NE .EXP.GNFS.ZS.

173 **$2.7 trillion:** "Foreign Direct Investment, Net Inflows," World Bank DataBank, https://data.worldbank.org/indicator/BX.KLT.DINV.CD.WD.

173 **almost doubled by 2016:** To some $2.7 trillion: "Aviation Benefits Report 2019," Industry High Level Group / International Coordinating Council of Aerospace Industries Associations, 17, https://www.icao.int/sustainability/ Documents/AVIATION-BENEFITS-2019-web.pdf.

174 **down to 54% in 2016 … look at the chart historically:** "Globalization over 5 Centuries," Our World in Data, "Globalization over 5 Centuries, World," Our World in Data, https://ourworldindata.org/grapher/ globalization-over-5-centuries?time=1945..2016. Data from Mariko J. Klasing and P. Milionis, "Quantifying the Evolution of World Trade, 1870–1949," *Journal of International Economics* 92, no. 1 (2014): 185–97; A. Estevadeordal, B. Frantz, and A. Taylor, "The Rise and Fall of World Trade, 1870–1939," *Quarterly Journal of Economics* 118, no. 2 (2003): 359–407, retrieved from http://www.jstor.org/stable/25053910); World Bank— World Development Indicators, http://data.worldbank.org/data-catalog/ world-development-indicators; Robert C. Feenstra, Robert Inklaar, and Marcel P. Timmer, "The Next Generation of the Penn World Table," *American Economic Review* 105, no. 10 (2015): 3150–82, available for download at www.ggdc.net/pwt.

174 **at great cost to American taxpayers:** Trump's tariffs will reduce average US household income by $1,277 in 2020, according to a study by the Congressional Budget Office: "The Budget and Economic Outlook, 2020 to 2030," "Trade Policies," Congressional Budget Office, January 2020, https://www.cbo.gov/publication/56073.

175 **in 1967, stood at 15%:** Organisation for Economic Co-operation and Development (OECD), "Tariff Escalation & Environment" (Paris, 1996), 15, citing UNCTAD (1968), "The Kennedy Round: Estimated Effects on Tariff Barriers," TD/6/Rev. 1, United Nations, New York, http://www .oecd.org/officialdocuments/publicdisplaydocumentpdf/?cote=OCDE/ GD(96)171&docLanguage=En.

175 **under 3%:** The 2017 global tariff average = 2.59%: "Tariff Rate, Applied, Weighted Mean, All Products (%)," World Bank DataBank, https://data .worldbank.org/indicator/TM.TAX.MRCH.WM.AR.ZS.

175   **dependence on foreign suppliers for vital medical products:** United States: "'Never again should we have to depend on the rest of the world for our essential medicines and countermeasures,' said Peter Navarro, President Trump's economic adviser": Sur, "The Coronavirus Exposed the US' Reliance on India for Generic Drugs. But That Supply Chain Is Ultimately Controlled by China"; India: Vindu Goel, "As Coronavirus Disrupts Factories, India Curbs Exports of Key Drugs," *New York Times*, March 6, 2020; and France: Rym Momtaz, "Macron Urges Massive Increase in Local Production of Medical Equipment," *Politico*, March 31, 2020.

176   **masks were running desperately low:** In the US, see: Farhad Manjoo, "How the World's Richest Country Ran Out of a 75-Cent Face Mask," *New York Times*, March 25, 2020; K Oanh Ha, "The Global Mask Shortage May Get Much Worse," Bloomberg, March 10, 2020.

176   **fifty-seven times:** Viswanath Pill, "Rising Inventory, Falling Prices Spook PPEs, Sanitizer Makers Who Jumped into COVID-19 Bandwagon," Moneycontrol.com, quoting Association of Indian Medical Device Industry (AiMeD), https://www.moneycontrol.com/news/business/companies/ rising-inventory-falling-prices-spook-ppes-santizer-makers-who-jumped -into-covid-19-bandwagon-5547681.html.

176   **mask prices fell 90%:** Heather Mowbray, "Trending in China: Wholesale Mask Prices Fall over 90% and Raw Materials Fall to Fraction of Peak Price," *Caixin Global*, July 15, 2020.

176   **never significantly replenished after the H1N1 outbreak:** Sarah Fitzpatrick, "Why the Strategic National Stockpile Isn't Meant to Solve a Crisis Like Coronavirus," NBC News, March 28, 2020.

177   **70% to 80% of global production:** "Made In China?," *Economist*, March 12, 2015.

177   **created incentives for firms to onshore production:** European Union: Flavia Rotondi, Piotr Skolimowski, Jeannette Neumann, and Joao Lima, "Europe Finds It's Not So Easy to Say Goodbye to Low-Cost China," Bloomberg, June 29, 2020; Japan: Isabel Reynolds and Emi Urabe, "Japan to Fund Firms to Shift Production out of China," Bloomberg, April 8, 2020.

177   **tax breaks to American exporters:** "Companies Get Leniency in Made-in-America Export Tax Break," Bloomberg, March 4, 2019.

178   **decline sharply since the 1950s and '60s:** See St. Louis Fed for US data, https://www.stlouisfed.org/on-the-economy/2017/april/us-manufacturing -really-declining; and decline since 1960 for other developed countries: Our World in Data, https://ourworldindata.org/grapher/share-of -manufacturing-employment-in-high-income-countries-1960–2011.

178   **"Made in the USA" version of the same pants costs about $350:** Dana Varinsky, "Here's What 5 of Your Favorite Products Would Cost if They

Were Made in the US," *Business Insider*, November 27, 2016, https://www
.businessinsider.com/how-much-products-would-cost-if-made-in-us-2016
-11#jeans-2.

178 **Smoot-Hawley Tariffs:** Chad P. Bown and Eva (Yiwen) Zhang, "Trump's
2019 Protection Could Push China Back to Smoot-Hawley Tariff Levels," Peterson Institute of International Economics, May 14, 2019, https://
www.piie.com/blogs/trade-and-investment-policy-watch/trumps-2019
-protection-could-push-china-back-smoot-hawley.

178 **stayed flat under his watch:** Excluding sudden fluctuations around Covid-
19, manufacturing jobs rose by half a million under Trump in absolute
terms. As a share of total employment, they have remained flat—started at
8.49% in January 2017, peaked at 8.55% in February 2019, down to 8.44%
in January 2020. For comparison, manufacturing's share declined by 3.5
points under George W. Bush. Data from: US Bureau of Labor Statistics,
All Employees, Manufacturing [MANEMP], retrieved from FRED,
Federal Reserve Bank of St. Louis; https://fred.stlouisfed.org/series/
MANEMP, July 15, 2020.

> For historical context, St. Louis Fed shows:
> 1980 = 19 million manufacturing jobs
> 2000 = 17 million
> 2010 = 11.5 million
> January 2020 = 12.8 million
> May 2020 = 11.7 million

Ronnie Polidoro, "Apple CEO Tim Cook Announces Plans to Manufacture Mac Computers in USA," NBC News, December 6, 2012.

178 **these facilities had never been financially viable:** Brooks Brothers CEO
Claudio Del Vecchio, in a *New York Times* interview: Vanessa Friedman
and Sapna Maheshwari, "Brooks Bros., 'Made in America' Since 1818,
May Soon Need a New Calling Card," *New York Times*, June 5, 2020.

179 **a custom screw:** Jack Nicas, "A Tiny Screw Shows Why iPhones Won't Be
'Assembled in U.S.A.,'" *New York Times*, January 28, 2019.

179 **"multiple football fields":** Ibid.

179 **production out of China—to Vietnam:** Yoko Kubota and Tripp Mickle,
"Apple Explores Moving Some Production out of China," *Wall Street Jour-
nal*, June 20, 2019; and India: Kim Lyons, "Apple Starts Making First
Flagship iPhone in India," *Verge*, July 25, 2020.

179 **Seventy percent of US GDP:** 70.4% as of Q4 2019. US Bureau of Economic Analysis, "Value Added by Private Services-Producing Industries as
a Percentage of GDP," retrieved from FRED, Federal Reserve Bank of St.
Louis, June 18, 2020, https://fred.stlouisfed.org/series/VAPGDPSPI.

179   **Four out of every five American jobs:** 80.2% of US jobs are in services: US Bureau of Labor Statistics, "Employment by Major Industry Sector," Table 2.1, September 4, 2019, https://www.bls.gov/emp/tables/employment-by-major-industry-sector.htm.

179   **70% of its economic output:** 69.3% of German GDP from services: Bruttoinlandsprodukt für Deutschland 2019 (Gross Domestic Product for Germany 2019), Federal Statistical Office of Germany (Statistisches Bundesamt), 11, https://www.destatis.de/DE/Presse/Pressekon ferenzen/2020/BIP2019/pressebroschuere-bip.pdf?__blob=publica tionFile.

179   **70% of...its jobs:** 74.5% of German jobs from services: "Persons in Employment and Employees by Sectors of Economic Activity," Federal Statistical Office of Germany (Statistisches Bundesamt), May 19, 2020, https:// www.destatis.de/EN/Themes/Labour/Labour-Market/Employment/ Tables/persons-employment-sectors-economic.html.

179   **less than 10% of GDP:** "Manufacturing, Value Added (% of GDP)— France," World Bank DataBank, https://data.worldbank.org/indicator/NV .IND.MANF.ZS?locations=FR. Note that the World Bank definition of manufacturing excludes construction. Including construction, all industry provides closer to 17% of French GDP, again per World Bank data, http:// wdi.worldbank.org/table/4.2.

180   **cross-border bandwidth grew ninetyfold:** Christine Lagarde, "Creating a Better Global Trade System," IMF, May 14, 2018, https://www.imf .org/en/News/Articles/2018/05/14/sp-lagarde-creating-a-better-global -trade-system. See also McKinsey: Cross-border data flows grew by a factor of 150 from 2005 to 2017. McKinsey Global Institute, "Globalization in Transition: The Future of Trade and Value Chains," January 2019, 72, https://www.mckinsey.com/~/media/mckinsey/featured%20insights/ innovation/globalization%20in%20transition%20the%20future%20 of%20trade%20and%20value%20chains/mgi-globalization%20in%20 transition-the-future-of-trade-and-value-chains-full-report.ashx.

181   **"South-South trade":** Susan Lund and Laura Tyson, "Globalization Is Not in Retreat: Digital Technology and the Future of Trade," *Foreign Affairs*, May/June 2018.

181   **less than 35% of Asia's GDP:** Organisation for Economic Co-operation and Development (OECD) Report: "Perspectives on Global Development 2019: Rethinking Development Strategies," November 2018, Figure 4.9, 164, http://obela.org/system/files/persp_glob_dev-2019-en.pdf.

181   **$120 billion:** Benn Steil and Benjamin Della Rocca, "Belt and Road Tracker," Council on Foreign Relations, Greenberg Center for Geoeconomic Studies, May 8, 2019, accessed July 13, 2020, https://www.cfr.org/ article/belt-and-road-tracker.

181   **495 million people:** "Overview and Benefits of the CPTPP," Government of Canada, February 11, 2019, https://www.international.gc.ca/trade-commerce/trade-agreements-accords-commerciaux/agr-acc/cptpp-ptpgp/overview-apercu.aspx.

182   **migrating out of Africa:** Cassandra Love, "In Their Footsteps: Human Migration out of Africa," *National Geographic*, January 18, 2019, https://www.nationalgeographic.org/article/their-footsteps-human-migration-out-africa/.

182   **the long process of globalization:** For a recent work that dates globalization substantially earlier than most accounts (globalization primarily within the Old World of Africa-Eurasia, but including Norse expeditions to Iceland, Greenland, and Canada), see: Valerie Hansen, *The Year 1000: When Explorers Connected the World and Globalization Began* (New York: Scribner, 2020).

182   **"most important events":** Adam Smith, *The Wealth of Nations*, Volume II, Chap. VII, Part III, "Of the Advantages which Europe has derived From the Discovery of America, and from that of a Passage to the East Indies by the Cape of Good Hope," referenced in Kevin H. O'Rourke and Jeffrey G. Williamson, "When Did Globalization Begin?," *European Review of Economic History* 6, no. 1 (April 2002): 23–50, https://doi.org/10.1017/S1361491602000023, building on the work of J. D. Tracy (1990), "Introduction," in *The Rise of Merchant Empires*, edited by J. D. Tracy (Cambridge: Cambridge University Press, 1990), 3.

183   **"all the different nations":** Smith, *Wealth of Nations*, "Of the Advantages which Europe has derived."

183   **"big bang":** O'Rourke and Williamson, "When Did Globalization Begin?"

183   **cost of shipping rice ... freight rate on coal:** Ibid., "IV. The Second Era: 19th Century Transport Revolutions and Commodity Price Convergence."

183   **world shipping almost tripled:** Eric Hobsbawm, *Age of Empire: 1875–1914* (New York: Vintage Books, 1987), 350, citing Mulhall, *Dictionary of Statistics* (London, 1881) and *League of Nations International Statistical Yearbook 1913*, Table 76.

183   **broad rise in incomes:** Our World in Data, "GDP Per Capita, 1870 to 1914," https://ourworldindata.org/grapher/average-real-gdp-per-capita-across-countries-and-regions?time=1870..1914. For the most globalized regions, Western Europe and "Western Offshoots" (i.e., US, Canada, Australia, New Zealand), note the more-than-doubled GDP per capita during the period of the first wave of globalization. Data from: Maddison Project Database, version 2018. Jutta Bolt, Robert Inklaar, Herman de Jong, and Jan Luiten van Zanden, "Rebasing 'Maddison': New Income Comparisons and the Shape of Long-Run Economic Development," Maddison Project Working Paper 10 (2018).

184 **5 million international students:** UNESCO, "Outbound Internationally Mobile Students by Host Region," accessed June 18, 2020, http://data.uis .unesco.org/Index.aspx?queryid=172.

184 **270 million migrants:** United Nations Department of Economic and Social Affairs, "The Number of International Migrants Reaches 272 Million, Continuing an Upward Trend in All World Regions," https://www .un.org/development/desa/en/news/population/international-migrant -stock-2019.html.

184 **1.5 billion tourist trips each year:** UN World Tourism Organization, "World Tourism Barometer," January 2020, https://www.unwto.org/world -tourism-barometer-n18-january-2020.

185 **"The inhabitant of London":** John Maynard Keynes, *The Economic Consequences of the Peace* (1920), Chapter II: "Europe Before the War."

185 **increased fivefold:** Maurice Obstfeld, "Globalization and Nationalism: Retrospect and Prospect," University of California, Berkeley; Peterson Institute; CEPR; and NBER Italian Economic Association Annual Meeting, Palermo, Italy, October 24, 2019, https://conferences.wcfia.harvard .edu/files/peif/files/globalizationandnationalism.pdf.

185 **"fast becoming one people":** Lord James Bryce, The Romanes Lecture, June 7, 1902, Oxford University. (The lecture had the cringeworthy title, "The Relations of the Advanced and the Backward Races of Mankind.")

185 *The Great Illusion*: Norman Angell, *The Great Illusion: A Study of the Relation of Military Power in Nations to Their Economic and Social Advantage*, 3rd ed., 1911, https://archive.org/details/greatillusion00angeiala.

186 **return to the peaks:** Obstfeld, "Globalization and Nationalism."

186 **rise of a new great power and the unease this creates in the existing hegemon:** see Thucydides, "It was the rise of Athens and the fear that this inspired in Sparta that made war inevitable," as quoted in Graham Allison, *Destined for War: Can America and China Escape Thucydides's Trap?* (London: Scribe, 2017).

Lesson Nine: The World Is Becoming Bipolar

187 **"failed state":** George Packer, "We Are Living in a Failed State," *Atlantic*, June 2020.

187 **"secular stagnation":** Lawrence H. Summers, "Reflections on Secular Stagnation," February 19, 2015, remarks at Princeton University's Julis-Rabinowitz Center for Public Policy and Finance.

187 **highlighted rising inequality:** See, inter alia, Thomas Piketty, *Capital*

in the Twenty-First Century (Cambridge, MA: Harvard University Press, 2013).

187 **"deaths of despair":** Anne Case and Angus Deaton, *Deaths of Despair and the Future of Capitalism* (Princeton, NJ: Princeton University Press, 2020).

188 **Fintan O'Toole:** Fintan O'Toole, "Donald Trump Has Destroyed the Country He Promised to Make Great Again," *Irish Times*, April 25, 2020. O'Toole's column has caught the eye of other writers, and has been quoted by several, including Maureen Dowd in "Double, Double, Trump's Toil, Our Trouble," *New York Times*, August 1, 2020.

188 **lockdown on 800 million:** James Griffiths and Amy Woodyatt, "780 Million People in China Are Living Under Travel Restrictions Due to the Coronavirus Outbreak," CNN, February 17, 2020.

188 **an essay in *Foreign Affairs* in 1988:** Samuel P. Huntington, "The U.S. — Decline or Renewal?," *Foreign Affairs*, Winter 1988/89.

189 ***The Collapse of British Power*:** Correlli Barnett, *The Collapse of British Power* (Amherst, NY: Prometheus Books, 1986).

190 **sometimes an order of magnitude more:** "Firearms: Global Mortality from Firearms, 1990–2016," Global Burden of Disease 2016 Injury Collaborators, *JAMA* 320, no.8 (2018): 792–814, https://jamanetwork.com/journals/jama/fullarticle/2698492; prison: Eurostat, "Prison Statistics," https://ec.europa.eu/eurostat/statistics-explained/index.php?title=Prison_statistics; and Drew Kann, "5 Facts Behind America's High Incarceration Rate," CNN, April 21, 2019.

190 **expanded over the last decade:** In 2010, US GDP as share of world GDP = 22.7%; in 2018, it was 24%: World Bank DataBank, https://data.worldbank.org/indicator/NY.GDP.MKTP.CD.

191 **nearly ties China:** 2016 Global Manufacturing Competitiveness Index, Deloitte, https://www2.deloitte.com/global/en/pages/manufacturing/articles/global-manufacturing-competitiveness-index.html.

191 **almost 90% of all currency transactions:** 88% of all foreign exchange trades conducted in US dollars in April 2019: "Foreign Exchange Turnover in April 2019," Triennial Central Bank Survey, Bank for International Settlements, https://www.bis.org/statistics/rpfx19_fx.htm; and 85% of foreign exchange transactions conducted in US dollars as of June 2020: Committee on the Global Financial System, Paper #65: "US Dollar Funding: An International Perspective," 3, https://www.bis.org/publ/cgfs65.pdf.

191 **"until around 2050":** Ruchir Sharma, "The Comeback Nation: U.S. Economic Supremacy Has Repeatedly Proved Declinists Wrong," *Foreign Affairs*, April 31, 2020.

191 **than the next ten countries combined:** US military spending in 2019 =

$732 billion, total military spending of next 10 nations (China, India, Russia, Saudi Arabia, France, Germany, UK, Japan, South Korea, Brazil) = $725.8 billion: "Trends in World Military Expenditure, 2019," Table 1, Stockholm International Peace Research Institute, https://www.sipri.org/sites/default/files/2020–04/fs_2020_04_milex_0_0.pdf.

191   **"soft power":** Term first coined by Joseph S. Nye, *Bound to Lead* (New York: Basic Books, 1990).

191   **Nye ... has warned in recent years:** "The evidence is clear. Donald Trump's presidency has eroded America's soft power": Joseph S. Nye, "Donald Trump and the Decline of US Soft Power," *Project Syndicate*, February 6, 2018.

192   **64% for Obama:** Richard Wike, Bruce Stokes, Jacob Poushter, and Janell Fetterolf, "U.S. Image Suffers as Publics Around World Question Trump's Leadership," Pew Research, June 26, 2017, https://www.pewresearch.orjg/global/2017/06/26/u-s-image-suffers-as-publics-around-world-question-trumps-leadership/.

192   **29% for Trump:** Richard Wike, Jacob Poushter, Janell Fetterolf, and Shannon Schumacher, "Trump Ratings Remain Low Around Globe, While Views of U.S. Stay Mostly Favorable," Pew Research, January 8, 2020, https://www.pewresearch.org/global/2020/01/08/trump-ratings-remain-low-around-globe-while-views-of-u-s-stay-mostly-favorable/.

192   **"rise of the rest":** See Fareed Zakaria, *The Post-American World* (New York: W. W. Norton, 2008).

193   **economic output has quintupled:** World Bank DataBank, Turkey GDP since 1990: https://data.worldbank.org/indicator/NY.GDP.MKTP.CD?locations=TR.

193   **per capita GDP has tripled:** World Bank DataBank, Turkey GDP per capita since 1990: https://data.worldbank.org/indicator/NY.GDP.PCAP.CD?locations=TR.

193   **now it accounts for 16%:** World Bank DataBank, China and World GDP, 1990 to 2019, https://data.worldbank.org/indicator/NY.GDP.MKTP.CD?locations=CN-1W.

193   **number one trading nation in goods:** As of 2013; see "China Eclipses U.S. as Biggest Trading Nation," *Bloomberg News*, February 9, 2013, https://www.bloomberg.com/news/articles/2013–02–09/china-passes-u-s-to-become-the-world-s-biggest-trading-nation.

194   **roughly constant since 1980:** In 1980, US GDP as share of world GDP = 25.4%; in 2018, it was 23.9%: "GDP (current US$)—United States" and "World GDP (current US$)," World Bank DataBank, https://data.worldbank.org/indicator/NY.GDP.MKTP.CD.

194   **shrink from 30%:** Mikkel Barslund and Daniel Gros, "Europe's Place in the Global Economy—What Does the Last Half Century Suggest for

the Future?," "Figure 5: Regional GDP Shares in US$, 1965–2030," in "50 Years of European Integration," *Intereconomics* 51, no. 1 (2016): 5–11 (ZBW—Leibniz Information Centre for Economics and CEPS—Centre for European Policy Studies), https://www.intereconomics.eu/contents/year/2016/number/1/article/europes-place-in-the-global-economy-what -does-the-last-half-century-suggest-for-the-future.html.

195 **No two bipolar systems are the same:** For a detailed discussion of the differences between US-Soviet bipolarity and US-China bipolarity, see: Øystein Tunsjø, *The Return of Bipolarity in World Politics: China, the United States, and Geostructural Realism* (New York: Columbia University Press, 2018).

195 **destined for conflict:** See, for example, Graham Allison, *Destined for War.*

195 **"power transitions":** See ibid., and Harvard Belfer Center, "Thucydides's Trap Case File," https://www.belfercenter.org/thucydides-trap/case-file.

195 **"Chimerica":** Niall Ferguson in conversation with Nathan Gardeis, "Niall Ferguson: Is U.S.-China Economic Marriage on the Rocks?", *HuffPost* blog, May 25, 2011, https://www.huffpost.com/entry/niall-ferguson-is-us -chin_b_245470.

196 **Xi Jinping, who came to power in 2012:** Although Xi assumed the presidency in 2013, he was de facto ruler since 2012 when he became general secretary of the Communist Party and chairman of the Central Military Commission: John Rutwich, "Timeline—The Rise of Chinese Leader Xi Jinping," Reuters, March 16, 2018, https://www.reuters.com/article/us-china-parliament-xi-timeline/timeline-the-rise-of-chinese-leader-xi -jinping-idUSKCN1GS0ZA.

196 **"Wolf Warrior":** Ben Westcott and Steven Jiang, "China Is Embracing a New Brand of Foreign Policy. Here's What Wolf Warrior Diplomacy Means," CNN, May 22, 2020.

197 **In fact, US contributions:** US State Department cites $2.4 billion in congressional allocations "to support health systems, humanitarian assistance, and economic, security, and stabilization efforts worldwide": US Department of State, "Foreign Assistance for Coronavirus (COVID-19)," https://www.state.gov/foreign-assistance-for-coronavirus-covid-19/.

197 **Beijing won this round of public diplomacy:** A global survey of 124,000 people in fifty-three countries in spring 2020 found that just two countries thought the US did a better job than China of responding to the Covid pandemic. One was the US and the other was the long-running China rival, Japan. See: "Nearly all countries say that China's response to the COVID-19 is better than the US's," in Democracy Perception Index—2020, https://daliaresearch.com/blog/democracy-perception-index-2020.

198 **on his first workday in office:** Peter Baker, "Trump Abandons Trans-Pacific Partnership, Obama's Signature Trade Deal," *New York Times*, January 23, 2017.

199   **Xi's rhetorical embrace of multilateralism:** Xi Jinping: "We should
       adhere to multilateralism to uphold the authority and efficacy of multi-
       lateral institutions. We should honor promises and abide by rules. One
       should not select or bend rules as he sees fit," CGTN America, "Full Text
       of Xi Jinping Keynote at the World Economic Forum," January 17, 2017,
       https://america.cgtn.com/2017/01/17/full-text-of-xi-jinping-keynote-at
       -the-world-economic-forum.
200   **"'hostile foreign forces'":** Orville Schell, "The Death of Engagement," *The
       Wire—China,* June 7, 2020, https://www.thewirechina.com/2020/06/07/
       the-birth-life-and-death-of-engagement/.
200   **"new era":** What Xi calls "an era that sees China moving closer to center
       stage and making greater contributions to mankind": Xi Jinping, "Secure
       a Decisive Victory in Building a Moderately Prosperous Society in All
       Respects and Strive for the Great Success of Socialism with Chinese Char-
       acteristics for a New Era," Delivered at the 19th National Congress of
       the Communist Party of China, October 18, 2017, *China Daily,* http://
       www.chinadaily.com.cn/china/19thcpcnationalcongress/2017–11/04/
       content_34115212.htm.
200   **notably silent on this abuse:** If former national security advisor John
       Bolton's account is to be believed, Trump actively courted China's elec-
       toral assistance in the agricultural Midwest. John Bolton, *The Room Where
       It Happened: A White House Memoir* (New York: Simon & Schuster, 2020),
       excerpted in the *Wall Street Journal,* https://www.wsj.com/articles/john
       -bolton-the-scandal-of-trumps-china-policy-11592419564:

>   Trump then, stunningly, turned the conversation to the coming
>   U.S. presidential election, alluding to China's economic capability
>   and pleading with Xi to ensure he'd win. He stressed the importance
>   of farmers and increased Chinese purchases of soybeans and wheat
>   in the electoral outcome. . . . At the opening dinner of the Osaka
>   G-20 meeting in June 2019, with only interpreters present, Xi had
>   explained to Trump why he was basically building concentration
>   camps in Xinjiang. According to our interpreter, Trump said that
>   Xi should go ahead with building the camps, which Trump thought
>   was exactly the right thing to do.

200   **become more ambitious:** "As America Gets Tired, China Gets Busy,"
       Economist, June 18, 2020.
200   **outnumbers the US four-to-one:** "Who Runs the World?," *Economist,*
       June 18, 2020.
201   **a developing country:** See, for example, Stefan Link and Noam Maggor,
       "The United States as a Developing Nation: Revisiting the Peculiarities of

American History," *Past & Present* 246, no. 1 (February 2020): 269–306, https://doi.org/10.1093/pastj/gtz032.

201 **not even among the world's top five economies:** Top economies as share of world GDP circa 1820: #1 China (38.7%), #2 India (16%), #3 France (5.4%), #4 UK (5.2%), #5 Russia (4.5%) . . . #9 USA (1.8%), from Angus Maddison, *Monitoring the World Economy, 1820–1992* (Paris: OECD, 1995), 30, compiled by Vincent Ferraro, Mount Holyoke College, https://www.mtholyoke.edu/acad/intrel/ipe/topten.htm.

203 **sleepwalk into war:** Christopher C. Clark, *The Sleepwalkers: How Europe Went to War in 1914* (London: Allen Lane, 2012).

204 **June 2020 border skirmish:** Jeffrey Gettleman, Hari Kumar, and Sameer Yasir, "Worst Clash in Decades on Disputed India-China Border Kills 20 Indian Troops," *New York Times*, June 16, 2020.

204 **once unimaginable:** Military partnership: "U.S. Security Cooperation with Vietnam," US Department of State Bureau of Political-Military Affairs, Fact Sheet, May 21, 2019, https://www.state.gov/u-s-security-cooperation-with-vietnam-2/.

206 **bipolarity without war:** For more on the stability of bipolar systems, see Kenneth Waltz, *Theory of International Politics* (Long Grove, IL: Waveland Press, 1979).

206 **lost around 25 million:** Estimates of Soviet casualties in World War II vary widely—"There are no reliable figures," according to *Britannica*. For the estimate of 25 million including battle deaths and civilian deaths (but excluding loss in population from those who would have been born, but for the war), see: Warren W. Eason, "The Soviet Population Today: An Analysis of the First Results of the 1959 Census," *Foreign Affairs*, July 1959, https://www.foreignaffairs.com/articles/russian-federation/1959-07-01/soviet-population-today#:~:text=(1).

207 **"Market Leninism":** Kristof, "China Sees 'Market-Leninism' as Way to Future."

207 **rarely went above $2 billion a year:** See US Census, "Trade in Goods with the USSR, Years 1985–1990," https://www.census.gov/foreign-trade/balance/c4610.html.

207 **$2 billion—*every day*:** $737.1 billion trade in goods and services in 2018, $2.02 billion per day. $737.1 billion from: Office of the US Trade Representative, "The People's Republic of China: U.S.-China Trade Facts," https://ustr.gov/countries-regions/china-mongolia-taiwan/peoples-republic-china.

208 **"Britain has the earth":** Woodrow Wilson, in conversation with Britain's ambassador Walter Hines Page: Wilson in August 1916 "spoke of England's having the earth and of Germany wanting it," recorded in Page's diary. Quoted in Adam Tooze, *The Deluge: The Great War, America and the Remaking of the Global Order, 1916–1931* (New York: Penguin/Viking

Press, 2014), Chapter 1, footnote 39, compiled in *The Papers of Woodrow Wilson*, 69 vols., edited by A. S. Link et al. (Princeton, NJ: Princeton University Press, 1966–94), 36:120.

208 **"Both rivalries":** Markus Brunnermeier, Rush Doshi, and Harold James, "Beijing's Bismarckian Ghosts: How Great Powers Compete Economically," *Washington Quarterly* 41, no. 3 (Fall 2018): 161–76, https://www.tandfonline.com/doi/full/10.1080/0163660X.2018.1520571.

209 **"easy to join and hard to overturn":** John Ikenberry, *After Victory: Institutions, Strategic Restraint, and the Rebuilding of Order After Major Wars* (Princeton, NJ: Princeton University Press, 2001, new edition 2019), Preface.

Lesson Ten: Sometimes the Greatest Realists Are the Idealists

211 **"China has to be by itself":** Mu Lu, "Mastering Advanced Tech Protects National Security," *Global Times*, March 18, 2020.

211 **restricted exports of key medical supplies:** Pamela Boykoff, Clare Sebastian, and Valentina Di Donato, "In the Race to Secure Medical Supplies, Countries Ban or Restrict Exports," CNN Business, March 27, 2020.

211 **reduce its dependence on China:** Ari Altstedter, "India to Spend $1.3 Billion to Boost Pharmaceutical Production," Bloomberg, March 22, 2020.

211 **develop drugs:** Devjyot Ghoshal and Sachin Ravikumar, "Health Experts Cast Doubt on India's Timeline for COVID Vaccine," Reuters, July 3, 2020.

211 **manufacture crucial supplies on its own:** "I see people thinking *kaash* (I wish) we were self-reliant in medical equipment, I wish we were self-reliant in manufacturing PPE kits. . . . I wish we were self-reliant in manufacturing all that we buy or consume. . . . The solution to all this can only come from *atma nirbhar Bharat* (self-reliant India)," said Narendra Modi at the inaugural address of the 95th annual plenary session of the Indian Chamber of Commerce: *Deccan Chronicle*, "Turn Crisis into Opportunity, Says PM Modi; Reiterates Self-Reliance," June 11, 2020.

211 **over 150 million dead:** Based on the most commonly agreed-upon estimates for the death tolls of these 1914–45 atrocities: 20 million in WWI; some 50 million of the Spanish flu (and perhaps up to 100 million); some 80 million in WWII, including those who died in the Holocaust and other victims of the Nazi death camps; some 5 million dead in Stalin's mass killings (the Great Purge and the "Holodomor" famine in Ukraine).

211 **killed nearly 20,000 British soldiers . . . to gain just three square miles of muddy ground:** 19,240 casualties, according to the BBC, "WW1: Why

Was the First Day of the Somme Such a Disaster?," https://www.bbc.co
.uk/teach/why-was-the-first-day-of-the-somme-such-a-disaster/zn3hwty.

213 **"Locksley Hall":** Alfred, Lord Tennyson, "Locksley Hall," *Poems* (1842).
This poem notably provided the title for Paul Kennedy's history of the UN,
The Parliament of Man.

213 **copied out the following stanzas:** John Hersey, *New Yorker*, April 7, 1951,
https://archives.newyorker.com/newyorker/1951–04–07/flipbook/050/.

214 **read them Tennyson's lines:** "Caught in the Middle," *Economist*, July 13,
2006.

214 **Eisenhower explained to Cronkite:** "Eisenhower Recalls the Ordeal of
D-Day Assault 20 Years Ago," *New York Times*, June 6, 1964.

215 **"cross of iron":** Dwight D. Eisenhower, "April 16, 1953: Chance for
Peace," University of Virginia Miller Center, https://millercenter.org/the
-presidency/presidential-speeches/april-16-1953-chance-peace.

215 **"United States of Europe":** "Speech of Sir Winston Churchill, Zurich,
19th September 1946," Council of Europe, Parliamentary Assembly,
https://archive.is/20130218054245/http://assembly.coe.int/Main.asp?link=
/AboutUs/zurich_e.htm#selection-653.1–661.27.

215 **"put your countries first":** Donald J. Trump, "Remarks by President
Trump to the 72nd Session of the United Nations General Assembly,"
White House, September 19, 2017, https://www.whitehouse.gov/briefings
-statements/remarks-president-trump-72nd-session-united-nations
-general-assembly/.

216 **constrained America's unilateral power:** Ikenberry, *After Victory*.

216 **not even bothering to inform his closest European allies:** David E.
Sanger, "For Trump, a New Crisis and a Familiar Response: It's China's
Fault, and Europe's," *New York Times*, March 12, 2020.

217 **"vocal for local":** "'It's a Great Service to the Nation': PM Modi Urges
People to Go Vocal About Local," *Hindustan Times*, June 28, 2020.

217 **brought out nationalism even in . . . Europe:** Giulio Sabbati and Costica
Dumbrava, "The Impact of Coronavirus on Schengen Borders," European
Parliament, Members' Research Service PE 649.347, April 2020, https://
www.europarl.europa.eu/RegData/etudes/BRIE/2020/649347/EPRS_
BRI(2020)649347_EN.pdf.

217 **credulously accepted Beijing's claim:** Kathy Gilsinan, "How China
Deceived the WHO," *Atlantic*, April 12, 2020; for WHO credulity of
Chinese claims, see: World Health Organization, "Novel Coronavirus—
Thailand (ex-China)," last updated January 14, 2020, https://www.who.int/
csr/don/14-january-2020-novel-coronavirus-thailand-ex-china/en/.

217 **delayed declaring the virus as a pandemic until March 11:** World Health
Organization, "WHO Timeline—Covid-19," last updated April 27, 2020,

https://www.who.int/news-room/detail/27–04–2020-who-timeline--
-covid-19.

217   **a tiny budget:** $4.4 billion in 2018–19, WHO, "Programme Budget
2020–21," 7, https://www.who.int/about/finances-accountability/budget/
WHOPB-PRP-19.pdf?ua=1.

217   **cannot even shame its more powerful funders:** Note that during the 2003
SARS epidemic, when China was substantially less wealthy and influential,
the WHO did indeed shame Beijing over its epidemic response: "China
was rebuked by the World Health Organization for its handling of SARS,
a black eye from a United Nations agency that rarely confronts member
states": Joseph Kahn, "China Discovers Secrecy Is Expensive," *New York
Times*, April 13, 2003; see also "China's failure to admit the true extent
of the SARS outbreak drew severe criticism from governments and from
WHO's Director-General Gro Harlem Brundtland," Isabel de Bertodano,
Bulletin of the World Health Organization 2003, 81 (8), https://www.who
.int/bulletin/volumes/81/8/News0803.pdf.

218   **eagerly accepted supplies from China:** Alexandra Stevenson, Nicholas
Kulish, and David Gelles, "Frantic for Coronavirus Gear, Americans in
Need Turn to China's Elite," *New York Times*, April 24, 2020.

218   **provided 1.5 million test kits:** "Strategic Preparedness and Response Plan:
Data as of 22 April 2020," WHO, https://www.who.int/docs/default-source/
coronaviruse/covid-19-exr-srp-infographic-.pdf?sfvrsn=6f7a7e58_11.

218   **far more travelers from China:** Pre-pandemic, Taiwan had 5,700 monthly
flights from China, versus some 1,300 flights to the US. South Korea
received some 480,000 Chinese visitors in January 2020. Taiwan flight
data: NPR, "With Odds Against It, Taiwan Keeps Coronavirus Cor-
ralled," March 13, 2020; US flight data: Lin Yang, "China Flights Increasing, but American Carriers Still Left Out," *Voice of America*, June 12, 2020;
South Korea tourism data: Korea Tourism Organization, "Monthly Arriv-
als," January 2020: China, http://kto.visitkorea.or.kr/eng/tourismStatics/
keyFacts/KoreaMonthlyStatistics/eng/inout/inout.kto.

219   **"in no way holy, nor Roman, nor an empire":** "*le saint empire romain n'était
en aucune manière ni saint, ni romain, ni empire*": François Marie Arouet
de Voltaire, *Essai sur l'histoire générale et sur les mœurs et l'esprit des nations*
(Essay on Universal History and the Manners and Spirit of Nations) (1756),
Chapter 70.

219   **Hugo Grotius:** for Grotius's contribution to the origins of international law
and the foundations of a more peaceful global order, see: Oona A. Hatha-
way and Scott J. Shapiro, *The Internationalists: How a Radical Plan to Out-
law War Remade the World* (New York: Simon & Schuster, 2017).

219   **Immanuel Kant:** in his 1795 "Perpetual Peace: A Philosophical Sketch."

219   **"equal rights of all nations":** William E. Gladstone, "Third Midlothian

Speech, West Calder, 27 November 1879," *English Historical Documents*, 1874–1914, edited by W. D. Hancock and David Charles Douglas, citing *Political Speeches in Scotland* (1880), 1:115–17.

220 **deeply mercantilist as well:** As with, for example, the "Imperial Preference" system of reduced tariffs between Great Britain and its colonies. See: Brian Varian, "Britain's Post-Brexit Trade: Learning from the Edwardian Origins of Imperial Preference," *VoxEU*, Center for Economic Policy Research, June 23, 2018, https://voxeu.org/article/what-imperial -preference-can-teach-us-about-post-brexit-trade-deals.

220 **first modern arms control agreements:** Notably the Hague Conventions of 1899 and 1907.

221 **seventy-two times:** Lindsey A. O'Rourke, "The U.S. Tried to Change Other Countries' Governments 72 Times During the Cold War," *Washington Post*, December 23, 2016.

222 **top twenty-five markets for foreign direct investment:** A. T. Kearney Foreign Direct Investment Confidence Index, 2020, https://www.kearney .com/foreign-direct-investment-confidence-index/2020-full-report.

222 **a 2015 report:** Michael O'Sullivan and Krithika Subramanian, "The End of Globalization or a More Multipolar World?," Credit Suisse Report, September 2015, https://www.credit-suisse.com/media/assets/corporate/ docs/about-us/research/publications/the-end-of-globalization-or-a-more -multipolar-world-report.pdf.

222 **"about half of China's growth slowdown":** Nicholas R. Lardy, *The State Strikes Back: The End of Economic Reform in China?* (Washington, DC: Peterson Institute for International Economics, 2019), 31.

223 **passed the $10,000 milestone:** According to the Director of China's National Bureau of Statistics, Ning Jizhe: "China's Per Capita GDP Crosses USD 10,000-Mark for the First Time," *Economic Times*, January 17, 2020, https://economictimes.indiatimes.com/news/international/ business/chinas-per-capita-gdp-crosses-usd-10000-mark-for-the-first -time/articleshow/73329871.cms.

223 **marked decline in war and annexation since 1945:** Mark W. Zacher, "The Territorial Integrity Norm: International Boundaries and the Use of Force," *International Organization* 55, no. 2 (Spring 2001): 218, "Table 1: Interstate Wars by Historical Era, 1648–2000," https://www.jstor.org/ stable/3078631.

224 **58% of the global economy:** The United States and listed US allies have 57.7% of world GDP: $50.6 trillion in total GDP of $87.7 trillion world GDP, per World Bank data as of 2019.

224 **Chinese attempt at a full "breakout":** see Ikenberry, *After Victory*, preface to the 2019 edition.

225 **America's abdication:** See Ivo H. Daalder and James M. Lindsay, *The*

Empty Throne: America's Abdication of Global Leadership (New York: Public-Affairs, 2018).

225 **Trump's instincts are Jacksonian:** Walter Russell Mead, "The Jacksonian Revolt: American Populism and the Liberal Order," *Foreign Affairs*, January 20, 2017.

225 **abandoned the field:** Daniel W. Drezner, "This Time Is Different: Why U.S. Foreign Policy Will Never Recover," *Foreign Affairs*, May/June 2019.

225 **pull troops from European bases:** "Donald Trump's Baffling Proposal to Withdraw Troops from Germany," *Economist*, June 27, 2020.

225 **end of a seventy-year Atlantic partnership:** For a somewhat more sanguine account of transatlantic tension, see: Karen Donfried and Wolfgang Ischinger, "The Pandemic and the Toll of Transatlantic Discord," *Foreign Affairs*, April 18, 2020.

226 **"for the U.S. only":** Aitor Hernández-Morales, "Germany Confirms That Trump Tried to Buy Firm Working on Coronavirus Vaccine," *Politico*, March 15, 2020, citing Jan Dams, "Diese Erfahrung wird Europa so schnell nicht vergessen," *Die Welt*, March 15, 2020, https://www.welt.de/wirtschaft/plus206563595/Trump-will-deutsche-Impfstoff-Firma-CureVac-Traumatische-Erfahrung.html.

226 **swooping in on deals:** Richard Lough and Andreas Rinke, "U.S. Coronavirus Supply Spree Sparks Outrage Among Allies," Reuters, April 3, 2020.

226 **saving up to 18 million lives:** According to the State Department: "The United States President's Emergency Plan for AIDS Relief," US Department of State, https://www.state.gov/pepfar/; see also Anthony S. Fauci and Robert W. Eisenger, "PEPFAR—15 Years and Counting the Lives Saved," *New England Journal of Medicine* 378 (January 25, 2018): 314–16, https://www.nejm.org/doi/10.1056/NEJMp1714773; and "The U.S. President's Emergency Plan for AIDS Relief (PEPFAR)," Kaiser Family Foundation, May 27, 2020, https://www.kff.org/global-health-policy/fact-sheet/the-u-s-presidents-emergency-plan-for-aids-relief-pepfar/. Even less dramatic estimates are in the neighborhood of 3 million lives saved: see Dylan Matthews, "George W. Bush Was a Much Better President Than Liberals Like to Admit," *Vox*, July 8, 2015.

226 **Other nations donate:** Europe does give a vast amount in foreign development aid, far more than the US by some metrics. As of 2016, the US gave some $30 billion annually, while EU institutions together with France, the UK, and Germany contributed around $60 billion, according to OECD data: http://www.oecd.org/dac/stats/ODA-2015-detailed-summary.pdf.

226 **raging across most:** The US hit a new all-time high for daily Covid-19 cases (over 75,000) on July 16: Lisa Shumaker, "U.S. Shatters Coronavirus Record with over 77,000 Cases in a Day," Reuters, July 16, 2020.

227 **"Once there was the United States of the Berlin airlift"**: Kevin Rudd, "The Coming Post-Covid Anarchy," *Foreign Affairs*, May 6, 2020.

227 **a series of multilateral groups:** In Latin America, engagement with the Community of Latin American and Caribbean States (CELAC) via the China-CELAC Forum since 2015 (http://www.chinacelacforum.org/eng/ltjj_1/P020161207421177845816.pdf), in Central and Eastern Europe with the "Visegrad Group," and the so-called 17+1 format (Albania, Bosnia and Herzegovina, Bulgaria, Croatia, the Czech Republic, Estonia, Hungary, Latvia, Lithuania, Macedonia, Montenegro, Poland, Romania, Serbia, Slovakia, and Slovenia, joined by Greece in 2019): Emilian Kavalski, "China's '16+1' Is Dead? Long Live the '17+1,'" *Diplomat*, March 29, 2019.

228 **former Soviet republics in a defense treaty:** The Collective Security Treaty Organization (CSTO), also called the Tashkent Pact, from 1992, originally including Armenia, Kazakhstan, Kyrgyzstan, Russia, Tajikistan, and Uzbekistan, adding in 1993 Azerbaijan, Belarus, and Georgia. CSTO, "From the Treaty to the Organization," https://en.odkb-csto.org/25years/.

228 **wary of tying themselves to Moscow:** "The crisis over Ukraine became the E[urasian] E[conomic] U[nion]'s birth trauma." Evgeny Troitskiy, "The Eurasian Economic Union at Five: Great Expectations and Hard Times," Wilson Center, January 14, 2020, https://www.wilsoncenter.org/blog-post/eurasian-economic-union-five-great-expectations-and-hard-times.

228 **play its own independent role in the world:** Ivan Krastev and Mark Leonard, "Europe's Pandemic Politics: How the Virus Has Changed the Public's Worldview," European Council on Foreign Relations, Policy Brief, June 23, 2020, https://www.ecfr.eu/publications/summary/europes_pandemic_politics_how_the_virus_has_changed_the_publics_worldview.

228 **"face China, the United States, and global disorder":** Emmanuel Macron, "Addresse aux Français," https://www.elysee.fr/emmanuel-macron/2020/06/14/adresse-aux-francais-14-juin-2020.

229 **survive the end of American hegemony:** For more on the idea of the US-crafted order outliving the state power that created it, see Ikenberry's 2019 preface to *After Victory*.

230 **Venus:** Michael Cabbage and Leslie McCarthy, "NASA Climate Modeling Suggests Venus May Have Been Habitable," NASA Goddard Institute for Space Studies, https://climate.nasa.gov/news/2475/nasa-climate-modeling-suggests-venus-may-have-been-habitable/.

Scientists long have theorized that Venus formed out of ingredients similar to Earth's, but followed a different evolutionary path. Measurements by NASA's Pioneer mission to Venus in the 1980s first suggested Venus originally may have had an ocean. However, Venus is closer to the sun than Earth and receives far more sunlight. As a result, the planet's early ocean evaporated, water-vapor molecules were broken apart by ultraviolet radiation, and hydrogen escaped to space. With no water left on the surface, carbon dioxide built up in the atmosphere, leading to a so-called runaway greenhouse effect that created present conditions.

232 **"numbing, boring, and impressive"**: Paul Kennedy, *The Parliament of Man: The Past, Present, and Future of the United Nations* (New York: Random House, 2006), 283.

Conclusion: Nothing Is Written

238 **its first official public opinion poll:** Frank Newport, "75 Years Ago, the First Gallup Poll," Gallup, October 20, 2010, https://news.gallup.com/opinion/polling-matters/169682/years-ago-first-gallup-poll.aspx.

238 **strongly against the EU:** "One opinion poll in late-March suggested that 72 per cent thought the EU had not contributed 'at all' to addressing the pandemic, and trust in the EU had slumped to 25 per cent from 34 per cent before the pandemic struck." Luigi Scazzieri, "Trouble for the EU Is Brewing in Coronavirus-Hit Italy," Centre for European Reform, April 2, 2020, https://www.cer.eu/insights/trouble-eu-brewing-coronavirus-hit-italy, citing ADN Kronos, "Il sondaggio: fiducia in Ue crolla anche fra europeisti," https://www.adnkronos.com/fatti/cronaca/2020/03/29/sondaggio-fiducia-crolla-anche-fra-europeisti_4SqDLxMTeNlpRJsz9jEwzK.html.

239 **an accord was struck:** Jan Strupczewski, John Chalmers, and Robin Emmott, "EU Reaches Historic Deal on Pandemic Recovery After Fractious Summit," Reuters, July 20, 2020.

240 **many biologists believe:** For example, Robert Boyd and Peter J. Richerson, "Culture and the Evolution of Human Cooperation," *Philosophical Transactions of the Royal Society of London, Series B, Biological Sciences* 364, no. 1533 (November 12, 2009): 3281–88, https://www.ncbi.nlm.nih.gov/pmc/articles/PMC2781880/; a theory popularized recently in Rutger Breman's *Humankind: A Hopeful History* (New York: Little, Brown, 2020), trans. Erica Moore and Elizabeth Manton.

240 **"Men make their own history":** Karl Marx, *The Eighteenth Brumaire of Louis Bonaparte,* translated by Saul K. Padover (1852), Chapter 1.

240 **"God's footsteps":** A slightly different formulation of this Bismarckian

dictum was offered by Henry Kissinger in "Otto von Bismarck: Master Statesman," *New York Times*, March 31, 2011.

240 **Dr. Viktor Zhdanov:** This account of US-Soviet collaboration on smallpox comes from the Harvard historian Erez Manela, in his excellent and authoritative "A Pox on Your Narrative: Writing Disease Control into Cold War History," *Diplomatic History* 34, no. 2 (April 2010), https://scholar .harvard.edu/files/manela/files/manela-pox-dh.pdf. He quotes Thomas Jefferson's letter to Edward Jenner, May 14, 1806, The Thomas Jefferson Papers, Series 1, General Correspondence, Library of Congress, Washington, DC.

241 **officially eradicated:** "Smallpox," US Centers for Disease Control and Prevention, last reviewed July 12, 2017, https://www.cdc.gov/smallpox/ index.html.

Credits

Portions of "Lesson Nine: The World Is Becoming Bipolar" and "Lesson Ten: Sometimes the Greatest Realists Are the Idealists" draw on "The Self-Destruction of American Power." Reprinted by permission of FOREIGN AFFAIRS, July/August 2019. Copyright 2019 by the Council on Foreign Relations, Inc. www.ForeignAffairs.com.

A portion of "Lesson Nine: The World Is Becoming Bipolar" draws on "The New China Scare." Reprinted by permission of FOREIGN AFFAIRS, January/February 2020. Copyright 2020 by the Council on Foreign Relations, Inc. www.ForeignAffairs.com.

This book draws on the author's previously published work, notably his columns in *The Washington Post*, all of which are available at https://www.washingtonpost.com/people/fareed-zakaria/.

THE POEMS OF EMILY DICKINSON: READING EDITION, edited by Ralph W. Franklin, Cambridge, Mass.: The Belknap Press of Harvard University Press, Copyright © 1998, 1999 by the President and Fellows of Harvard College. Copyright © 1951, 1955 by the President and Fellows of Harvard College. Copyright © renewed 1979, 1983 by the President and Fellows of Harvard College. Copyright © 1914, 1918, 1919, 1924, 1929, 1930, 1932, 1935, 1937, 1942 by Martha Dickinson Bianchi. Copyright © 1952, 1957, 1958, 1963, 1965 by Mary L. Hampson.

Chart on p. 173 excerpted from "Globalization over 5 centuries, World," Esteban Ortiz-Ospina and Diana Beltekian, Our World in Data, published 2014, revised October 2018, https://ourworldindata.org/grapher/globalization-over-5-centuries?time=1945 ..2016. Data from Mariko J. Klasing and P. Milionis, "Quantifying the Evolution of World Trade, 1870–1949," *Journal of International Economics* 92, no. 1 (2014): 185–97; A. Estevadeordal, B. Frantz, and A. Taylor, "The Rise and Fall of World Trade, 1870–1939," *Quarterly Journal of Economics* 118, no. 2 (2003): 359–407, retrieved from http://www.jstor.org/stable/25053910); World Bank—World Development Indicators, http://data.worldbank.org/data-catalog/world-development-indicators; Robert C. Feenstra, Robert Inklaar, and Marcel P. Timmer, "The Next Generation of the Penn World Table," *American Economic Review* 105, no. 10 (2015): 3150–82, available for download at www.ggdc.net/pwt. PWT v9.1.